REAL
OF THE KINGDOM

Volume I

IAN CLAYTON

TRANSCRIBED, EDITED & PRODUCED BY
REVELATION PARTNERS

Second Edition
Transcribed, Edited and Produced by Revelation Partners
Published by
Son of Thunder Publications Ltd 2016
www.sonofthunderpublications.org

Cover design by Gabrial Heath, Design Lead Aspect Reference Design
caleb.gabrial@clear.net.nz

Gateway diagrams by
Iain Gutteridge, I.G. Design
www.ig-graphic-design.co.uk

Seven Spirits of God diagram by Adam Butterick, Third Realm Studios
www.thirdrealmstudios.com.au

Typeset by Avocet Typeset, Somerton, Somerset TA11 6RT
www.avocet-typeset.com

First published by Seraph Creative 2014
www.seraphcreative.org

Formatting first completed by Freedom Publishing LLP
www.freedompublishing.org

Each chapter in this book is an edited and updated transcript taken from messages given by Ian Clayton at different times over a four year period. There are some minor differences from the audio messages the reader might have listened to before.

Published in the United Kingdom
for world-wide distribution

ISBN 978-1-911251-01-9

Contents

ACKNOWLEDGEMENTS

Partnering with Ian Clayton to write this first volume of his revelatory teaching has been an honour and a privilege. Thank You Papa God, Your encouragement to see this book written has been our constant companion, with visions of the heavenly city and a new awareness of the Seven Spirits of God and the angelic amid the battles. Recording prophecy and inspirational teaching has always been our heart passion, but there has never been a speaker whose words have inspired us in the creation of a book until Ian Clayton was invited to Wales a number of years ago. Our thanks and tribute go to Justin Abraham and COBH community for their pioneering walk, pushing through the religious constraints we knew, to find a new level of victory through intimacy with Jesus and experience of functioning from heavenly realms. Our greatest goal in seeing Ian Clayton's work published, is to unlock the experience of this reality for those wanting to find it.

It is a great pleasure to realise our long standing wish to publish this second edition of Realms of the Kingdom Volume 1, to complete the presentation of some of Ian Clayton's foundational work, including the chapter 'Using the Word as a Doorway'.

We want to honour the support, friendship and dedication of our former publisher Seraph Creative and the hours of detailed attention given to the original formatting of the book for hard copy by David Powell of Freedom Publishing, which were invaluable. The inclusion of the preface, inviting readers onto the life changing journey this revelation offers, is also something we felt would be helpful for people starting to walk into heavenly realms, as Ian gives further guidance about how to more fully engage and get the most out of this teaching. Anyone who wishes to take a step into discipleship in this walk can find details about Ian Clayton's NEST programme through his website at: www.sonofthunder.org. Our thanks go to Paul Medcalf of Avocet Typeset for the diligent care he has taken in typesetting this second edition for us. Also the graphic design expertise of several talented team members, especially our design lead Gabrial Heath of Aspect Reference Design, who created the cover for us, Iain Gutteridge who helped us with the Gateway diagrams and created the inspired flow diagram and Adam Butterick of Third Realm Studios for his excellent work on the "Seven Spirits of God" diagrams.

We cannot give adequate thanks to the numerous precious sisters and several dedicated brothers who walked with us along the journey of creating this book, including proof readers, intercessors and friends of wise counsel, without whom this book would still be a vision. They have chosen to remain anonymous but they continue to be counted with affection as part of the Revelation Partners family.

We also want to express our love and gratitude for the kindness and encouragement of many which has opened doors along the way, including Mike Parsons; Jonathan & Helena Cavan; Matthew & Pearl Nagy and the wonderful Kingdom family in Horsham; Liz Wright, Lulu, Ann and precious prayer community; Lindi Masters, Pastor of Well Church, Teresa Withams, beloved Funmi and the community of faith in Guildford; faithful intercessors and friends Michelle Beare; Heiko and Susanne Schneider, Regina Frohms,

Manfred Mayer and kind friends in Germany, especially Gabriela and Katja; – thank you so much for your loving support for this work as we walk into heavenly realms together.

Finally, we want to express our affection and gratitude to Ian Clayton, his family and team, especially Karl Whitehead, for their wisdom, support and oversight of this labour of love.

Revelation Partners
United Kingdom

ENDORSEMENTS

It is a delight for me to be able to write about my friend Ian Clayton. It has been seven years since our friendship began. What can I say? He is a son – no question about it! He knows the Lord intimately and has studied to show himself approved to God. I have found he walks as Yeshua walked with both the favor of God and man. His materials have come to provoke sons into the study of the word as well as to cause them to rethink how we have lived and behaved as we have sought to live our lives to serve the Father.

Ian not only teaches how to live as a son, he lives it. Revelation 3:11 states, "I am coming soon. Hold on to what you have, so that no one will take your crown." This is an important study – to look at which crowns we have and how not to get them taken, as well as how to get them back! This study and more are all important in our journey as we finally reach maturity and learn to walk as Yeshua walked.

As you read through and study his material may your destiny and purpose be revealed as you look to Jesus the author and finisher of your faith!

Shalom

Michelle Tidball
Abundant Ministries, USA

Ian Clayton is a true forerunner of a new order. He has opened a way for many to follow. This has enabled many who have had involuntary heavenly encounters to develop a lifestyle of living and ruling in dual realms.

Following many personal heavenly encounters in 2010, listening to Ian's teaching gave a context for a lot of my experiences. Ian is an invaluable resource to the body of Christ.

Mike Parsons
Freedom Church, UK

Finally – Ian Clayton! "Realms of the Kingdom"!

One of the most significant leaders of our time, releases, in book-format, portions of the revelatory treasure he has been receiving and cultivating for decades. What a gift!

For years, my wife and I have been privileged to sit at Ian's feet to learn. We have also been honored to be Ian Clayton's friends.

The subject matter of the following pages is life-changing, on all counts. It comes from a pure source who is always full of the wisdom, power, and counsel of God.

I wholeheartedly celebrate Ian and his most eagerly-anticipated, "Realms of the Kingdom"! May it have the greatest impact imaginable! Glory to Glory

Marios Ellinas
Connecticut, USA & Pera Pedi, Cyprus

In the summer of 2011 I was taken into Heaven. I found myself standing in front of Jesus and to the left hand side of Ian Clayton. He was bowed before the King, his whole being surrendered. The love between them was overwhelming. In that moment I was permitted to experience a glimpse of the intimate relationship Ian has with Jesus and who he really is in Christ.

I saw the Spirit of Might being released to him, the Spirit Ian later shared with me he has been permitted to minister in.

I am so thankful for this true father to the Body of Christ. For the insatiable hunger Ian has to know the heart of God and the reality of His Kingdom.

For him going ahead of so many of us to enter into new realms of wisdom and for providing us with a glimpse of what it means to be a true son of the Kingdom. He is a man who genuinely lives and moves and has his being in Christ, not only revealing the virtue of His nature but with much fruit to evidence the power the sons are to operate in as we begin to enter into effective governance, bringing the Kingdom on earth. Ian is a living epistle showing us the reality of just how much authority can rest on a life that is fully yielded, who forsakes all other loves and becomes a friend of God.

As you open your spirit now to read through the pages of this exceptional book, the wisdom, love, power and hope that will be imparted into you will literally transform your life. I encourage you to embrace the paradigm shifts, and as you allow your being to become expanded, you will enter into a greater experience of who you really are as a new creation – an experience I know Ian pours out his life to see become our full reality.

It is my honour and privilege to recommend this book to you.

Liz Wright
The Bridal Company, UK

FOREWORD

Justin Abraham

Ian Clayton is one of the most inspirational voices of our generation. His teachings are saturated with years of intimate face-to-face encounters with heaven. Ian is on a passionate quest to know the Mystic Secret of God, which is Christ. He is one of the burning ones that has an insatiable passion for friendship with God. His messages drip with life and hope that we can really be where God is and see His glory. We can live beyond the veil in a fantastic world of awe and wonder.

This first book is a rallying call to begin to learn how the unseen works, what I call 'the science of the unseen'. Each chapter has a wealth of step by step practical insights and activations to help you engage new creation realities; to disconnect and un-tether from the cares and worries of the world, and the limitations of your past and to be drawn into an expansive place of beauty and joy from which you can never return. Once you've tasted that new world there truly is no going back. The Lord himself begins to teach you and the whole unseen world comes to life.

We are in a new mystical era, and Ian Clayton is one of the catalytic voices to reposition the church into a place of acceleration, change and breakthrough. I can honestly say that getting to know Ian and progressing through his teachings has rocked our world. Our whole community has been radically changed. We are experiencing progressive expansion of our hearts and heavenly revelation to impact and shape the world around us. This revelation is powerful and active, a tangible superior reality invading the earth.

Heaven is at hand right in front of you and around you. It is not far away but inviting you every day to enter in. All sense of distance and delay is just an illusion. The truth is that you are a new creation in Christ, seated with Him in heavenly realms, fully able to access and enjoy heaven on earth now. It is not a work thing, it's a grace thing. Jesus invites us and provides the means for us to enter in as a pure gift.

You are made for this amazing new era, living in the right place at the right time. Engage with this beautiful and timely book. Work through the teachings that have come from years of encounter. This kingdom power will change you if you engage it (and as Ian says practise, practise, practise) stepping into it by faith. Choose to take God by the hand and walk arm in arm with him like Enoch. Become His best friend. This is the most exciting life you can imagine, a life of abundance and eternal joy. Be blessed as you read this book.

Justin Abraham
Company of Burning Hearts, UK

PREFACE

One of the key things that God is doing on the face of the earth today is empowering us as believers to become more than many of our churches had defined us in the past. One of the greatest struggles the church has had is with the revelation that God wants to bring, about the Kingdom realm, about who we are and our mandates, both on the face of the earth and in the heavens. The enemy has put blocks around us: through the way we have been trained to think, the way we believe, the way we feel, and the things around us, which has created a massive hindrance.

I was in Africa recently at a conference where we had thirty-five leaders who were associated with the Council of African Apostles. I spent five minutes around a table with these people who have been studying for twenty years. In just five minutes someone was shaking his head and saying, "Ian you have just undone twenty years of study in what you've told me today. You have wrecked everything that I've been studying!" I am saying this to prepare you for the journey that lies before you as you read this book, because you will probably feel the same way. There are strongholds inside our minds that have been a castle against the moving of the glory of the presence of God in and around our lives, not only in us but strongholds that work through us into the atmosphere over us and over the earth, into the galaxy and the whole capsule of creation that God has put in place.

I grew up a Baptist. My first engagement in any church circle was in a Baptist church. I was a bit of a radical, but praise God I got saved out of a lot of rubbish and got some good doctrinal foundation. I then went to a Pentecostal church, and God continued showing me some radical things that I could not talk to people about.

It is unimportant to me what your persuasion is; the key issue now is what are you doing with what Father God has given you? What are you doing with the measure that has been laid out before you in the scroll He wrote for you before the foundation of the world began? God is asking us today, "What are you doing with what I have given you?" Because to the measure and the power that you have been given, there is much responsibility, to see the Kingdom of God come on the face of the earth.

One of the key things for me as a believer is being able to understand who we are. Many in the church do not know who they are. They have no idea of the Kingdom they represent or what they are in that Kingdom. God says in the Bible, *"Let Us make man in Our image, according to Our likeness"* (Genesis 1:26).

The Bible says "God *is* Spirit, and those who worship Him must worship in spirit and truth" (John 4:24).

So if I am made in the image of God, and God is a spirit then I am a spirit. I am not a human being that has a soul and lives in a physical body, nor am I a human being with a soul that has a spirit somewhere. I am a spirit being that has a soul that lives in a physical body. The problem is that not many of us believe the truth of who we really are. You are a spirit, a supernatural spirit being *first.* You are not a human being first. You were born on the dispensation of your parents as a human being. But the day you were born again you were born of an incorruptible seed. *"We know that whosoever is born of God sins not; but he that is begotten of God keeps himself, and that wicked one touches him not"* (1 John 5:18 KJ2000). So the day you are born again you have a seed that is put inside you that the devil has no legal mandate to touch. However, that is what goes on in your spirit. But the problem is the issue of reconstruction of your soul that needs to go on, so that what is in your spirit man can begin to transform your soul, and translate your body, because whatever goes on inside you is reflected in your body.

If I am a spirit being then there is a Kingdom that I belong to. We need to understand that as spirit beings, we are in the earth but of a different Kingdom - I am a sojourner in the earth. I originally came out of a Kingdom and I am called to be a king in the Kingdom I came from.

Jesus is the King of Kings and the Lord of Lords. God is looking for kings and for lords to come into the stature of sonship so He can rest His government upon them and put them in a position to rule. You and I were not made to be servants. We were made to be rulers, kings and priests of our God. But we need to understand that either the kingdom of self or the Kingdom that we have been bought into will manifest through our lives.

In the Old Testament, long before the Holy Spirit was given through Christ, David said, *"Do not take Your Holy Spirit from me" (Psalm 51:11)*. David lived out of the dispensation of the future. He could live out of his day in victory because he had already seen the future, and that is why he was not afraid. Our role as kings is to live out of the future in our day. David lived out of a future where he could see himself as king, so he was not afraid of facing the trials of his day. That is why he could face Goliath, because he knew he would not die.

There have been so many people that can name, frame and blame every single demonic thing but they have no idea about the angelic arena. I do not need to find the darkness to discover the light. If I uncover the light I will see the darkness. We have in us the capacity to release the heavenly Kingdom into that arena, to establish the dominion of Jesus' Kingdom into the kingdom that is in darkness. It is not the kingdom of darkness, but it is a kingdom in darkness (Colossians 1:13). Nothing can be created by Satan; he can only copy what is already there. The darkness has just copied the truth, and told the church we cannot do that. (We will look at this in more depth in Chapter 14.) I am looking forward to the day that I can levitate, walk through walls and disappear and then reappear, as Jesus did.

This is the Kingdom that we are going to inherit, the Kingdom that the cross has bought us into, the Kingdom that God is wanting to manifest around us and Jesus has delivered to us. This is the Kingdom that you and I have been given the privilege to reveal, been mandated to be kings and lords in; this is the Kingdom that is operating around our lives.

We can choose to receive it or reject. But if I have a Kingdom that is within me, that Kingdom must be revealed through me and must come out from within me. If I have a Kingdom that is within me, that Kingdom needs to manifest through me, so the glory follows my life.

The church is facing a big question today: how big do you think you are? Because as the Bible says, "...According to your faith be it unto you" (Matthew 9:29 KJ2000). That is why the church is not living in victory, because it does not believe. It gives lip-service but denies the Kingdom that flows from within us. God wants us to live out of a Kingdom that is very real.

Adam was made in Heaven to be manifested in the earth; Jesus was made in the earth to be manifested in Heaven; now you and I are being manifested in Heaven to be revealed on the earth.

I would like to give you some basic keys that I call terms of engagement for the Kingdom realm that will help you to get the most out of your journey as you walk with the Lord through this book:

1) **Set yourself.** It says in scripture that David set himself to seek the Lord (2 Chronicles 26:5). When you set yourself, it is a determination from within to engage all the possibilities of what you can be in Him. It is like two wrestlers who come together and engage (Genesis 32:24-30). You set yourself to engage the Kingdom of His destiny – not your destiny; His destiny. We need to remember that *"We are His workmanship, created in Christ Jesus for good works, which God prepared beforehand that we should walk in them"* (Ephesians 2:10). Before the creation of the world, you agreed to fulfil things on the face of the earth. You were a spirit being in what was, before you were here in what is. God and you had a meeting about all the things that you and He agreed together that you would fulfil on the face of the earth. You have a destiny written in Him before the foundation of the earth. And

so if I set myself to desire and engage that, then it will begin to manifest here. So it is important to set yourself and purpose in your heart to engage the destiny that He has prepared for you.
2) **Engage.** *"Whatever things you ask in prayer, believing, you will receive"* (Matthew 21:22). Engagement is by desire; it is not about my will, because my will is submitted to God. It is about desire and so you need to engage desire, the same way people engage any other passionate pursuit. You engage the whole arena around the desire to see yourself fulfilled in the presence of God, manifested in the Kingdom here and allow desire to dream about it. Desire comes from what you dream about.

Your heart is connected to the realm of your spirit. The seat of the government of God inside you is what enables your body to be programmed by your heart, *"For as he thinks in his heart, so is he"* (Proverbs 23:7). It is all about dreaming, and so when you engage, you set yourself out of engagement and out of desire. You set your heart to receive out of the realm of the Kingdom and it will flow through your life.
3) **Sow into your life by the words you speak and by your dreams**. *"Faith is the substance of things hoped for, the evidence of things not seen"* (Hebrews 11:1). Whatever you dream inside your heart will come into your mind and get fulfilled in your imagination. They are the things that you will fulfil in your life.
4) **Align yourself.** Aligning yourself is positioning yourself with purpose, and so aligning yourself does not just mean doing things with God, it means getting next to people that carry the glory and carry the purpose and desire of God. You align yourself next to them, laying hold of their mantle until you get what they have got. You do not want to be who they are; you want the mantle they operate in, which is the manifestation of the Kingdom of God on your life. When you have got that, they become your ground floor; that is why the Bible said that Jesus is the firstborn of many (Romans 8:29) - He is the first one that made a way.
5) **Serve the will of God.** You can only serve the will of God by engaging the purpose of God and you can only engage the purpose of God once you have set yourself. The will of God is

that you manifest his Son here on the face of the earth, period. People say to me, "Ian, I want to know what the will of God is for my life". Well, the will of God is for you to manifest Jesus; it is as simple as that. Whatever measure that means, wherever it means, into whatever it means, you are called to manifest Jesus. That is the will of God for your life, to be a second-born son of God. Full of grace, full of mercy, full of loving kindness, bringing the glory of Heaven into the face of the earth.

6) **Enlarge of the borders of your tent**. The only way you can do this is with revelation, not repackaged knowledge. Everything that is taught by and found in theological seminaries today is actually repackaged knowledge from the last 400 years. It is repackaged knowledge with no new revelation in it. A lot of what is done in our mega churches today is just repackaged knowledge, there is no Kingdom; I do not see much of the Kingdom of Heaven manifesting with healing and deliverance and the fruit of the Kingdom. We need to make a choice as a church to actually go after the Kingdom of God instead of becoming a mega-church. I am not a pastor and I am not in full-time ministry, I am a businessman. I employ a number of staff, I work in three businesses in between ministering, I have a family and I speak itinerantly world-wide because I want to see the Kingdom come.

I have found YHVH always gives a dispensation or period of grace so you and I can win. If you do not use and operate in the dispensation of the grace of God you will find that you constantly fail. The key is to ask for His grace while we grow and great grace will be given unto us to grow and become sons of the most high God.

The e-book version of this volume with links to 'pray with Ian' audio clips is available from Kindle and Apple ibooks. Further information is available from Seraph Creative at: http://www.seraphcreative.org/ian-clayton/

Chapter 1
Introduction – Accessing the Presence

One of the things we struggle with as believers is that we try to draw Heaven down to earth instead of allowing Heaven to draw us up from earth into Heaven. One thing I have recognised in churches is that we still try, through the religious processes and the ways that we have been taught, to take Heaven and pull it down, to put it into us. That is not the way it should be. Heaven should be released from inside of you, filling the atmosphere and then you carry that, or that carries you into the realm of the Kingdom. It is very important to understand that the God of the universe lives inside of you. What this means is that the very essence of the Person of God lives in your spirit. The first place for us to encounter God needs to be in our spirit. It is inside of you, not on the outside of you.

The reason we struggle with things of the spirit is because we have not understood this principle: God lives inside of us and we can touch Him on the inside of ourselves. In my Christian experience I want to know God as a friend. One way you get to know someone as a friend is to embrace them and say, "I love you". That is what you do as a family. I can remember one day praying, "God, I want to get close to You. Lord, I want to be loved by You, but more than that, I want to be known as Your friend. I just want to get hold of You somehow." The book of the Song of Solomon says:

"...when I found him whom my soul loves. I held him and would not let him go..." (Song of Solomon 3:4 AMP).

Well, I wanted to do the 'hold Him', let alone the 'not let Him go' part! So in the process of trying to understand this, the Lord said to me, "Give Me a hug." I said, "I am a physical being, You're a spirit being, what do you expect me to do?"

I have a relationship with God and He talks to me. It is okay that I speak to Him like that because He knows my heart's desire. In comparison to Him I am just this little dung beetle on the backside of the desert somewhere! (The backside of the desert is a good place to be because you are usually by yourself when you are in the presence of God). What God wants is a relationship and so He said to me, "Give Me a hug," and I said, "Yeah, right!" So God began to teach me by asking simple questions like, "When you hug your wife what do you do?" I said, "Well, I hug her" but actually I do not just hug her with my body, I take who I am, which is a spirit being, that has a soul, that lives in a physical body and my spirit being embraces her. The final result is my physical body doing what my spiritual being is doing.

When I hug my wife I do not stand there going, "Hi honey, nice to see you today." I would not have a relationship with somebody like that and yet many of us do that with God. We see Him living in this great big euphoric atmosphere. He dwells there, operates there and all we do is say, "Nice to see you God!" That is not how you relate with somebody. What you are supposed to do is take what you have inside you and put it over your partner and embrace them. This is what my family call 'a tank full' because it is two-way. You see, what God is looking for is a two-way relationship.

So I am embracing my wife, not just with my body but with my soul and my spirit. So that means my spirit can actually do something. It has the capability of embracing somebody. Understanding that, the Lord said, "Now give me a hug." Understanding as well that He does not just live out there in the realm of the Kingdom, but He lives in me. That means I have the ability to turn my soul and my spirit towards His presence inside of me and embrace Him.

I had to do a mental shift to understand that I could hug God.

Then I had to do another mental shift; what is going to happen when I hug Him? If it is a two-way street, what do I have to give Him? Actually, all He wants is our love. Our Dad just wants our love. He wants to be embraced. When my son or daughter comes home and comes to hug me, I hug them in response. When they come up to give me a hug, they hug me first and I respond by hugging them. If this happens in the natural, then when we reach out towards God to embrace Him, how much more is He going to embrace us, because finally somebody has understood the reality; "They can hug Me!"

So, some really simple steps are spending time praying in tongues, whilst working on my mind to believe:

1) That I can embrace God.

2) That I am a spirit being that has a soul and I can embrace His glory on the inside of me. I can actually lay hold of it on the inside of me and embrace Him.

3) I am going to choose to do that. You must make a choice to embrace the presence of God that is inside you.

So I began to pray in tongues. I did not know what else to do, so I would put my arms around my body and I would hug them over my body, with my hands wrapped around myself on each side. I was praying to make my body do what my spirit and soul were doing because the Bible says:

"every city or house divided against itself will not stand" (Matthew 12:25).

If my body is just standing there and it is not involved, my house is divided. My body and soul need to be actively involved in everything that my spirit is doing. So I would do as much as I could with my body to engage it in the process of what my spirit man was doing. I would walk around praying in tongues saying, "Lord, I chase Your presence. Father, today I take my spirit and my soul and I begin to entwine them around Your presence inside of me. Father, I take them and I begin to embrace Your glory and Your presence. I lock into it today and I embrace Your presence in Jesus' Name."

Now I am not looking out there for some great thing. I have turned totally to the inside, to the Kingdom of Heaven that is in me. I have turned to that realm inside of me where He lives. And what I have done is embraced Him. You can only join to God when you embrace Him as a spirit.

"the person who is united to the Lord becomes one spirit with Him" (1 Corinthians 6:17 AMP).

You need to embrace the presence of God. So I would practise that day after day. The first time I tried it I felt like a real idiot! I would hate to have seen somebody come when I had my arms crossed, walking up and down, praying in tongues. So walking up and down the room I would pray. It took about three days of persisting with it and as I began to practise, I ended up on the floor in a mess, because I embraced Him and then He embraced me! I got the better part of the deal. You see, a dad's covering comes over his children when they love on him. A dad's heart is extended towards his family when they love him. Love commands a response, both ways. Because I chose to embrace the presence of God, love commanded a response, as that is a spiritual law. I embraced Him in love and guess what happened; I got the better part of the deal!

It brings a security inside you, anywhere and often. After a meeting I will be standing around talking away, but I am drawing myself towards the presence of God. I have learned the process and I do not have to wrap my arms around me anymore to do it! I will be rattling away about some irrelevant thing and sometimes I am not even there. What God wants is to be real to us, because He lives inside us we can embrace His presence inside us. Here is the most exciting thing when you encounter the Kingdom of God that is within you. This Kingdom will transition you into the Kingdom of Heaven that is on the outside of you, without any struggle, because it is this Kingdom of God that transfers you into the Kingdom of Heaven. It is this Kingdom inside that seats you in another position. No longer is there wrestling in the realm of the spirit in going to the realm of heaven. No longer is there any struggle. Why? Because this Kingdom of God inside me takes me from here and puts me right over into the Kingdom of Heaven. When I am there I can enjoy it. I can enjoy what God does and I can enjoy the things of Heaven that are there. We have the capacity to do that, but it is a learned process.

So you need to practise. What I am going to get you to do is to hold yourself, like a hug. The reason I am doing this is not to make you feel stupid! It is actually for a purpose, so that your body is engaged in what you are doing. What I am going to get you to do is cross your arms around you and focus on the Kingdom of God that is within you; the realm where your Dad dwells, where His presence is inside of you. I am going to get you to pray in tongues and begin to focus there inside you. I want you to take your spirit and your soul, the same way as you would hug your husband or wife or your children, and begin to embrace Him with purpose, by your choice and start praying in tongues.

ACTIVATION

"Father, today I turn towards Your presence that dwells inside me. Father, thank You that You live in me and that You are a Spirit. Thank You, Lord, that it is spirit to Spirit that I can embrace your presence. It is spirit to Spirit that I can embrace Your glory. It is spirit to Spirit that I can touch Your presence. Lord, I take my soul with purpose and I turn my soul to embrace Your presence. I turn my soul to encompass Your presence and allow feelings of love to rush towards You. Lord, I want to be able to love on Your presence today, as I turn towards Your glory that dwells in me, Your omniscience, Your omnipresence and Your omnipotence.

Father, I turn towards that which is within the veil of my spirit. I turn towards You today, with my body, with my soul and with my spirit. I begin to entwine them into Your presence, Lord, folding them around You. I am embracing You with my heart, embracing You with my mind, embracing You with my will, embracing You with revelation and embracing You, Father, with my love. Lord, today I know that all You want from me is my love and today I choose that this emotion should flow towards you. I open the gate of love and allow that to flow towards You. Father, thank You. Thank You that You live in me. Thank you that this process enables me to become one with Your Spirit.

Lord, I want to be arm in arm with Your glory, able to dance with Your presence and hold You close, just to feel Your embrace. Today, Lord, I turn to Your glory. Thank You that You first loved me. Thank You, Lord, that You sent your Son so that I could do this, spirit to Spirit with Your presence, hungering and thirsting after You, panting after You. Father, now I ask You to release the River of Glory from the throne of Your presence inside me. Release Your abandoned and expressive love towards me as Your child that You would be my shadowing and my covering, my shield and my buckler and that I would be adorned with Your presence. Amen."

Chapter 2
Entering the Kingdom of Heaven

I want to teach about entering the Realm of the Kingdom of Heaven. There are some amazing things that you will be confronted with and will need to contend with as a believer, when you first start to explore the reality of the realm of Heaven.

The Kingdom of Heaven creates a greater awareness of the nature of sin, because of the greater light. You may feel unworthy, and the reality is that you are unworthy, but it is the Blood of Jesus that makes you worthy. That is why the Blood of Jesus Christ being applied to your life is so vital.

This unworthiness and a greater awareness of God make us aware of our own sin and the sin of those who are around us. Isaiah said:

"Then said I, Woe is me! For I am undone and ruined, because I am a man of unclean lips, and I dwell in the midst of a people of unclean lips; for my eyes have seen the King, the Lord of hosts!" (Isaiah 6:5 AMP).

When you go into the Kingdom of God it becomes light and the light exposes every point of darkness. That is why when we turn up in the Courtroom of Heaven we look filthy, and that is why God says, "New garments!" (Zechariah 3:3-5) because He knows we could not stand there without them.

We need to build intimacy with the presence of God before we can experience His presence. We need to build towards and hunger after Him and build a relationship before we will ever see or experience Him. When I first saw my wife she was roller-skating around a rink. I saw her and imagined in my mind what it would be like to get to know her. God gave me the object of my desire, which is my wife, although I did not know God at that stage.

To get to know someone, you naturally roll things around your brain like, "I wonder what she will be like to talk to? This lovely apparition that is roller-skating around, but I cannot compete with roller-skating speed". Then she just happened to fall over right in front of me! I will not tell you what happened next, but in my heart and mind I got to know her and I wanted to know her more.

The yearning and desire to 'get to know' opens the doorway to make an initial contact. This is what this is all about: to build a desire in you to make the initial contact. Did you know that it is a frightening thing for a guy to ask a girl out, in case she laughs and says, "Not interested, sorry!" It is the same in the realm of the spirit: we are afraid that God is going to say, "Not interested." This is because of the condition of the sin we live in. Whereas the reality is that God is already waiting at the door. He is already waiting there.

*"Then he dreamed, and behold, a ladder was set up on the earth, and its top reached to heaven; and there the angels of God were ascending and descending on it". (*Genesis 28:12)

This is the doorway of Heaven. God was already standing there saying, "Get up here if you can hear me!"

One of the big questions is, "Will it hurt?" So far, the only physical experience I have had from this realm of the Kingdom has been the tremendous sense of burning and heat. However, it is still only a sensation; my skin has not blistered from it yet. The fire of God changes what draws near to it. Often when I am preaching I will be sweating like crazy and everybody else will be cold. It is because of the glory that I have drawn near to in the realm of the spirit. The Kingdom realm will change you and you can draw on it and become one with it when you are in the middle of a group of people. It is really exciting!

Another question is, "Will I die?" Who knows! It does not really matter anyway because if you die, you die in the best place you can. Your soul and your body want to hold on to life and not let go of control, feeling that if the control is lost so is the power. You have to face the potential of death, the same as the High Priest. Every year he went into the Holy of Holies where he had to face the potential of being burned to a crisp. If the blood sacrificed was not good enough; or if the incense was contaminated with something or was not mixed correctly, he would go in there and become a crisp! The reality is that you face a potential that you may die, but also that you may live. You need to come to terms with that inside of you.

At times the power of revelation that is inside there will make us feel weak, but we must trust God that He knows better than we do. I call these the realms of thunder. That is why I have called my ministry 'Son of Thunder'. It has come out of the experience around the throne of God. The realms we go into with God are often fearful things when they initially happen. But if you can stay, it changes from fear to awe and wonder. The fear comes from your soul and your body and the record of what happened inside the nature of your sin, in the garden when God brought judgment. We are all afraid of that flaming sword that is going to kill (Genesis 3:24). That flaming sword of judgment is fire and it burns everything it touches. However, if I have drawn near to the source of the fire and I have taken on the image and the nature of the fire, do you think a fiery sword is going to be able to touch me when I am exactly like it?

That is why it is important for you to engage God on the earth, because it means when you go into the Kingdom realms you already resemble its nature and the sword is going to say, "Welcome home." It will not be able to touch you because you are already carrying the nature of the flame and the fire. So it is very important for us to come to grips with some of these things. You will find that they will clamour in your soul, because your soul will clamour for position and authority.

Genesis 3 talks about the angel that was put in front of the Tree of Life to guard the tree:

"So [God] drove out the man; and He placed at the east of the Garden of

Eden the cherubim and a flaming sword which turned every way, to keep and guard the way to the tree of life" (Genesis 3:24 AMP).

Revelation 2 tells us:

"To him who overcomes I will give to eat from the tree of life, which is in the midst of the Paradise of God" (Revelation 2:7).

You need to face the potential of death to eat true life. You need to face death and, on the way, you die and you get resurrection power. The angel that stands before that tree is an amazing creature. What it is actually doing is guarding against the nature of sin touching the tree.

That realm God took away from Adam, is returned in Christ, but we must be prepared to face the sword anyway. For seven days I had an encounter with the flaming Pillar of Fire in my room and I faced that judgment sword that came out of it. I am glad I did it then. One day I was asking God, "Lord, I want to know what it is to come into Your presence, but I am so petrified because I do not know what is going to happen." The fear of the unknown is the thing that will stop you from going into the realm of the Kingdom. It is that fear of the unknown that we have demonised and has stopped us from going where we should be going. It is the unknown that holds the anchor that keeps us on the earth. If you are held back by the unknown then you need to be known and you need to get your 'knower' knowing. You do that by meditation and worship so that the Kingdom realm is familiar to you and not unknown. So when you are told "This is what it is going to be like" you can enjoy it because you already know what it is going to be like.

There is nothing unknown in Heaven. All the anchors are in the Word. The Bible describes what it is going to be like. That is the known. I do not have to go there thinking "What is it going to be like?" I go there knowing what the Bible says, that is my picture, that is what it is going to be like. So I go there with the known. The reason you have a fear of the unknown is because you do not know the known; what the Bible teaches. That is the reality. These things are the things we have to contend with in the spirit.

1 Kings 18 records Elijah calling out to God:

"Answer me, Yahweh, answer me, so that this people may know that you,

Yahweh, are God and are winning back their hearts. Then Yahweh's fire fell and consumed the burnt offering and the wood and licked up the water in the trench. When all the people saw this they fell on their faces. 'Yahweh is God,' they cried, 'Yahweh is God!' Elijah said, 'Seize the prophets of Baal: do not let one of them escape.' They seized them, and Elijah took them down to the Kishon, and there he slaughtered them" (1 Kings 18:37-40 NJB).

Judgment requires a response. You need to face the wrath and the judgment of God to find the grace and mercy of God. The wrath and judgment of God releases His power, dominion and might. The grace and mercy of God releases His love, His wonder, His awe and His compassion. For me, I would rather have the wrath and the judgment hit me up front and the grace, mercy, wonder and awe that comes out the other side, than to stand here wanting to receive the awe, wonder, grace and mercy and have the judgment go somewhere else. I would rather be judged now than judged in that day.

All of us have to face these kinds of things that go on in the spirit around us. God is still crying, "Adam, where are you?" God is still crying out for a relationship, for more people who can come into intimacy with Him and share His life with Him. This is not just sharing your life with Him, you need to share His life. Then you get to know about Him, what His heart is and what He wants, what He says and what He does. It is exciting up there!

FEAR

Another thing that can stop you is the fear of the spirit world. Through the generations we have been taught by the media, by movies and demonic spiritual experiences, to fear the spirit world and any contact with it. This fear is a fortress mentality that greatly hinders our spiritual experience with God. The reason it is like that is because those things have presented a picture that the demonic world is stronger than the believers; and we believe it! I have watched the movie The Exorcist. It shows the believers as weak and vulnerable to the demonic world, when it should be that demons are weak and vulnerable to the Kingdom world. But this is the conditioning of the realm of the demonic so that they can maintain their position, because everything is about position in the spirit. So if they can keep us afraid of this realm, then they have the position and then they have the power and the authority. That is why they are still in the heavens. It is because we have not been there and confronted them.

For some of you this is really stretching your brain! It is good because it is frying some of the transistors of your religious processes and structures. God made the heavenly places and that is where Adam lived before he fell. He gave Adam authority over all of it. How do you think the devil got that power? How do you think he got the world? It is because Adam was booted out of it. If there is not somebody to guard it then something else will fill it, and the devil has just filled it. He has filled the seat of government.

'Heavenly Place' is what it is called. The only reason he is there is because we have not taken our place as sons of God in the 'Heavenly Places' in Christ Jesus and the anointing of the Son (Ephesians 2:6). It is the anointing that gives you access to have dominion. The anointing is the power that gives the tools from God and the mandate to do the work. People say you cannot do these things, but I have been doing them for over twenty-five years.

The fear that stops us from entering the realm of Heaven is the same fear that ties us to the earth. That same fear goes all the way back to the Garden of Eden when Adam and Eve sinned and they hid themselves from the presence of God. It is this same fear that we have to face today. Exactly the same thing: "I am a man of sin". Well, hallelujah! There is provision for that by the blood. Do something about it.

The difference between a demonic encounter and a godly encounter is that one is based on death and fear, but the other is based on life and abundance. The realm of revelation is the stepping-stone to the realm of visitation. Once we have been attuned, with our transistors and our mind tuned to the area of revelation, we receive from the Word by our process of learned extraction. We put it into our lives and receive revelation. Visitation is on its heels.

VISITATION

Revelation is all about you watching something happen. Visitation is all about you going there and doing something. I do not want to just watch something happen. I do not want to just watch other people do things. I want to go over there and do them first.

There is a restoration of lost things going on in the realm of the Kingdom right now that is preparing the church, for those who would receive it. One of the things that has been lost in the church is the arena of government. I mean world government, not just church government; but we have lost that too in many ways. God is dismantling the processes of some of the human structures that have been put in place, and there are other things that are already trying to fill it. Some of these human structures are just not right, they are okay but they are earthly. For those who experience the realm of Heaven, who chase after it to go into that place where God is, God is going to put you together because He wants a family. I do not just share my meal with just my son, or just one of my daughters or only my wife. I love the whole family. It is great being around the table when there is a group of you. Why? Because you can talk, you can share things and you can laugh together. Now if that is in the natural, how much more so in the realm of the spirit. God wants to take someone from Russia and China and America and New Zealand and put us together around the table. Why? So we can talk!

Within the next five to ten years you are going to find that there are things that suddenly crop up in the church all over the world. You will be saying, "Well, we did not know anything about this doctrine, but suddenly it is everywhere" It is going to be like that because there will be people who are going into Heaven and sharing revelation. There is going to be a standard set where true government is exercised in the spirit over the earth, and suddenly the earth is going to respond to it.

I have been in that room; it is an amphitheatre. When I was first there, there were three people sitting in an approximately 20,000-seater amphitheatre. I walked inside and wailed in shock and awe. They shouted back, "We have waited so long!"

There are things that God is unlocking to the church and it is all about the Kingdom. It is all about being in the Kingdom and experiencing the Kingdom. If some of this is going over your head, that is okay, just work on the little bit that triggers your soul and your spirit. Work on that little bit that is important to you and generates a sense of going somewhere with God. You work on that bit and allow God to develop the rest. All He is looking for is one channel and when one is open and tuned then the rest come easily.

So how do you become attuned? Easy; by being discipled by another person who goes there. You need to be taught, in the same way as I have been taught by the Spirit of Knowledge; by going to its classroom. There are now fifteen or twenty people who sit there from the world of believers, when I go there. You see, the classroom is omnipresent, but the Spirit of Knowledge is not, it is one Spirit.

Now, you cannot take someone to a realm or a world you have never been to yourself. Unfortunately, there are many die-hards who are trying to do that. It is okay for a season, but there will come a time when God will say, "No" and they will die, because God does not mess around with this kind of activity. He tolerates it for a season and then He says, "No, you come home now, it is your time."

Another way to become attuned is familiarity with what the Word says; you need to read the Word and meditate in the Word. You need to purify and cleanse your imagination so there is no garbage in it, keep short accounts when you find something that disturbs you. As a guy, I see certain types of magazines all over the place, you can walk into a shop and they are right in front of your face. But if I look at them, "Oh God, Blood of Jesus, cleanse it out," and that is finished. Where is its power? It is not the actual seeing but the response that is the key. What goes on in your heart is the key. If you desire holiness and purity then you keep short accounts.

Also, dreaming about that reality, allowing your heart and mind to be captivated is a problem. What do we do? Record, review and revisit is the cycle of revelation training. How do you revisit the things you have experienced? First you must open your spirit to that reality again. Many people have had encounters with the realm of glory but then twenty-five years pass and they have not had another one. For some people it was five years ago, for some people it was three weeks ago. You must go back and review and revisit that encounter. You do it by praying in tongues first, opening your spirit, activating and drawing on the memory of that last experience and all that was connected with it.

One day a woman from America saw an amazing prophetic person of God giving her a goblet and she drank wine from this goblet. It was the most amazing experience. When I asked her how long ago it was, she said it was about two years ago. I asked her what she did with it and she replied, "What do you mean?" I told her she had to go back and review, revisit and write it down because that is the doorway to the rest of it. I asked her, "Do you know what the hand was like that fed it to you? What do you know about the room that it was sitting in? In fact, do you know what was in the bottom of the goblet or what the colour of the wine was? Tell me what the goblet was like, tell me about the rings that were on the hand that fed you the goblet. What was the person like who fed it to you? What was the room like?"

Encounters with the realm of glory are doorways that open up possibility, but you can only go back when you revisit them. So I spend time praying in tongues, focusing on the recall of the last experience. That is fantastic. Then it develops and becomes exciting; then it becomes awe inspiring; then it becomes hard work because you need to write down how you did it. It has taken me twelve years to get some of this down on paper.

It is hard work going through the process of what to do; pray in the spirit, recall what happened in your imagination and make a choice to step back into that window of the experience. I can remember the first time I ever had an angelic experience. I was busy praying, "Father I thank You for Your Word that is like a sword. Father please show me what Your Word does when I am decreeing, 'You are defeated by the Blood of Jesus.' Show me what that does in the Spirit, please Father."

Then I found myself in another space, I was not in the room anymore, and there was a tall angel who smiled at me. He had a long sword on his side. He took the sword out. I had been decreeing in the realm of the spirit, "Father, it is finished!" When he took that sword out it had written on the sword, "Father it is finished!" The angel said, "You were the only person in the church who took that sword." The angel swung the sword and when it got to a certain point it went into eternity. Then it came back as a small sword again, he put it back in its scabbard and I was back in my room with my mouth open, catching flies, saying, "Wow!"

I could have just had that as a wonderful experience. I am very familiar with that angel now, it is great hanging around him, you do not feel scared of anything. But I had to make the choice to go back to that experience. I had to face the fear and the terror and the questions in my mind about what do I say and what do I do?!

Well, "Hi!" is a good start! You say "Hi!" and he says "Hi!" What do I say then? Well, you start talking, "Who are you?" That is another good thing; every angel has a name and the name represents who they are and their nature and character. If you find out their name, you become familiar with their nature and their character. Then when they are around, you can feel them in the atmosphere and they work on your behalf, because we are the heirs of salvation (Hebrews 1:14). They bring the liberty of Heaven when they come into a room. They only come in because you are familiar with them and they want to be a part of what you are doing. The angels want to look into the things we are looking into because they do not know about them, all they know is about Him. They are with Him, but they do not know about these things that have been destined for us that we investigate and find out about. They want to be a part of it, not only do they want to be a part of it, they want to help you into it. They are only too happy to help you into it, with cries of "let's go!" and you are out of there.

There is nothing like riding a fiery chariot. I said to the Lord one day, "Lord, I want to know what it is like when there are no demons around." Great question! What would it be like to not have the oppressive atmosphere anywhere? Then I started hearing a sound that told me that was a big mistake. It is called a fiery chariot and sounds like a steam train. It came into my room and I was going at the speed of thought away from the earth. I saw my city, my nation and the earth rush away from me to nothing. I was screaming! I love riding roller-coasters, they are the closest thing you can get to a fiery chariot ride in your life. I love them. In America I ride them over and over again! The most amazing thing is to end up in a place where the human eye has not been able to see, where there is no corruption. That amazing tranquillity and absolute peace is the realm that God wants us to walk in on the earth; having the peace of God just like that inside of us. The scariest thing is that they put me at the head, right on the front of the chariot.

When I was a kid I used to love riding yachts, ploughing through the water getting wet, then coming back, right on the front, with the coastline rushing into view. I saw our solar system, then the earth, and I was screaming and laughing, shouting, "Slow down!" I ended up in my room trying to catch my breath, you see, they enjoy relating with us. They think we are funny!

I can remember being in a church preaching the Word of God. The inside of the building had a great big beam that went across it. I was still learning about things in the spirit and about angels in those days. As I was busy preaching my eyes began to open and there was an angel, like one of those girls who swings around on gymnastics bars. Every time she reached the top she shouted, "Go Ian! Go Ian!" while I was trying to preach this serious message! The realm of the angelic is real. They are here because we are the sons of God and they want to be part of an inheritance. It is awesome.

Some of us might find feathers appear or other things because they will leave these little deposits. There is a door that the living creatures go through and when they go through it they move at lightning speed. When they go through the door they hit the side and there are feathers on the side. These feathers have eyes in them and because nothing dies they are still alive and you walk through it and all these eyes follow you! It is glorious – it is just great fun.

I talked before about trans-relocation so you can see that it is real. My first experience in this was probably around 1998 or 1999. What God is looking at doing is giving us supernatural capabilities that can override every single natural law. In one of the trans-relocation experiences I had with the Holy Ghost, He put me into a prison cell in an eastern country somewhere, and there was a guy who was a believer, beaten up on this bed, absolutely smashed – eyes, nose, teeth – just messed up. I did not know what was going on, nobody talked about trans-relocation in those days. I just turned up. I said to him in English, "I am here, God has put me here." He replied, "I know", through his broken teeth. I laid hands on him, and like a paintbrush going over him, everything in his body came into divine order. I am standing there saying, "Oh yes, bring it on Jesus!" and he is also saying, "Bring it on Jesus!" When you are in a prison cell you do not make a noise because you will get beaten more. But he had got his hands up over his head shouting in victorious joy, "Hallelujah I'm free, I'm healed!" I heard these heavy footsteps coming down the passageway. The door has a little spike on it that was turned sideways and an eye looked through. Then I heard this shout and a gun came out and I heard a shot. Now, am I in the spirit or am I in the natural?! I saw the bullet come out of the end of the gun and then everything slowed down. It started coming towards me and I was thinking, "God, get me out of here, now!" Then the whole spirit world 'flashed' and I was not there anymore.

God wants us to experience some of these things. I have also been trans-relocated into a place where I have not been taken out of the situation, and I have ended up with physical marks on my body. My kids have seen them. That is okay, it is part of the price of doing those kinds of things. But let me tell you, it is glorious!

Chapter 3
Unrepented Imaginations

I want to teach on the mind and the problems we have with the images inside our mind.

"Now faith is the substance of things hoped for, the evidence of things not seen" (Hebrews 11:1).

This can be translated as, "Faith is a tangible reality of the things dreamed about that are yet in vision form." God is looking to see what captivates your heart, because whatever captivates your heart you will begin to believe and then you will have faith for it to happen for you. That is why you need to allow the Word to captivate your heart.

Faith is a tangible reality of things we have dreamed about, illustrating the importance for us to dream about the realm of the Kingdom of Heaven. The only way you are going to dream about it is to have an anchor for that reality to come over and do what is needed. There has been much talk about our need to have faith but we want to know how to have faith.

I grew up in a Baptist Church and I was a deacon at the age of nineteen because I was out there on the edge, crazy for Jesus! I was un-tempered, wild and woolly haired. I used to love sharing and getting into discussions with the elders. I knew nothing about the Word except what I had seen. We would talk about Heaven and these guys would throw the Word at me and I had my answers. It was really wonderful, a great period in my life.

I can remember going to one of the elders, as God was speaking to me about faith and I needed to understand the issue of faith. I went to one guy and said, "Tell me about faith, what is it?" He patted me on the shoulder and said, "Oh brother Ian, you have just got to have faith." I do not know about you, but when I hear religious people I can feel so frustrated. So, I went home and began to get on my face and pray. When you begin to get on your face and pray you need to keep knocking. You do not just knock, saying "Oh God, I want this to happen today" and expect it to happen. It is in the persistence in pursuing God that God will answer with revelation. You need to chase Him.

It is like the parable Jesus painted:

"Imagine that one of your friends comes over at midnight. He bangs on the door and shouts, "Friend, will you lend me three loaves of bread? A friend of mine just showed up unexpectedly from a journey, and I don't have anything to feed him." Would you shout out from your bed, "I'm already in bed, and so are the kids. I already locked the door. I can't be bothered"? You know this as well as I do: even if you didn't care that this fellow was your friend, if he keeps knocking long enough, you'll get up and give him whatever he needs simply because of his brash persistence! So listen: Keep on asking, and you will receive. Keep on seeking, and you will find. Keep on knocking, and the door will be opened for you. All who keep asking will receive, all who keep seeking will find, and doors will open to those who keep knocking" (Luke 11:5-10 VOICE).

This is just a type of what we are supposed to do with God. If He does not answer, you carry on knocking until He does give you the answer.

My kids say, "Dad...Dad...Dad...Dad…Dad…Dad" In the end I say to them, "What do you want?" "Oh, I need this..." "Okay, here you are" just to get some peace!

How much more access do we have to God in the spirit to say, "Dad, Dad...Dad..." He will say, "Here, just give me some rest!"

What God is looking for is your persistence in faith. Without faith it is impossible to please Him, for you must believe that He 'is' (Hebrews 11:6). Faith is a tangible thing. It is not some fluffy, cloudy, wonderful thing out there; it is a tangible substance that is in the spirit. You have a spirit gateway of faith (more in the Gateways chapter). That gateway is supposed to function. The only way you are going to get it to function is if you begin to work with it. You can only work with it when you have the Word. You begin to believe the Word, you allow it to captivate your mind and you dream about it. Dream about going through doorways. It captivates me because it is my entry point into Heaven.

What captivates your heart will begin to be released around your life, because what captivates your inner man begins to become real for you. God wants you to be caught with the potential possibility of the things you are dreaming about. Faith is the reality of Heaven around your life.

Hebrews 11 is full of men and women who were captivated by a dream or a vision of what could be. It says they were sawn in half, they were chewed up by animals and they had their body parts cut off. There were the most horrendous things done to believers but the Bible says that they died believing. They did not see it in their day but they are going to see it in our day. They are called 'men in white linen' (Revelation 15:6; 19:8; 19:14) and they are coming back. It is another thing that God is going to reveal to the church. We have a part in their inheritance and they have a part in our inheritance. They died believing for another glorious encounter.

I love the life of Jesus. I meditate around what He does. Have you ever wondered what it would be like to walk through people? The Bible says all the people:

"were filled with wrath, and rose up and thrust Him out of the city; and they led Him to the brow of the hill on which their city was built, that they might throw Him down over the cliff. Then passing through the midst of them, He went His way" (Luke 4:28-30).

Jesus walked through them and they could not touch Him. It does not mean they made a pathway for Him to walk through. Imagine you have fifteen thousand people standing around you and you can walk through them as they cannot touch you! These are the things that you need to begin to dream about. They are in the Bible.

I want to be like some of these men of old:

"Then the Spirit lifted me up, and I heard behind me a great thunderous

voice: "Blessed is the glory of the Lord from His place!" I also heard the noise of the wings of the living creatures that touched one another, and the noise of the wheels beside them, and a great thunderous noise. So the Spirit lifted me up and took me away, and I went in bitterness, in the heat of my spirit; but the hand of the Lord was strong upon me. Then I came to the captives at Tel Abib, who dwelt by the River Chebar; and I sat where they sat, and remained there astonished among them seven days" (Ezekiel 3:12-15).

Why astonished? Because God had shifted him six hundred miles, just like that.

You need to allow the potential possibility of what is in the Word of God to captivate your heart with that reality. It is this reality that the church is missing: the reality of the realm of the Kingdom of Heaven. You need to allow Heaven to captivate your heart and captivate your mind. It can only captivate your mind by you dreaming and having faith that what the Word says is true and is possible.

Trans-relocation has been going on for me for about nine years now. It is a wonderful experience to go and do things in other nations without having to travel in an aeroplane. I cannot do it voluntarily yet, but it has been going on for me involuntarily, by the Lord, for over a decade. It took me three years of studying the Word to begin to believe that it could happen for me. It took me being captivated in my mind and heart, praying "God I thank You that I can be in the spirit: body, soul and spirit. Lord, just with my spirit You can shift me and move me. You did it in the Bible for Philip, You did it in the Bible for these men of old and You did it there for Jesus."

Have you ever tried walking on water? I have. It has not worked yet, but we need to dream about it. Faith is the thing that activates your dream; faith releases the power of God on your behalf to see your dream come to pass. The Bible says God grants us the desires of our heart (Psalm 37:4). So what are you desiring? Is it more money? Riches? To see angels? What are you desiring? Because what you desire will captivate your heart and release faith for you all around your life. Whatever gets released around your life will be displayed, first in the secret place, then openly. But you can only develop it by dreaming in the secret place, spending the time with

God passionately pushing in, with tongues. "Father You are going to shift me, I am going to go through a door. Because it happened to these other people, it can happen to me. Your Word says that everything that is in the Word is possible for me. Father, today by faith I step into that door. I step into that door in Jesus' Name." Begin to push into the reality of the potential the Word has painted for you. Then it becomes real.

Our biggest problem is what goes on in our minds. Uncontrolled reasoning destroys faith. You must understand that your soul does not want your spirit to have dominion. Your soul will do absolutely anything to reason away a miracle and say, "Oh, it is only for the spiritual few." What a load of religious baloney! One of our greatest troubles has been a false spirit like the Pharisees and Sadducees. Jesus said about them:

"But woe to you, scribes and Pharisees, pretenders (hypocrites)! For you shut the kingdom of heaven in men's faces; for you neither enter yourselves, nor do you allow those who are about to go in to do so" (Matthew 23:13 AMP).

There has been a doctrine that it is only for the select few. That is one of the biggest lies the enemy has propagated in the Body of Christ. They say it is only for the spiritual few, but we are all spirits. We all have access to the same thing. What God wants is for you to believe, and believing is based on dreaming. Dreaming goes on in your imagination. Your imagination is one of the key vital points of connection with the presence and the realm of Heaven. God always speaks in pictures. Man as a body worldwide, has taught the church how to hear, not how to see. Often in the Bible when you find an encounter with God, it says that "the Word of the Lord came" and "I saw", then "I heard" (Chronicles 9:6, Job 13:1, Matthew 13:17, Revelation 14:1-2).

We have taken the Word of the Lord as hearing the voice of God. It is not just hearing the voice of God. The Word of the Lord is a door that enables you to see and then you hear. The only reason we can hear so clearly is because we have been taught how to do it. The reason you cannot see is because you have not been taught how to do it. I am trying to give you some simple things that enable you to see. It is actually not hard. It is a learned process that goes, A-B-C-D-E and you get F. That is the way it happens.

"God....calls those things which do not exist as though they did" (Romans 4:17)

Right now you may not feel you are experiencing this, but the reality is that you are, because you are a spirit being. So you live in this trans-dimensional conflict, and because you have only ever experienced one dimension you never believe the other will happen. We need to begin to call the reality of the thing we are not experiencing as if it were.

It is actually all about faith, believing that what you are doing and what you are dreaming about is going to come to pass for you. God will do it, He will open the door, because:

"He is a rewarder of those who diligently seek Him" (Hebrews 11:6).

It requires you meditating and allowing your mind to be captivated by the Word of God. It is like sucking on a lolly. It is a lovely lolly, the potential inside it is just amazing, but we cannot taste it. Sometimes in fact it tastes pretty awful. The reason it tastes awful is because the wrapper has been left on. Many of us as believers have left the wrapper on the revelation of the Word of God. We want the goodness in it but we leave the wrapper on it. The wrapper is our religious behaviour and practices. God wants us to take the lolly out of its wrapper. You take it out by meditating and focusing on it and working with it. As we take the Word out of its wrapper it looks fantastic. We can look at it all we like, but we will not taste it until we put it into our mouths. Many believers are at that stage; they need it out of the wrapper and they are going, "Wow! That can happen, look at that. Whoa! what a wonderful vision I have had." But it is not until you take it by faith that you have the full experience.

Many of us do not believe the Word is true. We do not believe the Word will do what it says it is going to do. We do not believe it is going to activate what it says it is going to activate and what it says is possible for you and me. So we leave it nicely wrapped up in a nice little container so we can control it. God wants us to die to controls. He wants us to be free because:

"where the Spirit of the Lord is, there is liberty" (2 Corinthians 3:17).

Dreaming does not just involve your imagination. You are a triune being. You have a spirit, a soul and a body. When I am dreaming I get my whole spirit man involved in my dream. I make my soul do what my spirit man wants it to do. How do I do this? I do it by practising. I make my soul bow the knee to my spirit. I can pray in tongues aloud or quietly, with nothing coming out of my mouth. What God is looking for is submission and surrender. When you are submitted in surrender you will then have the resurrection of the surrender. It is faith in the Word of God that enables that surrender to happen. It is you exercising the muscles of your spirit until your soul says "I give up". The most wonderful thing is that your spirit will transform your soul.

Our biggest struggle is with sin. The reason we struggle with sin is because we try to discipline it from the outside in, instead of transforming it from the inside out. If you struggle with areas of sin in your life you need to get the flow of the glory of God going from your spirit man into those areas. You will see what happens then. God wants to change and transform these areas of your life, change the nature of the way they function. It can only change when fire comes near. God wants the fire near the areas of our struggle. He wants the glory because the glory will change our nature, but you are the one who has the choice to let the glory in.

"Casting down arguments and every high thing that exalts itself against the knowledge of God, bringing every thought into captivity to the obedience of Christ" (2 Corinthians 10:5).

The issues in our minds that we struggle with are things that are in high places that exalt themselves against the knowledge of God. Knowledge of God is based on faith and revelation. It is based on the reality of what the Word says; not just written knowledge, but revelation knowledge. The Bible says to cast down everything that exalts itself against this revelation knowledge. Some of the biggest struggles we have are in our imagination. You are busy praying and the glory of God is in your room, then a picture appears in your mind and the spiritual atmosphere dispels. We want to deal with those pictures, because it is these things that stop us from receiving revelation. That is the high thing that has got to submit to the glory of God that is inside of you. You do not submit it by controlling it; you submit it by burning it and purifying it.

Years ago a young woman who was a prostitute came to me.

She had been in that field of sin for about nine years. She got born again and God began to speak to her and she wanted to get married. I can remember praying with this woman and watching God cleanse and restore her life. I remembered going through my own imagination and cleaning it, so I passed this revelation onto her and said "This is what I want you to do: take as many of the people's faces you remember and bring them under the Blood of Jesus; wipe them with the Blood." She went away and three months later she came back to me. She said, "Ian, I am free!" Why? Because the Blood of Jesus had restored and healed her. All she had done was taken the reality that I had given to her and by faith applied it to her life. Then she met this guy, they got married, they went on their honeymoon and she said, "Ian, I was a virgin again on my wedding night with my husband!" God had restored her body to her again.

This is an amazing testimony. God is able to restore purity to a woman that has been defiled like that. I mean absolute purity, not just emotionally and spiritually, but physically as well. Praying with her before the wedding I was going to say some things to her about that but I thought, "No, you can't do that." It was just going beyond the boundaries of what my mind thought was possible. When it happened it blew me away. I had to actually repent for not speaking out the revelation at the time that would have encouraged her.

The things we are talking about are real. They are real keys. I have worked with them for twenty-two years and they work. Dealing with these images is vitally important to our lives. To be able to build faith you need to deal with the garbage. You need to take something out and then put something back in again. Taking the garbage out means I need to acknowledge that I have this area, this thing in my mind. I need to take that picture, cleanse and restore it and then take the Blood of Jesus and paint the picture out. Then it is gone.

I now know people who have worked on this and now cannot remember what actually happened anymore. That is what Paul says:

"Forgetting those things which are behind and reaching forward to those things which are ahead" (Philippians 3:13).

The word 'forgetting' means I cannot remember anymore. That is what you do when you forget. The only reason these people could not remember actual events was because of the glory; the work the glory had done in their life.

It is no different with us. The glory will work on your life when you give it the opportunity to do so. It does not matter what has happened to you, the Blood of Jesus can purify everything. This is one of the vital keys I use when I am counselling people. I give them homework consisting of going home and working with that Blood over their lives. I am not going to do it for them. I am not going to stand there and pray for them for hours and hours. They need to go and do their own work and get their own testimony. Until I started doing this nothing ever happened for me. The moment I chose to begin to work like this, my life began to change, because the Blood of Jesus sanctifies and takes away the dust and the mark of the devil on our lives. It is the Blood of Jesus that does that for us.

"If anyone desires to come after Me, let him deny himself, and take up his cross daily, and follow Me." (Luke 9:23)

Your cross is not your husband or your wife or your family. Your cross is the nature of sin that you wrestle with in your own personal life. That is what you need to carry. You need to take that to the Cross, bear it and exchange it. The Cross is a place of exchange, where you take your garbage and you put it on and into Christ. Then you take His resurrection, freedom and life, receiving it in exchange. As far as I am concerned I have got the better part of the deal.

Jesus has already done that for us, He has already accomplished everything in your life to full resurrection and full transfiguration. Jesus has already done it. We just might not have caught up with that reality yet. It is this reality that God wants to bring us into. So we are going to practise.

ACTIVATION

I want you to stand up, put your hands on your belly and pray in tongues for a couple of minutes. When you have done that, take an image in your mind that you have wrestled with. I want you to draw it to mind, look at it and acknowledge it. Not to sin after it, lust after it or to be controlled by it, but to acknowledge it as sin, because to own something means you can repent of it. You need to go through the process of repenting while you are still praying in tongues, because everything must happen in the spirit. Sometimes I transfer on and off from English to the spirit. I just work with the Holy Spirit because I have learned that I can pray in the spirit in English just as easily as I can pray in the tongue of an angel. It is just as easy to pray in tongues in English, it is something you can learn to do.

When I take an image I take that Blood of Jesus in my imagination and a paintbrush, painting out that original poster. You can do whatever will work for you in your imagination. I have meditated around this process for so long that I am absolutely captivated by it and I know in my own life and experience of other people that this works.

I want you to take that picture and hang it in the spirit realm and look at it. Then take the Blood of Jesus and begin to paint that picture out with the Blood.

Now, praying in tongues, turn towards Heaven, the Kingdom that is in you. "Father, I thank You that I am a spirit being, thank You Father that my spirit is the candle of the Lord and is alive to Your presence. I thank You, Father, that Your authority and dominion, the realm of Heaven, lives inside of my spirit."

After about two minutes, keeping your eyes closed and still praying in tongues I want you to take another image of a thing that you struggle with. I want you to take it, pin it up in your imagination, acknowledge it as sin and repent of it. While still praying in tongues and holding it up, I want you to take that Blood and begin to paint it out, redeeming it by the Blood of Jesus Christ. I will give you some examples of how I pray through this process.

"Father, today, in the Name of Jesus I take the Blood that redeems. Father there is power in that Blood to restore my soul. There is power in the Blood of Jesus to cleanse me from the defilement of the controls of my soul. Father, today I take that picture in Jesus' Name. I take the Blood and I begin to paint it with the Blood. Thank You Holy Spirit. Jesus I wipe that picture out with Your Blood. I speak to that picture and declare today that you are redeemed from the power of the enemy and I am redeemed from your influence today. I decree today that I am redeemed by the Blood from its power; I am redeemed from its influence. I am free from its hold over my life today, in the Name of Jesus Christ!"

You can then take another image and repeat the process. When you can walk through this process you can keep short accounts and it makes it easy on your life. Do not forget to celebrate the victory – shout His praises – Hallelujah Lord Jesus!

Chapter 4
Using the Word as a Doorway

I love using the Word of God as a doorway or entry into the realm of Heaven. The Word is a barometer and the plumb line to all that is spiritual. Almost every spiritual experience, whether via revelation or visitation, in some way is anchored in the Word. What I mean by an anchor is a foundation or basis for an experience to stand upon. The Word of God must become the doorway of our entry into the realm of Heaven for our experiences to be legitimate. It is a wonderful thing to walk in Heaven with God, but it is not just to make us feel good. I never ever chase the experience, I chase God who gives the experience. There are two ways to pursue seeing God; one is with your spirit, and the other is with the Word of God. In this chapter I want to help you to use the Word as a doorway of entry into the realm of Heaven.

Although the Bible is the key that unlocks Heaven, it does not tell you everything that goes on in Heaven – that is our job to discover. The Bible says very clearly, *"There are many other things Jesus did. If every one of them were written down, I suppose the whole world would not be big enough for all the books that would be written"* (John 21:25 EXB). Not everything that goes on in Heaven or everything I have seen in Heaven is in the Bible. But the Word of God needs to be the anchor for our experiences of Heaven and the place that we begin our experiences.

I can remember working with the Word and trying to understand how this process happens. Reasoning with our human minds destroys faith when used in a negative manner. So many people are so full of the Word, they reason with the Word, and they reason away faith. They reason away the belief that we can enter the Kingdom. I have people say, "You gotta have the Word, brother", and I say, "I gotta have the revelation of the Word, brother." Unless you get revelation of the Word, you will be feeding from something dry. I need the revelation that brings the Word alive. Using the Word as a door opens access points so I can enter into the spiritual arena. You need to understand that what you see around you came out of the realm of the spirit. Every single thing in nature had its origins in the realm of the spirit.

The Bible describes being in the spirit, John says, *"I was in the Spirit on the Lord's Day"* (Revelation 1:10). You can be present physically in the earth but present with the Lord in your spirit. There is a difference between being in the spirit with your spirit, being in the spirit with your spirit and your soul and being in the spirit with your spirit, soul and body. So there are three different dimensional realms we can walk in as believers.

God's objective is to bring revelation about the realm of Heaven to the body of Christ. If we only do what we have always done, we will only get what we have always got. I do not know about you, but I am tired of what we have got. Trans-relocation is not a problem for God. It is our problem because we are not going there and doing that.

The Bible says, *"For we do not wrestle against flesh and blood, but against principalities, against powers, against the rulers of the darkness of this age, against spiritual hosts of wickedness in the heavenly places"* (Ephesians 6:12). The Bible also says, *"He raised us up with Him and seated us in the heavenly realms..."* (Ephesians 2:6 VOICE). They are the same realm – it is a place of dominion where authority is exercised. The only reason they are there is because you and I do not go there.

When I was in Canada leading an intensive conference, this guy who was a three day old believer came to the conference. No one had ever said to him 'you can't see in the spirit'. He was in the meeting saying, "Wow can you guys see that?" And the others were asking, "See what?" He was saying "wow"... All he needed was permission and someone to say, "You can see, I can see – yes, look at that, I can see." It was really astonishing to me that without all the doctrinal garbage this young man experienced the glory, and over a two day intensive he went from a new son into a mature son. God changed his life radically, because he could see, engage, encounter and participate with what was going on in the Kingdom world. I asked him if he was afraid of demons and he said, "What demons? I don't see demons, I just see the glory and I see the angels". Why? Because that is what I told him he was going to see. So that is all he looked at. He was not interested in the other stuff. It is the church and the religious system that seem concerned about that stuff. The religious system has told us that we cannot use our imagination, because when we do we are going to be deceived, and when we are deceived God will hate us. So we become more afraid of deception than we desire the truth.

The Bible says, *"I chased my enemies; I caught up with them and did not turn back until all were conquered. ...I placed my feet upon their necks. ... My enemies quail before me and fall defeated at my feet"* (Psalm 18:37-39 TLB). And when John turned he saw, *"One like the Son of Man... His eyes like a flame of fire; His feet were like fine brass, as if refined in a furnace..."* (Revelation 1:13-15). When you have brassy feet the enemy cannot deal with and bruise your life, but you certainly can crush his head.

POLLUTION OF THE SOUL

The Word of God needs to be the place that anchors our imagination. There is a lot said in the body of Christ today about fear of the imagination. The reason some of us are afraid of the imagination is because of the pollution that the imagination is caught in. The imagination is very important in the realm of the spirit. It is a screen in your mind, but an unsanctified imagination with all the garbage that sits on it stops the flow of the glory. We looked at how to deal with this in Chapter 3, *Unrepented Imaginations.*

There can be other barriers inside our lives. Often it is the destructive controls that we have allowed to be exerted through Adam's sin in us that resists and hinders the Kingdom realm becoming real and ours. Often your soul will not want to have anything to do with God because it must surrender control and dominion over your spirit for Holy Spirit and the Kingdom to manifest. The Word says, *"For the word of God is living and powerful, and sharper than any two-edged sword, piercing even to the division of soul and spirit..."* (Hebrews 4:12). The Word is the basis that divides the control of your soul from your spirit. Your spirit must have dominion. God changes our spirit, transforms our soul, and transfigures our body. We are a spirit being first, which means that our spirits must have the supremacy and authority.

The problem is that the destructive controls of the nature of the body that we live in, the thing that we are currently subject to, is the thing that controls the flow of the spirit. You need to take the Word, which is where meditation comes in. Meditation allows the Word to become a divider and break the control of your soul off your spirit. Your body and your soul wrap around your spirit and hold on tight when you are on the earth because your soul does not want to surrender its power. Your soul has got to be crucified. It is called the natural or carnal man and it has to die. *"And those who are Christ's have crucified the flesh with its passions and desires"* (Galatians 5:24). You need to go and visit the cross, without the cross there is nothing, absolutely nothing. Without the Blood of Jesus there is no purity, absolutely none. Jesus has done everything He can. Jesus even tore the twelve inch thick woven veil in Jerusalem, which was solid material, so that you and I could come in and experience the realm of Heaven. Not just one or two people or high priests. The Bible calls us a kingdom of priests. We are a kingdom of priests that have a right. We have a legal mandated right by God to go into Heaven.

INTERNAL WELLSPRING

Have you ever seen those old clunky western pumps? When someone pumped the handle, water would come out. But would you like to drink the first flow of water that comes out? No, none of us would. Well your life is no different. You have had a still well sitting in your life for years. When you first start to prime the pump you are going to have all sorts of rubbish and little worms come out. But if you carry on clanking the pump, pure water will start coming out. Then you can drink it. But you have got to prime the pump, because when you first start this process your mind will start to interfere, all this stuff will start happening, and the worms will start saying, "You can't do this, you can't do that.... how dare you do that". You might have this conversation with a demon inside your brain, because it wants to stay buried inside your imagination so it can use you to do what it wants to do. So you have to prime the pump of your spirit man to get the water flowing again and take the rocks out of the well. There are different kinds of wells we have in our life. We each have a wellspring – we have to take the rock and the cap off the wellspring and get it flowing. But once the gateway has been opened you begin to learn and enjoy it. Then you can start getting into the flow of participating in it and building the whole arena of the Kingdom around your life.

Once practised this process is a lot easier to facilitate us entering the realms of God. When you first start as already discussed in Chapter 3, often unbidden invasions happen through old patterns inside your mind, because your mind does not want to let go of its control over your spirit. The key to overcoming this is dealing with it and staying focused. Too many of us are still trying to get information flowing from the outside in, instead of from the inside out. This is because we are still trying to feed from the tree of the knowledge of good and evil, instead of the tree of life that is in the midst of us in the paradise of God. God may speak in word pictures when He speaks. Often unless His voice is very clear He will speak in vision or in word pictures inside your head.

The Bible says that Jesus is the high priest of our confession. Confession is *homologeo* in the Greek, meaning to say the same thing as another, or to agree. So if Jesus is saying the same thing as you are saying, why do we talk about our crud so much? The church is unthankful. We have too much on our list of struggles. The enemy has us too focused on our struggles because we have not been into Heaven to be cleaned from them. You go into Heaven to get cleaned. When you are there you become clean, and you become the righteousness of God on the face of the earth (see Chapter 11, *The Courtroom of God*). Everything gets removed.

Everything shifts. You start shifting from first gear to fourth gear and travelling 190MPH instead of 9MPH. It is like getting hold of a 5000 kilowatt power source as oppose to a 250 kilowatt power source. One will fry your hands, the other will fry your whole body. God wants us to be transformed into His image and it takes fire. Fire does not just burn, the heat changes the chemical formula and structure of whatever the fire is manifesting over. The chemical formula change releases gas, and the gas is displayed as flame, so that the subject's nature changes. That is why God is a consuming fire; He wants to change our nature. The function of God's fire is not just to burn, consume and destroy, but to change nature to bring life.

THRONE OF GRACE

The Bible says "*Let us therefore come boldly unto the throne of grace, that we may obtain mercy and find grace to help in time of need*" (Hebrews 4:16 KJ21). So does it mean to say you just sit there? No, it means you go in the spirit before the throne, and until you go you will never get hold of the government of the grace of God in your life, because you go to the throne of the government of God – of the grace of God, where the grace is released to your life, which is the power and the will to do His will. So I go to an arena of the government of Heaven where the grace can become mine. The Word says to go there, you come boldly to obtain the grace. The word *obtain* means to seize hold of and take. You have a right as a son to go into the supernatural world, into the arena of the government of God and seize hold of that government from the throne of the grace (unmerited favour), and pull it to yourself. Then you obtain the power and the will to do His will, and mercy to help in time of need. Notice your need comes right at the end. It does not say you come with your need before that throne. It says you come to that throne first, then maybe by the end you have not got any need left.

PERSISTENT PURSUIT OF GOD

When we first start using the Word it can take time to develop the anchors inside our head for the supernatural world to accumulate information on. Sometimes even up to three weeks for it to become a revelation for me. So I would focus on one passage of scripture, meditating around that scripture trying to imagine what it would be like to be there and revolve it around in my head until the dials and gauges began to lock in with the truth. Revelation takes persistence, and generally takes time, persistently pursuing the presence of God. It is about spending the time with God and making your mind conform to the Word of God, as the Bible says, "*...be transformed from the inside out by renewing your mind*" (Romans 12:2 VOICE). The only way you are going to be transformed is when your mind is renewed. God wants our minds to be changed. He wants us to persistently pursue Him with the knowledge that He wants to give us revelation and visitation. I have called it the passionate pursuit of the presence of the person of God for the promise of the power of the provision of God.

So what you find is that it is your pursuit of Him and the passion that gets released that releases the promise and the provision of the power that is ours. It is all about passion in the end, and passion comes back to Him. Everything comes back to intimacy, everything.

We must persistently gaze upon the door to the abode of God so that we can enter into the realm of God. The Word describes Jacob seeing the gate to the abode of God in Genesis 28. The real issue is that we must enter it, not just see it. God's cry is for us to come up to Him. From the day He put Adam out of the garden it has never stopped. God's cry is still for us to come into Eden and to enjoy the experience with Him as our Father and our friend; to walk with Him in His arena. The cry in the heart of God for fellowship, friendship, and relationship has never stopped. From the day He stood there in the garden calling Adam, "*Where are you?*" (Genesis 3:9), He was not saying "Adam why have you sinned", He was saying "I am separated, I cannot feel you anymore".

LEARN AND PRACTISE THE PATHWAY

If I were the first person coming into church and all the lights were off, it was pitch black and I had to walk from the front door to the auditorium but I did not know the building, I would walk through the door, hit the handle, hit the seats, knock my knee, stumble over a chair, hit somebody's bag and fall flat on my face trying to get there. But if I had been in the church for years, when I walked in and out of the building I would know the pathway. So if it were pitch black I could walk down the pathway not touching a single thing. Have you ever been inside a house you do not know and tried to find the restroom at nighttime? Whack.... Owwww!! The reason is you do not know the pathway.

The Bible says, *"The spiritual did not come first, but the physical, and then the spiritual"* (1 Corinthians 15:46 EXB). It is like that with us in the spirit. You have to learn and practise the pathway. You practise the pathway by having an anchor in the Word, by meditating on the Word, allowing the Word to captivate you and take you on a journey to the point of that door. Once you find that door then you go on to perfection. We must go on and not get stuck at one spiritual experience. Do not ever get stuck – there is far more in Heaven than your life could ever contain.

JESUS PAINTS PICTURES

It is amazing how the Bible has painted many pictures for us about somebody else's experience with the supernatural world, and yet very few believers have their own experiences, even though the pastel painted dimensional pictures have been presented to us in written form. Pictures are painted in the Bible by what is said and what is done. A picture is a doorway of entry for you to go into their experience and then use their experience to anchor your own experiences on. Then your own experiences become your anchor as you explore the Kingdom realm.

The only way that you are going to be able to see Heaven is to allow your mind to be captivated with the potential possibility of what Heaven is. That is why the foundation needs to be in the Word. Jesus spoke in pictures. Before there were written records of scripture on the earth, scripture was passed on orally by the spoken word and memorised, but the truth was never lost. The way it was described was in pictures because pictures carry a thousand words. Jesus painted pictures; that is what His parables were. Right from Genesis through to Revelation the Bible describes pictures, as it paints potential doorways for us to go through. Jesus, Father God and Holy Spirit have painted these pictures for you and me in the Bible and all we ever do is read them. We do not meditate around them, we do not spend time cultivating the potential possibility of what is there.

The Bible paints a single dimensional picture for us that reveals the possibility of what is behind it. I could describe a picture in a photograph to you – it is a wonderful picture of some wild lilies in another nation. Being in the place where we took the photo was an amazing experience, something like nine and a half thousand feet up in a mountain in Taiwan. The only reason you know it is in Taiwan is because I have told you, can you tell me which mountain it is? Can you tell me what the mountain looks like? You cannot because this is a single dimensional picture of what I saw when I was in Asia. But behind the picture is the mountain and behind the picture is the doorway to that nation. This picture is a part of that nation, you cannot see the nation but you can see the picture. The Word of God is like that, it paints a single dimensional picture for us, which, once you meditate around, becomes a door to the potential possibility of what is behind it. All the Word does is paint the potential for you. Your mind and your heart need to be captivated with that potential. Whatever captivates your heart will captivate your mind. Whatever captivates your mind will frame your actions and your being. *"For as he thinks in his heart, so is he"* (Proverbs 23:7). The Word of God needs to be the anchor. God paints with more than a third of the Bible – your choice is the pursuit of God. You pursue God through the pictures He has made for us to come through, to enter Heaven and to chase Him.

Jesus when he talked often talked in pictures. The Hebrews spoke in picture form, they did not speak in Greek (word) form, they talked in pictures. This is how information was passed on in the Jewish traditions. It was by verbal communication by painting pictures so the stories could be held in the imagination and the hearts of the Jewish people. The Word of God is supposed to be like that. When we speak it, meditate on it, declare it and hold it in our heart, it is supposed to become a source of life to us – pictures that create the environment for us to believe and to contemplate what it could be like. God wants to unlock the reality of what it means to imagine, which is to do with the activity of meditating: revolving the picture around until it engages your spirit and becomes a doorway of entry. The Word of God is a single dimensional pastel painted picture of the possibilities of what can be stored in remembrance in a written form. It is stored in remembrance in a written form so that you can take the written form and with the strokes of the passages paint the picture in your imagination, and it starts inside your head.

When we are inside the Word in meditation, often in one sense we are unable to grasp or perceive everything that goes on. This is usually because our brain is not being wired and taught how to retain the information that God is downloading from our spirit into our soul. The soul is a transistor for the spiritual information that God gives us from the inside. Our spirit man receives it and our soul has to decipher that information. But our soul needs an anchor for that information to be retained. Your past experiences with God become an anchor for that revelation to sit on. When you are not able to grasp everything you are perceiving, that is when you must go and record, review and revisit. I love the re-visiting process because it becomes easier as you practise.

Many of us have been given doorways into the realm of Heaven by revelation and had wonderful spiritual experiences – years ago. People often say to me, "I've never had another one since." I say to them, "You know why – because you haven't used the one God gave you in the first place".

The artist Akiane Kramarik was considered amongst the twenty top geniuses in the world of art at age twelve. She paints the most amazing pictures. This is because Akiane goes into Heaven and when she is in Heaven she sees and then comes back and paints what she has seen. Akiane is recording a door in a visual way. The Bible is a written record of a visual door. If you can get, this is a major key.

I had someone say to me a while ago, "I don't need all this stuff you talk about, Ian. I get it from the Bible – I'll just go into the Word, I don't need to go into the spirit". And that is okay, horses for courses, you do what God has called you to do. I know what I want to pursue: I do not want to turn up in Heaven and discover it when I die. I do not believe that is the Lord's plan for believers in the earth today. God's plan is for you and I to experience Heaven today and then to bring the reality of Heaven into the harvest field.

ASCENSION – JACOB'S LADDER

"Now Jacob went out from Beersheba and went toward Haran. So he came to a certain place and stayed there all night, because the sun had set. And he took one of the stones of that place and put it at his head and he lay down in that place to sleep. Then he dreamed, and behold, a ladder was set up on the earth, and its top reached to heaven; and there the angels of God were ascending and descending on it. And behold, the LORD stood above it and said: "I am the LORD God of Abraham your father and the God of Isaac; the land on which you lie I will give to you and your descendants. Also your descendants shall be as the dust of the earth; you shall spread abroad to the west and the east, to the north and the south; and in you and in your seed all the families of the earth shall be blessed. Behold, I am with you and will keep you wherever you go, and will bring you back to this land; for I will not leave you until I have done what I have spoken to you. Then Jacob awoke from his sleep and said, "Surely the LORD is in this place, and I did not know it." And he was afraid and said, "How awesome is this place! This is none other than the house of God, and this is the gate of heaven!" (Genesis 28:10-17).

Jacob rested his head on a stone, fell asleep there and then he saw a ladder extending from the earth, which was anchored on the earth into Heaven; then he saw a door in Heaven. But Father God did not come down the ladder. He stood at the top of the ladder in the door waiting for Jacob to ascend and Jacob said "this is the House of God".

The church has been waiting at the bottom of the ladder for the last 300 years. There have been a few people who have gone up the ladder but have not told us that we can go up as well, which is my job, to tell you that you can go up as well. We can ascend into the presence of God, which means going up and going into Him. Have you ever wondered what it is like when you go up and go into God? Where is the Father? He is sitting on the throne. So when I go up and I go into Him, where am I? I am sitting on the throne in the Father. Where did Jesus see what the Father was doing? He was in Him, sitting on the throne in Him – Jesus made a way for us to be in Him. *"...As You, Father, are in Me, and I in You; that they also may be one in Us"* (John 17:21).

VISITATION

There is a difference between revelation and visitation. Meditation opens the gate to revelation; revelation opens the door to visitation. Revelation is when you see something. Many believers stop at that arena of revelation when they have an experience of seeing something going on in Heaven. Revelation must move to visitation. Visitation is where you participate and are actively involved in what is going on. Revelation is the process of enabling you to see the realm of the Kingdom with the eye of your understanding, enlightened to know the depth and breadth of our calling in God. That is what the Bible is supposed to do – open up revelation to us so we can see. But God does not want it to stop there – He does not want you just to see – He wants you to go in. Just like John in Revelation, *"... A door standing open in heaven. And the first voice which I heard was like a trumpet speaking with me, saying, "Come up here..."* (Revelation 4:1). There is a cry in the heart of God today, "Come up here!" God is tired of a one way street in relationship with us as a church. When we say, "God fill the house with Your presence", He is starting to say, "I'm bored with doing that". All we are getting is the fragrance of His presence. What God is after is for you to go visiting. When the Bible paints pictures of the doorways of Heaven, He paints an access point for you and me. We must use those access points. I have gone through probably 2,900 of those in the last ten or eleven years and it is amazing how you go through one door that leads you to another and you find they are all webbed together.

In Revelation 4, John has a most amazing encounter and as he is in the spirit having this encounter he sees a door. He did not get stuck at that one spiritual experience for the rest of his life. It is a progression – everything in the spirit must progress from one step to another, glory to glory. There are some key things in this verse that help springboard us into the type of revelatory activity that we need to get hold of. First it says, "He looked". You must make a choice to actually look, just like when you use your eyes you make a choice to turn your gaze from here to there and look. The same principle applies in the spirit world: when you look in the spirit you must make a choice to turn your attention onto something. It is amazing when you study the word *look*. What it means is to look on something, to actually focus on it and to engage the object you are looking at. The implication is to gaze with eyes wide open with an earnest continued inspection. Do you know what trances are – "Wow! Look at that"? All they are is a continued inspection of the thing that opened up in revelation. Revelation will lead to visitation. As a church and as a body of Christ we have to have the visitation today. God wants you to look at the Word until it becomes a picture for you. Scripture says, John was in the spirit and he looked. So the key is being in the spirit, you cannot do it here, you need to be in the spirit, which means we engage with the person of God and transition into His Kingdom with expectation to encounter His presence and once you are there then you can begin to look around you.

"Lift up your heads, O you gates!
And be lifted up, you everlasting doors!
And the King of glory shall come in" (Psalm 24:7).

Doors are very important for our role as sons because doors are points of entry that are open to the earth. Unless we occupy a door and use it, something else will occupy it and shut it down. Our war is about those things seated in those doors – the heavenly places where the control comes from. *"For we do not wrestle against flesh and blood, but against principalities, against powers, against the rulers of the darkness of this age,[c] against spiritual hosts of wickedness in the heavenly places" (Ephesians 6:12).*

MAKE A JOYFUL NOISE

"Make a joyful noise unto the LORD, all you lands.
Serve the LORD with gladness:
come before his presence with singing" (Psalm 100:1-2 KJ2000).

The Bible tells us to make a joyful noise. It does not say sing in nice harmonized notes. I am a noise, in the natural as well as the spirit. When I begin to sing I come before His presence, He does not come before mine. So why do we always ask God to come down? We start worshipping with the expectation that He is going to come down, out of Heaven around us. He is already around us, all we need to do is go into Heaven. We are invited to come before His presence and when you start to sing you go somewhere.

Psalm 33:3 says, *"Sing to Him a new song; Play skilfully with a shout of joy"*. It has been amazing being around our brother, he says, "Angus I love you in the Lord, in the glory. I have such a precious place in my heart for you". What he is doing is playing skilfully with the presence of God, tuning the fork of Heaven to be revealed in Heaven. For by giving thanks for another's life, you enter His gates. *"Enter into His gates with thanksgiving, and into His courts with praise!"* (Psalm 100:4 KJ21). Notice that it is not your gates but it is HIS gates. We access the realms of the Kingdom, then we start to engage in thanksgiving. I come before His presence, then I can go into His gate, which is a door.

"The LORD is my shepherd;
I shall not want.
[2] He makes me to lie down in green pastures;
He leads me beside the still waters.
[3] He restores my soul;
He leads me in the paths of righteousness
For His name's sake.

[4] Yea, though I walk through the valley of the shadow of death,
I will fear no evil;
For You are with me;
Your rod and Your staff, they comfort me.

[5] You prepare a table before me in the presence of my enemies;
You anoint my head with oil;
My cup runs over.
[6] Surely goodness and mercy shall follow me

All the days of my life;
And I will dwell in the house of the LORD forever" (Psalm 23).

I have often found that putting myself in a natural environment illustrating the Word can help me create the anchor – the trigger that will produce a spiritual encounter. For example the Bible says, *The Lord is my shepherd.* I wonder what it is like to have a shepherd? Psalm 23 continues, *He makes me lie down in green pastures besides still waters,* so I went and lay down in a green pasture beside still water.

I had not previously had an experience of that in my imagination so I did not have a reality I could meditate around. The way to give your imagination an anchor for your spirit to get the revelation for the doorways is to put yourself in a position that frames the experience for your spirit to anchor into. So I went to my father-in-law's farm, down by a little river, which had this lush carpet of green over the top of this bank. I can remember lying down on the green grass just meditating, being captivated by the scripture, *He makes me lie down in green pastures, beside still waters,* and meditating, "Lord you make me lie down in green pastures beside still waters."

Once you have been there you can go back anytime you like. So I was laid out on grass meditating, putting myself in a natural environment for the potential reality, the possibility of what the Word paints to become real to me, using the natural environment as an anchor to accumulate the spiritual information, giving it somewhere to rest upon so it can become a permanent memory. So I am lying on this grass thinking about the water going past me. I had my eyes closed and I started thinking about Jesus walking amongst His sheep and wondering what He would do. How would He hold them? Praying in the spirit, listening to the larks sing, it was the most amazing moment God set up for me. When you desire these encounters, God will set up circumstances because He wants to bless you. I was lying on the grass and the sun was coming up and then the light of the sun changed. I was thinking that's really weird. I carried on thinking about all that was happening around me, and the stream changed its noise. I opened my eyes and I was no longer on the nice little green knoll. I was now somewhere that was full of light and there was a river that was running past me, moving with the sound of the voice of God that was in the water.

It was not difficult – I had given the spiritual revelation an information anchor to be based on. I began to realise that what I was lying on actually was a different paddock of grass. By then I was really curious. I opened my eyes and I sat up. When I looked behind me the grass was alive; the sand was moving and was alive; the water was alive around me. Nobody was around so I stood up and went to look at the water and when I touched it, it was amazing.

I gave the Word of God a doorway. So it went from revelation to visitation where I began to participate with the things of Heaven. It is not difficult. We have believed it is hard to reach because the people who have had it have been hard to reach. That was alright for a season and it needed to be like that, but the season is now changing. The day and the season is emerging, bringing access for everybody. Not just for one or two, or those who are endowed with a spiritual propensity to experience those things. It is our learnt view. You learn how to walk, you will learn how to talk, you learn how to write, you learn how to read. The realm of the spirit is no different – you learn how to be and how to walk with God in the spirit. You learn and practise the process. The only way you know the alphabet or how to count is because you practised. It is no different with the realm of the spirit. The Bible says, "Practise your profession". You must practise being a believer of Jesus Christ; that being a believer, I am a son. What God is looking for is sons and daughters who will say, "Yes Lord, I can do this".

I did the same thing with the water. There is this lovely place called White Palm Bush and there is a waterfall that comes out. When it is in flood it comes out of this little hole and it thunders down the hillside. There was nobody around and I was just imagining what it would have been like to be near the river of life, and not really paying too much attention to what was happening and then suddenly the noise changed, and as I looked everything changed. My spirit man had gone into the realm of the Kingdom and started to see the reality of what the Word says about that living water. It is not difficult, the problem is no one has told you that you have permission to go in. It is a daily walk of spiritual encounter that releases the experiences that can become your reality.

RECORD – REVISIT – REVIEW

We have told the church, "You can't go there." We really have, and the teaching and the process of control and religious instructions that we have given people in the church has told them they cannot go there. You and I, in the process of growing up, have been finding out that this type of experience in the Kingdom is not just for the select few, it is for every one of us as sons of God. A record paints the potential of what has happened and you write it down in as much detail as you can. The key is not just to have it as an experience, but to going back and review it. When I review something, I spend time reading the picture, reading the information that I have written down, and then I spend time praying in the spirit while I am walking and drawing on the memory of that past experience. I am reviewing it: going back to that point of encounter, going back to that place where God opened the door of Heaven for me, and I go in and re-visit it. That picture becomes the anchor and the doorway for my experience to go further into the realm of Heaven. When I am there I look around, mostly with my mouth open in amazement like catching flies!

God wants us to revisit time and time again. Heaven is our home – we are a spirit being that has a soul that lives in a physical body, and because we are a spirit being if I were only here for seventy years I would want to know all there is to know about Heaven in those seventy years before I go home. But I do not want to die to go home; why should I? Enoch did not die. *"Enoch walked [in habitual fellowship] with God...[in reverent fear and obedience] Enoch walked with God; and he was not [found among men], because God took him [away to be home with Him]"* (Genesis 5:22, 24 AMP).

All that you see around you came out of the supernatural world. $E=mc^2$. Energy equals mass times the speed of light squared (or multiplied by itself). God is all power, all energy and He is light. He produces mass. Can you imagine what it is going to be like to build a galaxy? What do you think you are going to spend your time doing on the seventh day? Have you ever wondered what it is going to be like forever building in Heaven by the blueprint of what is in the circle of the Heavens? This stuff gets me really excited!

MORE THAN JESUS DID

Jesus sets us a principle when He says, *"Most assuredly, I say to you, he who believes in Me, the works that I do he will do also; and greater works than these he will do..." (John 14:12)*. This principle should be a key factor within your spirit life. When Jesus says we will do the things that He has done, I cannot think of doing anything greater than Jesus did, but the Bible says we are going to do more, those things that are more are not recorded in the Bible. So it means that you and I must discover them and that we have to go about some way to discover the 'more'.

God is looking for this earth to come back under the dominion of the sons of God again. The Bible says " ...Creation eagerly waits for the revealing of the sons of God... the whole creation groans and labors with birth pangs together until now" (Romans 8:19,22). It does not just say the whole of the earth, but everything you can see with the Hubble telescope is groaning for our manifestation as sons. The only way you are going to manifest as a son is if you go into Heaven and train to become a son. The only place you can get trained to be a son is in Heaven. You can learn about how to be a son on the earth and you can learn about the processes of becoming a son, without actually being a son. The only way you will be a son is if you are in Heaven. That is why it is important for us to go and experience Heaven.

Remember these three things:

1) Meditation opens the door to heavenly realms

2) Revelation forms a pathway and becomes the anchor for the door

3) Visitation becomes the experience of participation. This kind of participation is not for the select few, it is for all those who are spiritual. It is for the believers today in the body of Christ –it is for every single one of us.

ACTIVATION

There are some exercises I will give you that I have learnt to do with scripture. Stand with your bible and walk in a circle. Turn in your Bible to Psalm 100 and as you walk, begin to read out loud from Psalm 100. It is important you move to get your body involved in this exercise.

Being triune beings we have a body, a soul and a spirit, which means that we can do more than one thing at once. Now I would like you to pray in tongues as your mind reads the verses, while you are walking.

What I want to do now is to take two verses and repeatedly read them out in English while you pray in tongues on the inside. This will stretch you beyond the level you are used to. These are spiritual activities that generate inside of us the ability to do two or three things at the same time.

Next take the same two verses and speak in tongues while you are reading them in English in your mind.

And now, close your eyes. I want you to pray in tongues while your mind is beginning to get caught up with the scriptures you have just been quoting. What I am looking for is revelation to start coming from the Word. So I am praying in tongues asking the Word questions in my mind: "Father what does it mean to make a joyful noise?"

I am making the Word come alive on the inside of me by exercising and breaking the control of my soul off my spirit so that my spirit rules, because my body and soul must do what my spirit is telling it to do. Now begin to pray in tongues and allow those two verses to begin to captivate your mind – Begin to think on these things.

Lastly, do not pray at all with your mouth or words coming out of your body. I want you to pray on the inside while you are meditating around the Word.

It is not hard. This is how you learn to meditate – you break the control of your body and your soul off your spirit. As you practise these exercises you are breaking the influence of control. Then your spirit man can stand and you can begin to meditate around the Word. When you start this process you will become captivated by the Word, it will become revelation, which produces visitation.

Chapter 5
Gateways

Gateways are a vitally important reality in our lives as believers, not only in our own personal lives but also in the realm of the spirit. Gateways are entry points; they are the things or places where we access the realm of Heaven. They are gateways or doorways and everlasting doors. Everlasting doors are the places that will release the glory onto the earth in the last days (Psalms 24). It is going to be our right as sons and daughters of God to open those everlasting doors. But the thing is, before we can go anywhere near those doors, it must first happen in our own life.

"...first here in Jerusalem, then beyond to Judea and Samaria, and finally to the farthest places on earth." (Acts 1:8 VOICE).

It must happen in you first before you try and do it somewhere else.

A problem we are experiencing in the church today is that we have intercessors who are trying to do things in the realm of the spirit that they have never experienced deeply in their own personal lives first. This is because of lack of teaching and that is okay, but the times are changing. God wants us to be able to activate the things in the spirit with knowledge and wisdom.

This is a process that I have worked with for years and it works. It has been more than just a diagram. It has been a life's work to get who and what I am manifesting on the outside so I can be present with you here, but also very present with the Spirit and the presence of God. It is a most wonderful thing to be able to understand the flow of the move and the presence of God and what happens to it. In my own life I can recall many experiences where I would be so hungry for the presence of God and yet my sin would be talking to me. I would be praying in tongues and the presence of God would be there but then a thought would flick into my brain and all the anointing would go out of the room like a balloon going down. I would think "What is the use of this?"

What began for me was a journey of trying to understand how to release the glory of the presence of God from the Kingdom of God that is within me. There are two realms that we encounter God in. One is the Kingdom of God that is within us. The other is in the realm of the Kingdom of Heaven that is on the outside of us. Everything between here and there is usually demonic. I do not know about you, but I am not interested in seeing the demonic.

People sometimes say to me, "Oh Ian, I saw demons last night" I reply "Well, I saw angels last night. How many did you see?" and they say, "I only see demons." I say, "Well, you are not seeing by the right eye then."

If you can see demons, you can see angels. The reason you cannot see angels is usually because the inside of you and who you are is not purified enough to be able to see the right thing. So what is happening is the flow of the information that your spirit man is receiving is going into your soul and your soul is corrupting it, making it do something that it should not be doing.

I want us to work our way through some of these doorways. I want to talk about them and I want to talk about the process. In my manual, Gateways of the Three-Fold Nature of Man I have some... helpful for you.

When the Bible talks about a principle, this can be applied to every single part of a person's life and activity that they are involved in. The principle in the diagram of the body, soul and spirit goes beyond just you. A family has a body life, a soul life and a spirit life. A church has a body life, a soul life and a spirit life. A city has a body life, a soul life and a spirit life and a nation has a body life, a soul life and a spirit life. A big problem in the church today is that we have never been taught how to take hold of our own body life, our own soul life and our own spirit life to release the glory through those doorways. We have never been taught to manifest Heaven, first in Jerusalem, then into Samaria and then into the outermost parts of our city (Acts 1:8). So many of us have been trying to go into the outermost parts of our city or world and, when we do, we get hit and wonder why. It is usually because Jerusalem is not purged yet. I want to talk about some of the processes that I have gone through.

Gateways diagram from the manual

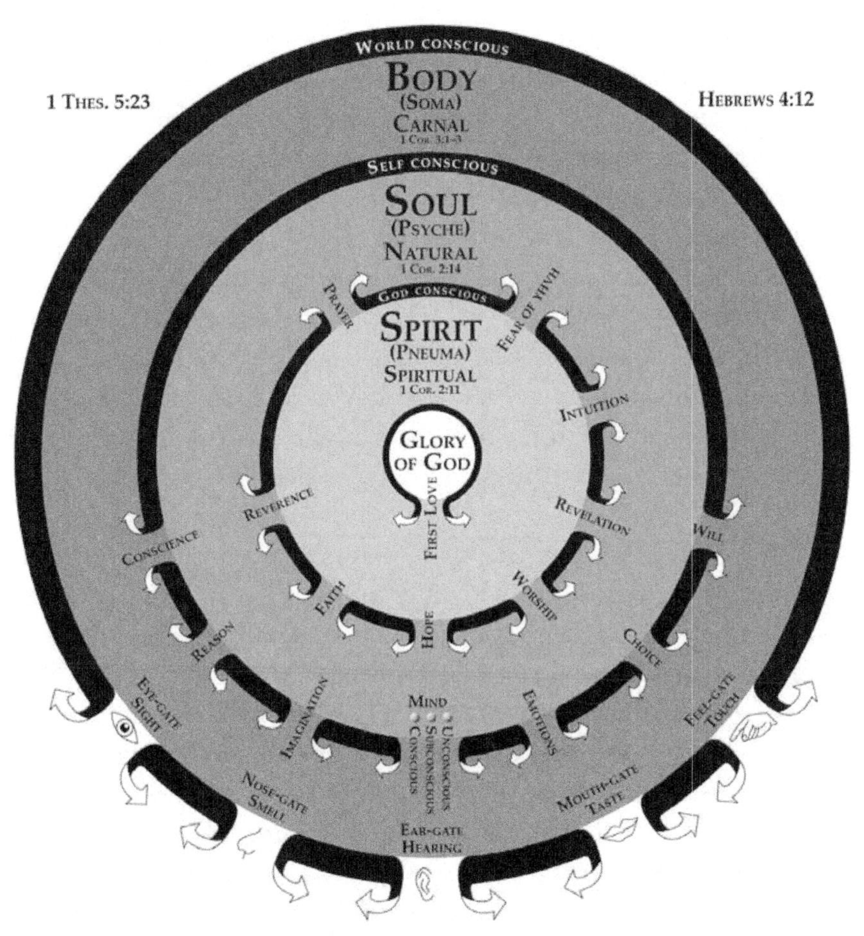

The influence of Christ extending outward to the world

THE GATEWAY OF FIRST LOVE

The Gateway of First Love is an amazing thing. In Revelation, talking about the Church of Ephesus, it says:

"However, I have this against you: you have abandoned your first love. Do you remember what it was like before you fell? It is time to rethink and change your ways; go back to how you first acted. However, if you do not return, I will come quickly and personally remove your lamp stand from its place" (Revelation 2:4-5 VOICE).

The Gateway of First Love is one of the most vital ingredients in a human life, enabling us to encounter God in a greater way. First love means abandoned love where there is no care for anything or anyone else but Him. Unfortunately, the devil's strategy is to shut out our ability to fall in love with abandon. This has happened in my own life and I am sure it has happened with you. If that ability can be controlled and shut and manipulated by the realm of the spirit, through what the devil wants to happen, then you will never fall in love with God the way you should do. So, for me, some of the greatest struggles have been in 'first love'.

First love is puppy love, love where you just do not care. In my own personal life I can remember very clear experiences I had as a young man growing up. I would be standing in class and this apparition of glorious wonder would walk into the room and my eyes could not move from her. You have these experiences where you are in love but you do not know it. That is the beginning of first love – that abandonment to love. The devil's strategy is to shut that down.

In my own life I can clearly remember several circumstances which shut that doorway down very effectively for me. I can remember one day at school writing a note to this lovely apparition of glorious wonder that came into my classroom. I can remember writing that note and thinking that when she walked out I was just going to slip it into her bag. I am not embarrassed to talk about it now because that is how you are supposed to be with God. The problem was that it fell out of my book onto the floor and the teacher picked it up and read it to the class! I can remember making an inner vow that day that no one would ever see me in love again.

About a year later I can remember being in physical education class with a girl. Do you remember getting in line just in case you might touch? And then, if you touch, the week of euphoria just because you touched?! I can remember being in this situation, trying to get myself lined up and it just would not work. Occasionally our eyes would meet and then "Wow!" For the next three and a half weeks it would be "She looked at me!" When God looks at you, that is the way you are supposed to return His love. I can remember waiting by the edge of this classroom hoping that she would walk past and our eyes would meet. Then I heard some people laughing and as I turned around there were these three guys from school laughing and saying, "Ha! Ha! Ha! Ian is in love!" I can remember making another inner vow that no one would ever see me in love again.

Then when I was about thirteen, I can remember going back to school for the first week, and there was this girl who I had always known, with long blonde hair and green eyes and I fell in love, abandoned love! My only reason for going to school was to sit behind her and look at her hair! Or to sit at the desk across from her, turn sideways and pretend I was writing, just to watch her! We had to wear this cap for school and I can remember coming home one day, walking up to the fridge, opening the fridge door, taking my cap off, putting it in the fridge and shutting the fridge door and walking away! My father started to laugh saying, "Ha! Ha! Ha! Ian is in love!" Again I made the inner vow that no one will ever see me in love again.

My life went on, I met my wonderful wife, had some wonderful children and I got born again. In my own spiritual life with God I would feel, "God I want to be in love with You. What is wrong with me?" I had been in the realm of the spirit and seen Heaven. I had even encountered Him and seen Him. (By the way, you can see God and live. I am a testimony to that, and I am not the only one in the world, but that is a subject for later on.)

So, I can remember going through my life as a believer, coming into church, wanting desperately to be in love with God, wanting desperately to experience God and know about God. I wanted even just to hear Him, because that is what it is all about anyway, isn't it? I would come into church and I would be sitting thinking, "Father!

Just to see You, Lord just to get one glimpse of Your glory, just to feel You come in, just to hear Your footsteps again... Father I am waiting, panting as the deer, panting for the presence of God..." I can remember thinking, "I must be a backslider, something is wrong." This began the journey of the arena of the Gateway of First Love for me.

I can remember one day the Lord spoke to me quite clearly. I was in the spirit and He put me in front of this door. It was the Gateway of First Love. (Doorways and gateways are the same thing and I will use the terms interchangeably.) I wanted that doorway to be clean through the process of working my way through the diagram of the Gateways. I wanted to fall in love with God. I wanted God! I can remember looking at this door and there were these wooden bars across it with twenty-five inch nails and great big pieces of chain with locks on them. I can remember thinking, "I am a born again believer, I have Jesus Christ residing in my life, I am an elder in the church and yet I have this garbage in my life."

Through a process, what God began to do was to take me back into memories, because you need to remember to repent. Following repentance comes restoration, following restoration comes renewal, and following renewal comes recommitment. So I began dealing with the bondages over the Gateway of First Love in my life. A gateway to me is just a door. Sometimes it is two doors, sometimes it is just one door. I do not really care; it is just a door, a point of entry.

The Bible says:

"However, the spiritual is not first, but the natural, and afterward the spiritual" (1 Corinthians 15:46).

Often it is natural things in our natural environment that become an anchor to the spiritual. I will be talking about that more later, in the chapter entitled 'The Human Mind'. To give you the basics, we need an anchor for the reality of the spirit world to hold onto, for us to be able to remember what is going on. I understood that at this stage, so I stood in front of a door and I opened the door and I shut the door, I opened the door and I shut the door saying "Father I open this Door of First Love and I shut the Door." You need to practise.

I can remember going through the process of restoration and dealing with the broken part of my life, the broken areas in the arena of First Love. Then I came to push through that door in the spirit and I can remember wondering and thinking, "What do I need to do? There is no handle on it". Then the Lord said to me, "Only those who touch the door will find the handle." In your pursuit of the door, once you find the door, you need to touch it and then you will find the handle. I did not know who you could talk to about these things.

I can remember standing in front of my Door of First Love in the spirit. Years ago I had seen the movie 'Backdraft', a horrible nightmare of a movie! There is a horrible scene with these fire-fighters in a high rise building. Inside, on one of the floors there is a room with a window and a door. A fire-fighter looks through the window and the room looks fine, all the carpet is there and all the furniture is there. As the camera stays there for a fraction of a second longer you see the room shimmering in the heat. The problem is that the whole room is on fire but there is no flame because there is no oxygen to feed it. There is just this little puff of smoke that comes under the door and then back again, puffs under the door and then back again. When the firefighter opens the door, oxygen will rush in and there will be a huge explosion. You are sitting on the edge of your seat saying, "Do not go in there!"

Well, I am now sitting on the edge of my seat in front of this doorway saying, "God I am going to be in love with You. This is it; I am finally going to get to a place where I can fall in love with You because I have dealt with my garbage. I am now in a place where I can open the door and begin to experience You." The Bible does say our God is a consuming fire! (Hebrews 12:29). I did not know that the whole of the inside of me was on fire, I just had not seen it yet. So I opened the door, and guess what happened? A Love explosion! It knocked me over. About an hour later I was still on the floor!

The Gateway of First Love is the key thing in every believer's life that the devil tackles first, hurting us when we fall in love as a young child. Because of lack of understanding, there is very little nurturing of our hearts, bringing government, and helping people to understand that it is okay to be in love like that. In fact it is a very precious thing to be able to be in love like that. My life with God began to change then, but that was only part of the journey.

The glory of God dwells inside us, as shown in the diagram on page 45, which is symbolic of the temple in Jerusalem. You have the Outer Court, which speaks of your body, the Inner Court, which speaks of your soul, and the Holy of Holies, which speaks of your spirit. Inside the Holy of Holies you have the dwelling place of the glory of God. We are set up in just the same way as the temple in Jerusalem was: we have an Outer Court, an Inner Court and the Holy of Holies. Inside the Holy of Holies is the dwelling place of the glory of God – the manifest presence of God that dwells inside of us. When you are born again, the omniscient, omnipresent and omnipotent God lives inside of you. It is that inner Kingdom of God that enables you to transition into the outer Kingdom of Heaven. It is only by that Kingdom of God inside of you, not by your efforts, but by the Kingdom. When that Kingdom is flowing from the Gateway of First Love, because it starts from the core of your being, the glory changes you. When you get born again your spirit is changed, then your soul begins to get transformed. Once your soul is transformed your body is going to be transfigured. I am not there yet, but I am on the pathway. It is very exciting, but it has all taken work. It all means work and lots of it; hard work.

THE GATEWAYS OF THE SPIRIT

Often with the Gateways of the Spirit (Revelation, Intuition, Reverence, Prayer, Faith, Hope, Worship, and the Fear of God) in most believers' lives we find three or maybe four of them operating. By looking at you I can tell which gateways inside your spirit man are functioning properly. Our spirit is the candle of God. If the candle is only lit on one side the candle is going to bend one way. So what happens is often Christians' lives are bent to one direction. Usually the areas we are bent towards are the areas of Worship, Reverence and Prayer. For people who operate in signs and wonders, Faith as well. So what happens in our lives is the other gateways are like muscles that have not been used. So when we try to release the glory of Heaven through our lives, it is what is in us that touches the world. You do not take Heaven by drawing it down and allowing it to touch the world. It is what is in you that comes out of you and touches the world around you. It is the glory of God that is in you that changes the world. It is this that is in you that changes the atmosphere. When you are in the spirit, your spirit cloaks your soul and your body. When you are in the realm of the spirit, you do not look the way you look in the physical. In Revelation 1, John says he turned and saw one like the Son of Man. He saw Jesus, but Jesus is the Son of Man. We are like him, so when John turned he saw what you look like when you are in the spirit. We can read in Revelation:

"*...clothed with a garment down to the feet and girded about the chest with a golden band* (The symbol of the hallmark of the investment of a King or a Prince). *His head and hair were white like wool, as white as snow, and His eyes like a flame of fire; His feet were like fine brass, as if refined in a furnace,* (to trample the devil) *and His voice as the sound of many waters; He had in His right hand seven stars, out of His mouth went a sharp two-edged sword, and His countenance was like the sun shining in its strength*" (Revelation 1:13-16).

This is what you look like! Not only that but if you have worked on the armour of light you will be encased in glory and have lightning coming out of you! The devil hates Christians being in the spirit, because it dispossesses everything that he is – he is darkness, light dispossesses darkness. Darkness in physics is described as the absence of light. That is the only reason for the kingdom in darkness, because of the absence of light. The devil does not like us going into the spirit realm because we are children of light. The problem is many people have gone from the natural realm into the spirit realm in order to get to Heaven and they have wrestled on the way there. It is the Kingdom of God that is within you – the glory that transitions you into the realm of Heaven. Then you bring that glory through the spirit realm into the natural realm. That is a different way of praying.

You will get impartation by the words you hear, because words are power and words are light. They will change who you are and make you something else. You have your own journey. You need to walk your own walk with God and become conformed into His image. It is all about His image in you manifesting so that the world can have that image and see that image displayed.

The Gateways of the Spirit are vitally important for us to exercise. If I did not do any exercise I would be as round as a keg. The problem is that if I go to the gym and start working on the weights, I cannot push 150 kg straight away. I need to work up from twenty kilograms, then to forty kilograms and increasing in this way it takes about six months to get there. By the time you have done this for six months you have built up the ability and it does not hurt any more. In the natural, atrophy of a muscle means that it loses its strength, power and ability. If you have not run for a long time and you go on a one kilometre run, you will be half dead by the time you get there. Three days later you will be feeling the aching muscles, because those muscles are not exercised, they are not used to doing the work.

In believers' lives many of the Gateways of the Spirit are exactly the same, because you have never been taught about them, or told you can use them. They are muscles that are atrophied. In our gateways, for some of us, there are no muscles there at all. It is just this little strand of sinew. So when you pray, "Father I want revelation of Your Kingdom", He says, "Is that right? Well, what have you done with the Gateway?" Unless you work on the gateway, do not expect the fruit of the gateway to manifest in your life.

When I began to work on my Gateways of the Spirit, my greatest problem was in my soul. As human beings we are a spirit being that has a soul that lives in a physical body. Some of our problems are because we do not believe that we are a spirit being, because we are encased in a body. We think we are a human being.

I went and had a blood test and the lady taking the blood asked me, "Are you a citizen of New Zealand?" I said to her, "No, actually I am a citizen of another world." And she said to me, "Really! That is interesting; what is that?" So I said, "Heaven!"

This is the reality we are supposed to live in. We are only sojourners on the earth, but citizens of another world. The reason I am a citizen of another world is because my spirit is engaged with the presence of God. This makes me a citizen of another world. If

I am a spirit being, then what goes into my spirit needs to be able to flow through my life to touch the world around me. Unless I am in the spirit, my spirit dwells inside of my body, not on the outside. When I am in the spirit, my spirit is on the outside of my body and the contents of my spirit are displayed for the spirit world to see. The devils hate it, but I love it! There is a part of me that is the lion and a part of me that is the lamb and we need to have that balance in our lives. I love trampling on the devil's head – it is the most wonderful exercise you can ever get – it is glorious! Do you know why it is glorious? Because you have feet of brass so he cannot bruise your heel. Hallelujah! God has given us all the tools but we do not always put them on. When we do not walk with God, we cannot experience the reality of the victories that He has given us. It does not mean you will not suffer, but in the suffering is the key: God will use your sufferings to drive you into intimacy in pursuit of Him. Use sufferings as a springboard.

Our soul is the greatest point of struggle and battle in our lives. The battle is for the possession of your soul. When people say to me, "I don't have demons", usually you lay hands on them and they start manifesting! When we get born again our spirit becomes alive and enlightened with the presence of God. The problem is that the reality of what is in our spirit is not transferred into the reality of what is going on in our soul. It is my soul that needs to be transformed and renewed. The Bible says:

"be renewed in the spirit of your mind" (Ephesians 4:23).

The flow of life is a renewing process, it is not something that goes 'bang!' I have only ever met two people in my life who went 'bang', and that bang lasted a year and then their soul was clean and they are now manifesting Heaven in a major way. I have only ever met two people like that. It is a gift from God because God has got a mandate for a specific season on a person's life. For most of us, however, we need to do the work. The problem is that it is cost up front, now. It is all cost up front and the reward comes later – but let me tell you, some of the reward I have tasted is glorious! The Bible says that Jesus:

"...endured the cross and ignored the shame of that death because He focused on the joy that was set before Him" (Hebrews 12:2 VOICE).

Do you know what His joy was? "I am going to make many like Me, the devil does not know that and he is going to flee!" That is what it is all about. It is bringing Heaven into your soul, because what goes on in your soul is going to be reflected in your body. The Gateways of your Body will reveal what goes on in the Gateways of your Soul. What comes out of your mouth, what you see, what you hear, what you speak, what you touch, what you taste, is going to come out of your soul. It either comes from inside out of you, which is the Tree of Life, or it comes from the outside into you, which is the Tree of the Knowledge of Good and Evil (Genesis 2:17).

THE GATEWAYS OF THE SOUL

From a child you are trained to receive information from the outside in. When we get born again we need to be trained to receive information from the inside out. The greatest struggle is what goes on in the soul.

For many of us, we know we have a soul but there is not much taught about it. In the diagram there are Gateways of the Soul. These are gateways that I have worked on. They are my revelation. They are things that have worked for me. I am not saying it is the entirety of the picture, it is just a picture I saw in the Scroll Room of Heaven from when God made the soul. You can call those gateways whatever you like. I found that the more specific I get in the arena of my soul and the more specific detail I can get about how to pray through it, the more effective it becomes in the process of changing us.

The gates inside your soul are the Mind, Conscience, Reason, Imagination, Emotions, Will and Choice. They are functions of your soul. Those functions of your soul can either stop the flow of the glory or release the glory to touch the world through your body.

Gateways are very important. The Bible talks about different transactions that occurred in the gateways:

2 Kings 7:1 (Business transactions)

Ruth 4:1-11 (Legal transactions)

Deuteronomy 25:7, 9 (Criminal cases in disputes and judgments)

Jeremiah 17:19-20 (Proclamations of the kings were declared)
Psalms 24:7 (Festivities were decreed)
2 Samuel 18:24-33 (Protection was given)

The Bible is full of references to the activities that go on in gateways. The most important thing to understand is that when we are in sin and trespass, other things control our Gateways. As an unbeliever I would have demon spirit forces that would be influencing and controlling the gateways of my soul. When I got born again my spirit came alive, the glory of God began to dwell inside of me and that glory wanted to get from inside of me to the outside of me. The problem is I have another gatekeeper sitting on those gateways. When you are dealing with spirit forces, everything with them is about legality. Every single thing about a demon spirit is about legality, so every chance you get, you need to be going into the Court Room of Heaven and dealing with garbage there (discussed in a later chapter). The spirit world contention is all over legality.

When you understand your legal rights as a son, who you are and what rights you have, you can stand against the greatest devil you can ever see in the world. When you understand the realm of Heaven, and who you are and when you have seen Heaven, you can bring Heaven to the earth. Heaven speaks about the dominion of God being brought back to the earth. That is what the earth is crying out for. That is what the spirit realm is crying out for; the devil does not belong there. The church has given the spirit realm to the devil because they are scared of him and that is because they have never been taught how to see into Heaven. Once you see into Heaven, the spirit realm is just a playground to bring the dominion of God into and it is wonderful fun! It is not hard, praise the Lord! For some of you, this is throwing your doctrine right out of the window.

DEALING WITH IMAGES OF THE MIND

The soul is very important for you to deal with. You cannot bridle the soul, it must be crucified and it must be made dead. In my own personal experience there have been many things I have wrestled with. One of them has been images in the mind.

These can be the things of the past, things that have happened to you, things that have occurred, things that you have seen that have polluted you. You will be praying away and this image will appear in your mind and all the anointing goes out of the window. The reason that happens is because those images are in your soul. People say to me, "The devil is trying to put them into my mind". No, what he is doing is using the playground that you have allowed him to play in.

As a young believer I used to pray over the Gateways of my Soul, like the Gateway of the Mind. There are three channels of the mind: unconscious, subconscious and conscious that work together in unison. If they are not under the Blood and not being worked on in your life then your spirit life will have trouble seeing, retaining what you have seen and wrestling with the experiences in your past.

One of the most important things for me has been to deal with the images in my mind. I would go to senior people in the church and tell them about an image that would come into my mind and just destroy everything. They would say, "Yes I understand, but you have got to stop it and resist it." So I would pray, battling in tongues. I would win for about three months. Then one day I would be doing something and suddenly it would come into my mind. I remember one day I was praying away in my bedroom, speaking into this thing that it would bow the knee, pushing it down and controlling it, when I heard God shout at me, "Hey, what are you doing?!" I said, "I'm sorry Lord, I don't understand – I need You to teach me". He said, "I am trying to get it out and you are trying to keep it in!"

God can see every single thing that is in your soul. When you participate in something in your soul, God can see, and if God can see it, so can the demons. People tell me demons cannot read your mind. Really?! I come from an occult background. They can read your mind all right. They know exactly what you are thinking because what you are thinking, the little pictures you have are called 'dust'. Dust is a record of the sin nature that you have experienced in your life. In Genesis 2 God gave Satan the dust of the earth. The dust needs to be brought under the Blood.

So I began a process of learning how to deal with those images. It is a very simple process

1) You need to acknowledge that you have got them and they are your responsibility, not God's.

2) You need to repent of them. (To repent of them you need to own them as yours. Remember, they are your problem, not God's. God has given you a way to deal with them.)

3) You need to bring them into the light and acknowledge them as sin.

4) You need to take and apply the Blood of Jesus to them.

In learning this process the Lord said to me, "Take a poster and put it on the wall. Take some red paint and paint the poster with the red paint." So I got this poster and painted it all with red paint. I sat there looking at this picture and there was nothing on it except red paint. The Lord said to me, "Can you see the picture anymore?" I said, "No, I have painted over it". He said, "Well, that is what my Blood does". It is the Blood that redeems you from the enmity of the record of sin that is against your life – the dust. It is the Blood of Jesus that redeems you from the dust of the earth and from the power that the devil has over that dust.

So a journey began in my life, over a long period of time dealing with the images of my mind, to the point where I came to be so preoccupied with it that I would look for every opportunity to go and meet with the devil and say, "Give me those pictures!" The reason why was because I was winning.

So I would go through the process: "Father, I take that picture, I own it, I confess it as sin. Today Lord I repent of its power. I bring it into the light and I acknowledge it and today, Lord, I take the Blood of Jesus and I cleanse it in Jesus Name."

The amazing thing is that when you practise something you find that you do it as second nature and it happens really quickly, to the point where it would take me one second to deal with an image, because I had practised the pathway. I had done the hard work of laying the foundation for the Spirit of God to move when an image would come into my mind and seek to destroy who I was.

The devil wants you to remember **what** you are; God wants to remind you **who** you are. The record of sin in your life reminds you of what you are; it reminds you that you are a person, a spirit in a temporal body. Who you are is a spirit being – you are a spirit being first.

I have some funny stories. As a manager of a swimming pool facility, I used to run all the swimming pools for the local District Council and my job was to mow the lawns. I told my staff, "If anybody mows the lawns you are in trouble!" I can remember mowing the lawns and getting so caught up in the spirit going through the images in my mind, praying in tongues (nobody could hear me because the lawn mower was making such a noise) to the point where I had finished but I was still standing there for fifteen minutes. One of my staff came up to me and seeing them I snapped out of it and walked off. I do not know what they thought of it, but I do not really care anyway!

COVENANT OF ADOPTION

Whatever captivates your heart will captivate you. I was caught by the potential possibility of being free and renewed in my mind. That Blood Covenant is based on the Covenant of Adoption, which is one of the principles that most believers do not really know about today. It is based on an adoption process that used to happen in a court of law in Roman times. When a person was brought into the court of law to be adopted by another family, two scrolls would be brought into the court. One would be a record of the old life with the old name on it and the record of every single thing about the person; who they were, where they were born, every criminal case, every single thing that went on in their life. Everything that happened with them would be written down on that scroll. On the other scroll would be their new name with the testimony of seven people who could testify to this person as being the adopted one (which for us are the seven Spirits of God, but that is another teaching subject).

The Roman judge would undo the scroll of the person's old life. In those days they did not have acid or solvent in their ink, so the Roman judge could take a damp rag and wipe the old scroll clean. From that point onwards the person did not exist in any court of law with that old name. His old life before the point of his adoption did not exist. This is why Paul could say:

"...forgetting those things which are behind ... I press toward the goal for the prize of the upward call of God in Christ Jesus" (Philippians 3:13-14).

The high calling is transfiguration; it is not just a nice experience. We are called to be transfigured sons of God. Ladies, I am sorry if you struggle being a son; I struggle being a bride! We have our own little problems in there! God has called us to be transfigured sons of God on the earth. If it happened to Jesus it will happen to you and me. It is just a process that we have not learned or been taught about. One of the ways of being transfigured is getting your life under the Blood.

I worked my way through my imagination, through the images in my mind, to the point where I would lay in bed and they would come, usually just before I went to sleep. The devil knows that, in the transition (of consciousness) just before going to sleep, you are on the edge of the realm of Heaven and you can either experience Heaven or get stuck on the earth trying to wrestle with the sin inside your life and the images that are there. So the wrestling goes on at night time.

I love going to sleep because I go into Heaven and I know that when I wake up I come out of Heaven having spent another seven hours with God. It is glorious! It is a practice – you can do this, it is not hard, it is a process you can learn. It is not a hard thing to do, but the church has never been taught how to do it. Well, it has, years ago in Paul's day, but not anymore. These scrolls have been locked up and they are now being chiselled open in the Court Rooms of God. We have access to get information out of them, bring them back to the Body and say, "Here is a present from Heaven!"

I am looking forward one day to having a meeting and saying, "You guys here, we have a meeting in Russia in about thirty seconds; I'll see you there!", then being relocated by God. This is what it is about. I have been there, Hallelujah! It is an exciting walk to allow Heaven inside your life.

So I began to work on images in my mind, to the point where I got right back to clear memories of being in my mother's womb and things that happened. God wants full restoration. I did not have to go and dig them up; I would be sitting praying in tongues waiting for them to come. I like doing this because we win! Most of us do not believe that because we are so used to the body and its control, power and assertion of authority over who we are, which is a spirit being. We are used to it controlling our spirit. But it is time our spirit got that authority and power back.

PRAYING THROUGH YOUR LIFE

So I began to work on these areas of my mind. The first one was these images; the next one was the record of my life. I began on a journey working on my life. One day you are praying and God says, "I want the first year". So you pray, "Lord by faith I give You the first year of my life, I bring it under the Blood of Jesus. Lord, I take that first year and I wipe it with the Blood". And you think that felt good! So you continue, "Father I take the next year of my life and I wipe it with the Blood of Jesus. Lord I take the next year, I wipe that with Your Blood and I redeem that year." I began to get excited because in the spirit world the testimony of the power of the devil over the arena of my life and the dust that was in my life began to come under the Blood and be redeemed by the Blood of Jesus, so the record of it was taken away from the devil's power.

I worked through the years of my life when I was about thirty, praying in tongues, every day five minutes a day for thirty days, praying, "I speak to that year, I command you to be redeemed, I wipe it with the Blood of Jesus. I decree today that this year of my life has been bought and redeemed by the Blood in Jesus' Name". By the end of those thirty days I felt good! It felt so good I decided to work on the months of the year. "Father, for the first month of the first year of my life, by faith I speak to that month in Jesus' Name, you are redeemed by the Blood of Jesus, I take that Blood and apply it". I did this each day, going through the first year of my life. Twelve days later I thought, "That felt really good!" So I began to work on every month in every year of my life. That felt so good I decided to work on every day of the year of my life. It is a work and a process, but there is a reward at the end, which is liberty. "Where the Spirit of the Lord is, there is liberty" (2 Corinthians 3:17). The testimony of Jesus Christ is His Blood on your life. The devil sees that testimony when you are in the spirit! Many believers are afraid of being in the spirit because they have never taken these simple things and put them into their lives.

After about three and a half or four months of praying through that, my spirit was alive and so I began to think, "Okay Father, first hour, of the first day of the first month of my life." So I began a journey over about a year and a half, praying through every single day of my life and bringing it under the Blood of Jesus Christ, taking that rag and wiping the slate with the record of the Blood of Jesus, redeeming the memory and the record of that away from the devil. When you have done that and you go into the realm of the spirit, guess who is going to win? This is one of about eighty keys. What God is looking for is a redeemed bride. It is the Blood of Jesus that redeems you. It is only the Blood. It is only the Blood of Jesus that can redeem you from the enmity of sin, nothing else can – not your works. I spent hours in prayer, I had to learn the process, and it took me four and a half years of work. I am giving you a key, but you are going to be responsible for it. I have given you about four keys for which you are now responsible, because you have heard it. God is going to say to you one day, "What did you do with that key?"

At the end of this teaching you will have a lot of things to do, but what I did was target the first one and I stayed with it until it was done and then onto the next one. A spider usually has five or six anchor points in its web. You can take two off and the web still stays in shape, but if you take three off the web implodes upon itself. I found that by the time I got to the third area of my life the devil's power over me began to implode and disseminate. The amazing thing is that if a spider is in the middle of its web and you cut three places simultaneously, the web will wrap itself up around the spider and kill it. First that which is in the natural, then that which is in the spirit.

These are some of the simple things that were just the Mind Gate. The conscience is another amazing thing. I can remember working on my conscience, going through the process of releasing the glory of God through the Gateway of First Love into the gateways of my spirit man of Revelation, Faith, Hope, Worship, into my soul, into the Gateway of my Conscience.

The Bible says that when you sin your conscience gets seared (1 Timothy 4:2). I can remember praying into my Conscience Gate and it was like a solid wall. I thought, "What on earth is this? It is supposed to be a gate". You need to dig, you need to make it work and make a hole. Water is very corrosive. It will eventually eat through anything given half a chance. So I began to dig into the area of my conscience, "Father where my conscience has been seared I dig today in Jesus' Name into that place of my conscience."

What began to happen was I felt the glory start like a trickle of water. When a trickle of water starts in a wall that has been dammed up it will eventually wear a hole. That hole will get bigger and bigger. All you have to do is give it a chance. By beginning to work and exercise into the area of my conscience it made me aware of sin and my need for a Saviour. It made me aware of the power of the realm of Heaven, to drive me into the Person of God, to come to know Him, because that is my job; I want to know Him. So I began to work on my conscience.

The river was only a stagnant pond, but if you go to the start of the stagnant pond and dig a channel, the most foul, stinking, smelly, filthy water is going to flow out first. Older folks may be able to remember those old priming pumps – the water that would come out when it first started was rusty, stinky, green and horrible. But if you carry on for two minutes, what comes out is pure, lovely, drinkable water.

It is no different in the spirit; I was priming the pump, getting into the area of my conscience, making it work, making it flow, making it become aware of holiness and righteousness and speaking purity into it because the reason our conscience is seared is a lack of purity. The person with a purified conscience will be a holy person. Every single human being has a conscience and that is how we will be judged. If you have never heard the gospel you will be judged according to your conscience because your conscience is God-consciousness of righteousness (Romans 2:14-15).

In the Gateways diagram the arrows flow from the centre outwards. That is the only way you will ever change your life, from the centre of your spirit, into your spirit, through your spirit into your soul, through your soul into your body and through your body into the world around you. It is the only way that glory will ever flow through your life, from the centre of your being. I do not want the glory to come out of Heaven and into me. It is already in me through Jesus Christ and my rebirth as a born again spirit. What is in me needs to flow through me into the world around me.

You need to go through that diagram and work on those gateways yourself. Some of the things we have worked through in this chapter are in the "Gateways of the Three-Fold Nature of Man" manual included and available from: www.sonofthunder.org

The diagram became like a Bible to me. I would just work on it and I have had people who have taken that diagram and three or four different pieces of cardboard, lining each gateway up with another one, working on the flow until it would flow properly. It is not important how you do it but we always go from the inside out. I would maybe first look at the Gateway of First Love into the Gateway of Hope (spirit), into the Gateway of my Mind (soul) and out of my Hearing (body), so that I could hear the words of God coming into my spirit. You could then look at the flow from the Gateway of First Love into the Gateway of Worship (spirit), into the Gate of Choice (soul), into the Gate of Touch, Taste, Smell, See, or Hearing (body). Each one of those gates is capable of flowing through another one of those gateways, but it goes from the inside out, not from the outside in.

ACTIVATION

For this activation, what we are going to do is work our way through a gateway. How I do this is by spending time praying in tongues. First I need to be able to see the diagram. (Page 45)

Then when it is embedded in my mind and I do not need the diagram anymore; I can close my eyes and see it in my memory. I know which gateway to work on; I know how they function and what they feel like when they are not flowing; I know when they get corrupted by my own choices or by the choices of others and I can work on them to keep them clean and pure.

We are going to work on one flow of direction. We are going to go from the Gateway of First Love to the Gateway of Worship (spirit), to the Gateway of Emotions (soul), to the Gateway of Hearing (body), to hear the voice of God. So the flow of God that I am looking for would come through the centre of my being, through the Gateway of Worship, into my Emotions, out into my Gateway of Hearing so I can hear the voice of God flowing from my spirit.

When you start to pray, do not try to reach for somewhere 'out there' for the Glory. I am not interested in it coming down. The days are gone when it is coming down, it is time for us to go up. It is time for us to be found in the presence of God, not for God to be found in our presence.

Focus on your belly, where the presence of the glory of God is, in the Gateway of First Love, that the glory would flow through from there into the Gateway of Worship, from the Gateway of Worship into the Gateway of Emotions to help us begin to express ourselves towards God; and through the Gateway of Hearing to begin to hear the voice of God. The changes happen from the inside out.

I want you to put your hand on your belly and start praying in tongues to stir the anointing within you. Inside you is a well-spring of life, it is that well-spring that needs to flow from your spirit into the world that is around you. The flow and direction we are looking for is from First Love, through Worship and Emotions, to the Hearing Gate, so that we can hear His voice speaking his love whispers to us.

We are going to pray in tongues for four minutes, focusing on each gateway for one minute. So it will be from your Gateway of First Love that the glory of God will flow to your spirit, through the Gateway of Worship into the Gateway of Emotions and through the Gateway of Hearing.

So the first one is the First Love Gateway of Glory. I want you to start praying in tongues (if you cannot pray in tongues you may want to get someone to lay hands on you in ministry and get you baptised in the Holy Ghost). I do not want you to reach out to Heaven, I want you to reach out to the glory that is within you. The Kingdom of God that is within you is where the presence of God is.

Chapter 6
The Human Mind

I want to teach practically, to give you some understanding of why we struggle with the spirit realm. The Lord has given me insights into how things work. When I was speaking in America, I did not know it, but I had a neurosurgeon in the meeting. I talked about this subject and he came up to me afterwards and said, "Ian, I only have one thing to say to you: 'Where did you get it from?!' I spent fifteen years of my life learning about this and you are not even a doctor!" I said, "Well, I asked the Spirit of Knowledge to show me how God created the mind and he showed me" (See Chapter on the Seven Spirits of God).

I have some idea of how it works, of some of the things that are behind it, why we as believers often struggle with seeing in the spirit and why we cannot retain the information. That is why each of these chapters links to one another, with activations and some teaching, to try and train your mind away from what it is used to doing.

I am going to give you a whole lot of terminology about the human mind and things associated with it. Then I want you to start to work with them so you get some understanding and revelation.

The Seven Spirits of God is something the church has really wrestled with. Some people do not understand it and really wrestle with it and that is okay. My experience has come out of Galatians 4:1:

"Now I say that the heir, as long as he is a child, does not differ at all from a slave, though he is master of all, but is under guardians and stewards until the time appointed by the father." (Galatians 4:1-2).

The human brain is like the latest huge shopping mall. If you could build a computer big enough to do the function of just the hippocampus area of the brain, it would be large enough to cover the whole state of Texas! It is like a hundred billion dealers on the Stock Exchange making transactions every second, and this is just a small part of what we use in our brain. Much of our brain is not even being used yet, because that is all connected to the realm of the spirit and the supernatural, and that has to be activated. Your brain is constantly storing, exchanging, cancelling, offloading, inverting, planting, recording, and analysing short-term memory. In the process happening every second of the day there are a hundred billion transactions that go on in the hippocampus area of the brain. That is just one part of the human brain – a hundred billion transactions!

Every skill we acquire and every memory stored is as a result of new connections being formed and built by the brain, which makes new connections in seconds and new memories in minutes. That is why you need to go and record, review and revisit your experiences in the spirit. Unless you use the memory, the brain will purge it and say it is irrelevant. This means you will never have an anchor for all the information that your spirit man is seeing to be retained, so it can never be stored in your memory. It just goes into the hippocampus and is destroyed. People say to me, "I do not see in the spirit." Well, actually you do, all the time, because you are a spirit being. You just do not store what you see, that is the problem.

When we are born, we are trained to receive information from outside us, into our soul. All our life we are trained how to receive information coming from the outside in. When we get born again the greatest problem and struggle exists because now we need to unlearn this process that has been established for years so that we can learn how to receive information from the inside out. Because you have a neuron functioning in one way with an impulse that will be travelling down one direction, you cannot make that impulse go backwards. You need to 'un-use' those memories and start new ones.

The new memories are built on revelation. They are built on meditating on the Word of God and being captivated. This builds new memories on the anchors of the Word. The Word of God then becomes the anchor to your next spiritual experience. Your spiritual experience then becomes anchored onto the Word of God. Each new spiritual experience is anchored and measured against your awareness at that present time. If there is no anchor for it in the present it gets shredded in your mind. So you end up struggling between what is real and what is not real, thinking you cannot see, your brain making you believe you will never see, when in fact you are seeing all the time. This is because you are a spirit being first, which has a soul (your brain's functions are part of your soul) and has a body. Because no one has ever taught you how to see, there is no relevant information for your spirit man to anchor new information on in order to retain it. So it goes into the hippocampus and disappears.

I have worked on this for eight years now, and the spirit world is as real to me as you are. It is so real that you can touch it, you can be in it, you can experience it and you can relate to it. What God wants us to understand is that we are still struggling with the temple we live in. The struggle is not that you do not see, the struggle is that you do see but you just do not retain what you see. I have given you some keys on how to retain some of that information, on purging images, meditating and things like that, in previous chapters. Each of these things builds on itself.

All the information that we have received from the time we have been conceived is received and processed from the outside in. When Adam was in the garden he did not live from outside information in, he lived from the information on the inside out. Every natural thing came out of the realm of the spirit. What we see around us came out of the realm of the spirit and therefore must be in, and have its birth in, the realm of the spirit. When Adam and Eve sinned with the devil it caused a depolarisation of the human mind (the Bible does not say they bit an apple by the way) and all that was connected with the realm of the spirit and the ability to retain information was cut off. The neurons that were going to that part of the brain were seared. That is part of what the flaming sword was doing at the Tree of Life (Genesis 3:24). So the human ability to retain spiritual information got seared.

The occult world knows about this. They teach their people how to see in the spirit. They teach them how to go in the spirit and they go. They are not afraid of it, they follow demons and the demons take them. But all they have done is taken what belongs to us, polluted it, poisoned it and made us hate it. They have made us feel it is not for the church because we are too spiritual for that! Well, really?! Hardly any of us are spiritual. We might think we are, but if you are spiritual then you do things that are spiritual.

When you can understand a little of how the human mind functions, it really helps to understand why we struggle with sin. The flow along the memory neural pathways that used to exist when Adam was in the garden, now no longer functions. When we get born again their ability to function is given back to us, but the same way as you learn in the natural, you must learn in the spirit. It must be line upon line, glory to glory, precept upon precept (Isaiah 28:10). It does not just happen by somebody laying hands on you and praying "Shundy bundy, you are blessed this Sunday – you are going to see for eternity!" I have only met two people in the world that were like that. One of them spent a year out in the spirit – every day drunk in the spirit, every day seeing, just absolutely captivated and God purged his life. Most of us will need to learn the process of seeing and activating, you need to learn the steps: A, B, C, etc. And the more you walk in it, the easier it is to activate it.

When we get born again there is already an established problem. The pathway of neuron functions and synapse impulses are so strained that, unless you make a conscious effort to give your brain something else to work with, you will only ever get what you have always got. You need to give your mind something to work with and that is why the Bible paints pictures.

Neurons store pictures, pictures create memories and memories create the 'now' as permanent memory. Memories that happen in the Word create the ability for the 'now', the present, to be stored in that memory. That is why you need to meditate in the Word of God and spend time going around it. The electrical receivers and pathways long unused by our spirit man need to be activated. As with a learned experience that creates a unique pattern of neurons, there is now a need to create a new pattern of neurons in your brain. That is why the Bible says, "And be renewed in the spirit of your mind" (Ephesians 4:23,). You need to be renewed in the pattern of your life. The word 'spirit' there comes from the word 'breath' or 'life' or 'movement of the wind of God'. You need to have a new mind in you, as the Bible says:

"Let this mind be in you, which was also in Christ Jesus" (Philippians 2:5 KJ21).

When the Bible talks about Christ Jesus (as opposed to Jesus Christ) it is not talking about the person of Jesus, it is referring to the anointing of the Son of God, which is what Christ Jesus is. It is only in the anointing of the Son of God that our mind can be renewed. It is only as we abide in that anointing that our mind can be transformed.

When the Bible talks about transforming, it is talking about the process that happens with a caterpillar. This beautiful little thing comes out of its egg and gorges itself until it becomes barrel-shaped. Then it sits on the side of the leaf and the sun comes out and it thinks, "One day I am going to spin this wonderful woolly blanket and I am going to spend the rest of my life soaking in the sun; wouldn't that be idyllic?!" We are going to do that one day. Hopefully we will be too busy creating universes to do that!

So, the caterpillar spins this blanket, it does not know that it is going to die. To understand the Bible when it talks about being transformed, it helps to understand the process that happens with a caterpillar. The complete DNA strand of the caterpillar disassociates so that there is not one single strand of DNA record in the memory of that caterpillar's structure. The heat of the cocoon does that and it is the way God has made it. We can see in nature what is supposed to happen with our brain. God wants new DNA to start in our brain. It is the heat in the caterpillar's cocoon that enables the creation of a new DNA strand. When it gets to a certain temperature, suddenly a new DNA strand starts to form and it is called a butterfly. We need to see that God wants us to go from the worm to the butterfly, where we can fly. We see first that which is natural and then that which is spiritual.

In the natural world there are things that give us the secrets of the spirit. Inside our minds God wants new DNA to start forming that comes out of the life of Heaven that is already inside of us. We release it from our spirit man, into our soul and into our mind. We release it by meditating, by worship, by the things I have talked about in previous chapters.

The world is waiting for you and me to come into divine order. I had the opportunity to be in the River of Glory that has been dammed up from when Adam fell. Did you know, the River of Glory still flows in the spirit realm? The devil has just surrounded it and shuts believers out. When Jesus was taken up into the exceedingly high mountain (and when you look at that phrase, it actually means the edge of the atmosphere, not a physical mountain), and the devil showed Him the kingdoms of this world (Matthew 4:8, Luke 4:5). Which world was that? It was not this world, but the world in the spirit realm, because everything that controls the spirit realm controls what goes on in the earth. Everything in the coming years in the church is going to be wrestling with the spirit realm and the control that goes on there. That is the heavenly place. That is where Adam got kicked out of when his role there got destroyed by his sin with the devil.

We are able to retrain our mind to captivate things of the spirit, because all the information that comes in through our natural senses is processed, logged, stored or shredded. The normal pathways of spirit information never become experience in our lives. We are never able to decipher that information, or process it, or store it, because we have never given it an anchor to remain on, to accumulate the 'now'.

I am talking about the rule of your spirit over your soul. You must dictate to your soul, because what comes out of your spirit will change your soul and make your body come into obedience. For example, in the last week and a half I have had three hours sleep a night. I actually had four hours sleep last night, and I do get tired, but I can make a choice. I either live out of another kingdom and the realm of that kingdom, draw on it as my source and as the government of my soul and my body, or I subject myself to this world and shut that out. You choose which master you serve. I love the realm of the spirit because there is power in the realm of the Kingdom for you and me to stand in who we are. I am looking forward to being like Paul. Well, I am and I am not! He can preach all night and walk all the next day and preach all the next night, without sleeping! I know I can stay awake for 48 hours when I go to the United States. But that is pretty hard work when you need to teach and deal with spiritual issues for the next 12 hours! You make your body do it, as Paul says:

"I pummel my body into submission" (1 Corinthians 9:27).

You need to pummel your body and make it do what your spirit wants it to do. In the same way as when you are quietly reading the Word, you do not actually have to say anything to make it happen, but you stand up on the inside and claim it with your heart. Your body will come into line. You need to practise that. It is not hard once you have practised.

David had found some wonderful keys to bring some of this about in his life:

1. Meditating
2. Worship
3. Spending time in the presence of God:

"For a day in Your courts is better than a thousand [anywhere else]" (Psalms 84:10 AMP).

David found being in the presence of God was a key. Worship was the thing that opened the doorway for him. David knew what it was to be in the spirit. All these men in the Old Testament knew about the spirit world. The Bible says about Abraham that he encountered God and then he was sitting in the door of his tent (I wonder which tent he was talking about). It says he lifted up his eyes and he saw three men coming towards him (Genesis 18:1-2). He knew who they were. Why? Because he had already seen them and encountered them before this time; he knew who they were – Melchizedek and two men in white linen (Revelation 15:6; 19:8; 19:14). Melchizedek is the king of the treasury room of Heaven.

Intimacy with God is vital in all the areas pertaining to spirit life.

We must deal with our imagination. You need to go through the process of redeeming your imagination, as I have already taught in a previous chapter. You need to build your faith. The last thing is to practise. I always come back to this. Everything in the spirit is a learned process. The personal gifting that is on our lives enables us to activate some things better than others, but all of it is a learned process. That is why we have classrooms at school, because everything is about learning something. There is no difference in the spirit. You need to learn about the ways of the spirit. The ways of the spirit are all to do with pathways and repetitive activities that enable your mind to store information and to be able to retain it; to be able to accumulate the 'now' in the spirit and to be able to store it, so that you can receive and experience it now.

The only way to do it is by practice. You need to practise meditating on the Word of God. I practise and I do things. The Bible talks about Ezekiel's river (Ezekiel 47); it talks about how it went to his ankles, then to his knees, then to his hips, then to his shoulders and finally over his head. Well, I have got a snorkel and a weight belt. I went to Lake Taupo (New Zealand) and stood on the side of the lake with my feet up to my ankles in the water. What I am doing is giving the 'now' in the realm of the spirit something to anchor the reality onto of the Word painted in Ezekiel's experience in the river, because I want the same thing he had. So I was praying in tongues as I allowed my body and my spirit to accumulate the information of what it would be like to stand in the River of Glory. Then I went up to my knees, praying in tongues for ten minutes, accumulating the information of what it would be like to be in that River of Glory. Then up to my waste praying in tongues, another ten minutes accumulating the information. Then up to my shoulders praying in tongues another ten minutes and then I was up over my head praying in the snorkel. I do not really know what the people thought on the beach! I really do not care. I had transitioned from the natural because the supernatural had something to anchor the memory and the information on.

It is the most wonderful thing to go and bury yourself in the River of Glory and swim upstream at will! To float and watch the glory flicker on the surface or go down and get some big gems and stick them in your belly. You need to enjoy it. That is what the Kingdom is about, to enjoy! That is why God made it, for us to enjoy. It was not hard. I take that information, write it down, take it into my quiet time and, praying in tongues, begin to draw on the memory of what happened, to give it a 'now', more relevant information to anchor on. I was in my bedroom an hour and a half later and realised I was on my floor laying backwards, but I do not have any record of falling backwards on the floor, because I was in the spirit. My body will not get hurt when I am in the spirit. That is why they could not touch Jesus when they took Him to the edge of the cliff (Luke 4:29-30), because he was in the spirit. That is why the devils cannot touch you when you are in the spirit, because the glory of God surrounds you.

These things have mostly been hidden from the church, but they are real. I have been there and I know others who have been there, and we have struggled to try and put some teaching process in place that will help you to believe. I have hungered after the Cloud of Glory. I wanted to know what the Cloud was like. I have a friend who takes me flying and one day we went with my father-in-law. They did not know what I was doing, but we flew straight through some of these clouds and I was busy looking, thinking, "I want to go in the middle of that. How do I get into the middle of that in my body? What do I have to do?" So one day, when everybody went out, I was praying and the Lord said, "Go into your shower and turn the hot tap on." So I went into the bathroom and turned the hot tap on. At this stage the bathroom was half the size it is now and the shower was on, so it was really nicely filled up with steam. As the water kept coming out and the room started to fill up with steam I began to think, "Well Lord, You are cheating me out of a shower tonight, that means I am going to have to have a cold shower! But I will put down my own ideas and focus on what I am doing here now." What happened was that the room got so full of mist that I could not see the other side of the wall. In fact, when I held my hand in front of my face I could not see my hand because of the steam that was in the room.

I closed my eyes and began to allow my body to feel what the steam was like while my mind was beginning to be caught up in the Word, of the Cloud of the glory of God descending on Mount Sinai – what it would have been like to be like Moses walking into that cloud, experiencing the revelation of the thunder and the beauty and the majesty of God. The Lord said to me, "Turn the light on." I turned the light on and the whole room went absolutely white because every drop of mist reflected the intensity of the light bulb.

There is no diminishing in the reflection; that is why we are going to be the reflection. That is why when the Bible says we are going to be caught up in the clouds to meet the Lord in the air (1 Thessalonians 3:17), it is not those fluffy things up there, it is the reflection in us that is going to be revealed to the world around us. God wants to reveal His sons on the earth, to the earth (Romans 8:19), so that the earth will know that there is a God in Israel. God made these statements:

"And I will sanctify My great name, which was profaned among the heathen, which ye have profaned in the midst of them;" (Ezekiel 36:23 KJ21).

"…and the heathen shall know that I am the LORD, the Holy One in Israel" (Ezekiel 39:7 KJ21).

God wants the realm of the spirit to be real to us so that the heathen will know that there is a God in the church. I do not know about you, but I am not satisfied with what I have and what I see in the church. It is up to us as individuals to cultivate a life with Heaven, the realm of God and with the angels that walk there. Angels are amazing to be around. I have encountered twenty-seven types of angels and there are about another fourteen to fifteen different types of creatures that are in Heaven. They are not all mentioned in the Bible and I do not care because I know what is around the Throne and when something flies around the Throne you need to believe it is of God!

God never stops creating, just because of who He is, what He is and what cascades off Him, in His Glory. There is a continual flow of glory coming off Him; it is the residue of the power that has been unused. That residue of power forms a River. Where that River comes out from under the veil it comes out as diamonds and oil and eventually turns into water that we can live in. It is alive. I teach on being baptised in that River (Chapter 9) because

we need to identify with the Father. I have been there and it has changed my life. There is a River and it is for you and me to enjoy. It is the residue of the power of God. God wants the supernatural to be real. He does not want it to be some fluffy thing that is out there and when people come around you they say, "Oh.... you are spiritual!" What a load of religious baloney! We are all called to be spiritual, because we are spiritual beings. We are all called to be with God and walk with God because we are the sons of God.
God wants us to know that Heaven is accessible now. I have tried to give you some understanding of why you would struggle seeing. It is basically because of the established processes of your brain and the way it has been trained to think. You have to 'un-train' it by retraining it to do something else. The most amazing thing is that when a neural pathway is not used for a long period of time it disconnects and the synapses break off and the neurons disconnect. That only happens when you have established new pathways, then the old one does not exist anymore.

We can use our pain as a springboard, instead of going down the pathway of sin. I go down the pathway of using that pain as a springboard to encounter, because I am establishing a new neural pathway to a place of encounter. I persistently use it until it is established as permanent memory. Then other things can be retained on that. Then it springboards off there and creates a whole synapse field and tree of its own with experiences of the realms of Heaven. This is how God has created us, with the ability to experience Heaven and make Heaven real.

Your experiences of the realms of the Kingdom of Heaven are not just to make you feel good. They do make you feel good and they are the most wonderful things that could happen, but people want to know about the realm of the spirit. That is why there are so many occult things going on – people are absolutely fascinated with it! I can think of one particular story of witchcraft for children, which came out of the mouth of a dragon! It is one of the greatest introductions to the occult world I have ever seen. If you have read the books you need to repent.

One of the things God wants is for the natural world around us and the environment we live in to see that the realm of the

Kingdom is real. We need to work in Words of Knowledge. The only way you can work in Words of Knowledge is if you have a relationship that knowledge can flow from. The only way you will work with miracles is if you work with the realm that the miracles come from.

A famous pastor was doing an overseas conference and a sister of faith sat next to another lady who had a dead knee, which had been welded together. This sister saw the lady's new knee in Heaven. There is a room of body parts in Heaven. This lady went into the room in Heaven with the body parts and said, "Yes, I will have her knee, thanks". No big "shundy-bundy" fluffy prayers. She just said, "There we are, a totally new knee, able to bend". Whatever you see in Heaven you can bring to the earth. Not what you hear from Heaven, but what you see in Heaven, because only what you see can you have. It gives you something to run towards. It is all about seeing and then hearing; seeing and releasing; seeing and bringing it down. I love bringing the glory and the thunder of the presence of God through the spirit realm back to the earth. I love it because it wrecks the devil in the spirit realm! There is nothing they can do about it, because light destroys and disperses darkness.

Darkness cannot penetrate light, you go out as a child of light carrying the glory, it spirals down and the devil gets wrecked, and anything that tries to touch it gets singed to a crisp! It is wonderful! But that is the way it is supposed to be, instead of us trying to fight through the darkness and get to Heaven, Jesus transitions us there because we are in Him.

Seeing in the spirit realm is the key to releasing the Kingdom. Renewing your mind is the key to seeing the spirit realm.

Chapter 7
How to Build a Strong Spirit

It is very important for us to have a strong spirit and be able to contain some of the things that will happen with us. The reason you need to build a strong spirit is because, when the glory comes in the market place, you do not want to be incoherent and you do not want to be falling all over the place shouting so people think you are mad. (They may think you are mad anyway, so it is not going to make much difference! But you know how it is.)
Because your spirit man is the thing that encounters the glory of God, you must build it to a point where your spirit can handle the presence and manifestation of the presence of God. Being in the spirit is a wonderful experience, but I do not chase being in the spirit, I chase God. I chase the glory of God. I chase and I want Him. So my desire in everything I do with my spirit man, including the building up of my spirit man, is to pursue God – to get to be with Him more. I want to spend as much time as I can with God. Even when I am talking with people I am very present with them but I am seeing something very different and I am very aware of things that are going on.

As I teach this in conferences, saints of old come into the meeting and deposit scrolls of revelation of the things I have been teaching into people's lives. You need to know that because some of you are sitting there going, "I can't do all this." That is okay, you cannot do it, but the Holy Ghost can. God's Word does not return to Him without bringing back fruit from the earth (Isaiah 55:11). So, when we are speaking like this in the spirit, the spirit world translates it and deposits it into our lives. You do not have to understand everything here, you just need to open your spirit and receive from the presence of God.

You should be able to live in both worlds quite easily. To be present in the natural and to be present with Jesus in the spirit world. But, because many of us have not exercised our spirit to be able to be present with someone and to also be present with God and the Holy Spirit and see what is going on in that world, because your spirit is not built to a place of being able to do that, you may think it is impossible. It is not impossible, it is a learned process and there are things that you can do to activate yourself towards it. I want to talk about how to build a strong spirit, because there are some really simple keys.

When God made Adam in Genesis it says:

"And the LORD God formed man of the dust of the ground, and breathed into his nostrils the breath of life; and man became a living soul" (Genesis 2:7 KJ21).

So, right there in Genesis we have the foundation for a body, a soul and a spirit. What dwells inside our spirit is the presence of God; that keeps our spirit. You see, your spirit is who you really are. My soul is a reflection of who I really am; it is my soul and my spirit that will go into Heaven. My spirit is going to carry the image of my soul so people will know who I am. I have met people in the spirit and I know who they are by that image. They look a little bit different because their skin is not the same, they carry different garments and they move and talk differently and that is okay, that is what it is all about.

Your spirit needs to be developed with some simple things. This is really the lion part of your life. There is the lamb part of being in love with God, walking with God, experiencing God and doing all those lovely things with Him. But there is also an aggressive side and the lion and the lamb must lay down together in your life. You must have both. You cannot just have one; you must have the other as well.

If you are too aggressive there will be a devil under every tea pot! If you do not have aggression in your life and it is all worship, everything will be fluffy and lovely and your soul will really be in charge of what is going on. What you need is a balance of both of these things inside your life. It is developing both, where there is the tenderness and the love and passion for God and the aggressiveness and the pursuit of obtaining the desire to get hold of the realm of Heaven. You must have both of these, the surrender and the victory – both sides.

When God made Adam a living soul in the garden He would come through Eden and walk with Adam in his garden. Then Adam would go and walk with God in Eden, which is God's garden. In that translation place the life of God and being near the person of God would be part of who Adam was because Adam had that breath in him. When Adam sinned he literally lost that breath and so the sustaining of who we are is now done by the soul when you are in an unsaved condition. When you get born again that breath comes back into you again and you get re-birthed into the reality of what Adam had! But our problem is we do not understand what Adam had. We do not even know what it was like there – but scripture paints little pictures of what it is like and we will talk about some of those.

I love walking in Eden. I love walking in the garden. I love that whole realm and what it is about because then I can speak to God as a Father, not a God who is on the throne, omniscient, omnipresent and omnipotent. If you do not know what those words mean, they mean all-knowing (omniscient), everywhere and in everything (omnipresent) and being all-powerful (omnipotent).

To build my spirit is vitally important in my life and walk with God. To be able to build something you need to give it the right kind of food. I have been involved in working in gymnasiums. If you work out and do not eat properly you will die because your body will 'rob from Peter to pay Paul', (an English idiom) when you are not getting the right nutrients inside your body. So, first in the natural, then in the spirit world. It is no different in the spirit world; you need to feed your spirit with the right nutrients for it to grow. If you are just going to push iron and push it and push it and not eat properly you will find your body starts to atrophy and you will not build big muscles. You have to eat the right food to build big muscles. What God is looking for is you giving yourself the right food, the opportunity and doing the preparation. You see, when preparation and circumstance meet, you then have the miracle. What God is looking for is the right circumstances in your preparation – and it is the preparation of your spirit that is important.

The first thing that is important in your spirit life is the issue of meditating. The Bible says:,

"...Man shall not live by bread alone, but by every word that proceeds from the mouth of God" (Matthew 4:4).

The Word of God, the enriching Word of God has come out of the mouth of God and has been written by the hand of man. God did not stand there and write the Bible; men did. It was inspired by God, but written by the hand of man. So the Word of God needs to be the basis of our meditation. Meditation according to Strong's concordance means, 'to ponder, to imagine, to revolve around your mind, to mutter like a sheep'. Over in New Zealand we know what sheep are. When you understand what a sheep does, then you can understand how the process of meditation works for you. In the morning when the sun comes up, a sheep will go and eat as much grass as it can and fill its gut. Then, when it is full, it will go and find a lovely, sunny place in the middle of the paddock or it will go and lean against a fence and get this kind of glazed look in its eyes. Then it will stand there chewing over and over. When the Bible talks about meditation that is what it means: to mutter; to mumble over; to chew.

This sheep wants to get every bit of energy out of the grass, so it takes its time with the grass. It is like us, we read the Word and we gorge ourselves and then we go away. It just passes straight through you because you have not worked with it. Many Christians' lives are like a drainpipe – it goes in and goes out and does nothing in between. Meditating on the Word of God is getting the in-between thing. It is taking the Word of God and taking your time with the Word. I cannot just read the Bible. It is impossible for me to read the Bible anymore, because I know the moment I start to read it

I am going to get caught by a scripture. It is going to go into my brain, I am going to get captivated by it and within fifteen minutes I am going to be looking at a doorway, because the Word paints a door. But that is practice and the reason it happens that quickly is because I practise doing that.

Meditating is vitally important in our lives. When you meditate you must seek to understand what the Word means, to understand how to apply it to your life or understand what implication it has for you, to understand what response you need to make and to understand what your role is in the Word. You see, if you are in Christ Jesus you have a role in the Word. You have a role to play in the Bible. Did you know that? There are things that only you can do. The Bible says there are things in Heaven, a record. God says He has written down things that He has dreamed about for us (Psalms 40:7; Hebrews 10:7). They are already written and each of us has a scroll that is like that. On the day when we die and go to be with God and see Him face to face He is going to unroll your scroll and you are going to see everything you could have had – everything that He had dreamed about for you. He dreamed about it and it was, before the 'is' existed. Wherever something 'is' He dreamed about it and it 'was'. The Bible says before the foundations of the earth He dreamed (Ephesians 1:4; 1 Corinthians 2:9). So that means before everything, before the record of what we call time ever started, God was already dreaming about you and He already had your scroll all wrapped up and done.

When a person remains in sin that scroll is in the trophy room of the devil. When a person is in an unsaved condition that scroll is in the trophy room of the devil. That is why the devil is trying to get as many kids aborted as he can, because their scrolls go into his trophy room. It is then lost to the earth, because each of them is a part. God then restores these children in Heaven and grows them into a son and their scroll burns in fire and gets destroyed out of the trophy room. They are just things that happen. I cannot show you them in the Bible, it is just the way it is; it is just what happens. Building your spirit man is very important. Meditating on the Word; you need to draw out of it, like with a lolly.

The second key to building a strong spirit is worship. In John it says:

"God is a Spirit, and they that worship Him must worship Him in spirit and in truth" (John 4:24 KJ21).

Worshipping does not mean just having a loud, clanky, happy time. It is vitally important you enter into the courtroom of God. The Bible says:

"Enter into His gates with thanksgiving, and into His courts with praise!" (Psalms 100:4 KJ21).

So you come before the Lord with singing, enter His gates with thanksgiving and His courts with praise. Singing and thanksgiving are supposed to be a part of worship. Coming into His courts with intercession is actually how to enter the courtroom of God and do business in the court room of God. What I want you to see is that worship is vitally important to you as a believer. It builds intimacy with the presence of God. If you just have a 'happy clappy' time in church then that is all you will ever have. There is no intimacy built in only 'happy clappy' times. Desire is built in the happy times, but intimacy is built out of worship, out of yearning, out of a longing. Basically, what worship means is I yield and bow down to someone who is greater than me. Worship means absolute surrender – it means I am giving all that I am to God in surrender. I am submitting, I am surrendering and I am looking to God to come and touch me and fill my life as I surrender.

It is a two-way street: I go, You touch me Lord, and I come back; I go, You touch me, I come back. That is what worship is supposed to do. There is supposed to be an encounter with the presence of God in worship. It is very important in your personal life. If you do not spend time worshipping then part of your spirit will be deeply inhibited because you will not be getting the nurture and the love of the presence of God into your life in a personal way.

I get frustrated when I come into church and everybody in church is trying to take the presence of God out of the atmosphere to fill them. They have been too lazy and have not been worshipping at home so they could bring that with them to fill the atmosphere. The first part, when people come and they want to pull out of the atmosphere, is the carnal. That is the natural. That is the soul wanting dominion and, because the soul is all people have ever been fed, that is what you get. That is why you cannot just have 'happy clappy' times. You need to have strong worship, which your soul uses to engage God and then you have intimacy, which builds a relationship with God. There is a difference between engaging somebody and getting to know them, hugging them and telling them you love them. That is the difference between what worship does and what a 'happy clappy' time does. Can you see the difference? It is very important for us to have a balance of this in our spirit life. In your personal time it is very important to spend time aggressively pursuing God in worship and then tenderly submitting to Him in worship.

Worship is a vitally important part of our life as a believer to grow our spirit. We must worship with our spirit. Strong's Concordance references John 4:24 to worship in spirit and in truth and the word 'truth' there is given as "without concealing or hiding anything." It means that I can come with all my garbage. With anything that could ever insult God I can go there and I can engage Him. The moment you turn up there you change – just by turning up there. You do not carry what you are into the realm of Heaven. You become who you really are when you go into the realm of Heaven. That means when I go into the realm of Heaven I transform into who I am, which is something totally different from what I am now. That is why I can come boldly, because His glory in me transforms me into the image of the Son, which enables me to present myself before Him. That is why worship is important, because it is a transforming and changing process inside of us. Isaiah says:

"*...they that wait upon the LORD shall renew their strength; they shall mount up with wings as eagles, they shall run and not be weary, and they shall walk and not faint*" (Isaiah 40:31 KJ21).

I can remember being in the spirit one day. I went through a doorway and I was standing on the edge of this precipice and there was just nothing in front of me except I could hear one of the spirits of Heaven blowing the wind. I knew what it was because I had been meditating on mounting up on wings like an eagle. I had done a study on eagles and the way they feel the wind underneath them in the morning so they can rise on the wind. I can remember standing on the edge, just nothing in front of me, except I could hear the wind blowing and I could feel it was coming. I remember standing with arms outstretched like an eagle, waiting to feel the wind blow under me and it happened. I got lost, totally lost for about an hour and a half, just being tumbled about by the glory and the wind of God. It happened again at night. There are just wonderful experiences that we are supposed to enjoy! We are supposed to have them; that is what our life is all about.

You need to wait on God. The word 'wait' is an interesting word (in the original) because it means "to bind together with twisting or to entwine together". When you are waiting on God in a place of worship you are twisting yourself into His nature. You are entwining yourself into His character. You are entwining yourself in and around His glory and His presence and you become one with Him. The Bible says:

"But the person who is united to the Lord becomes one spirit with Him" (1 Corinthians 6:17 AMP).

Many believers seem to have taken that out of their Bibles because their religious concepts say "I cannot be like God." Well, I am sorry, you are going to be like God because you are His son and you carry the same DNA as His. You are going to be like Him and there is nothing you can do about it! The way to develop your spirit is by twisting and entwining yourself around the presence of God until you become one with Him.

There is a place of intimacy. It is one of the four chambers of the heart called the 'dance floor'. On the dance floor you entwine yourself and become one with the presence of God and are led by Him in a dance in the realm of the Kingdom. The dance floor is the most amazing place to be with God, twirling around in the arms of God as a father, as a friend and as a lover. Often when we say these kinds of words our brain has a 'fleshy' concept and thinks "No, that can't happen!" Well, yes it can because we actually become one with the Spirit of God and join our soul with His.

It is really important for us to get to grips with how to build our spirit. Another way is fellowship. In Proverbs it says:

"Iron sharpens iron; so a man sharpens the countenance of his friend" (Proverbs 27:17 AMP).

You need to have fellowship with one another and I do not mean just "Hi, how are you today, nice to see you." That is not having fellowship; that is just saying hello. Fellowship means becoming acquainted with someone – "Hi, how's it going there Jane? Tell me what's happening in the spirit, etc." That is how you become acquainted. You see, when you are acquainted with someone you can love on them. This is the testimony of Jesus Christ in the church: That the world may know them by this love, one for another (John 13:35).

It is the fellowship that enables all of us to come out of our sin and to expose ourselves and to be vulnerable. One of the reasons I believe that the devil mocked God was because of His vulnerability as a child with Adam and Eve, playing in the garden with them. I love playing with my kids and wrestling them, I have wrestled Jesus. We do things like that and it is really cool!

What God is looking for is fellowship in the body, proper fellowship. Fellowship produces unity. Where there is unity God commands a blessing. Where there is unity, where everyone dwells together in union, then the power of God will be displayed. If you want the power of God displayed in your church you need to find that unity in fellowship. And it does not just mean saying hello to everybody on Sunday. It means getting knitted in with others in the body because each group is supposed to be knitted in with another group. Each one is supposed to have connections within the house of the Lord so that you have unity in the house of God. If you want the glory you need to get into unity.

But it is important to be cautious with people. You need to be cautious because not everybody is the same as you and not everybody has the same integrity as you. Sometimes you will find people with mouths that run off, so you need to be careful. There are boundaries that need to happen as well within the fellowship in unity. It is not just telling everybody your secrets. It is getting to know them and you being known by them as you begin to share. I love having some of these guys who come with me, because they get to see me in my humanity. They get to see who I really am.

I am not a spiritual geek, but I am a spiritual freak! There is a difference. One is a thing I can choose to do; the other is a thing I just am. What I have hungered for is relationship and you only build relationship when you spend time with someone.

I love going fishing with my friend Rob, and we yank away and we catch fish and it is just glorious! We go fishing and we talk away, catch fish and talk a bit more. It is one of those things you just do. That is what the Bible is saying about fellowship: to get linked together. It is the linking process that brings the glory of God. What happens is my gate links with your gate, and our two gates link with her gate, and our three gates link with his gate, and our four gates link with their gate and there is an exponential rise in the presence of God. It goes one times, ten times, a hundred times, a thousand times. One shall put a thousand to flight, two shall put ten thousand to flight (Deuteronomy 32:30); it is just a spiritual principle. When you are linked together properly there is an exponential increase in the flow of the presence of God into a meeting. That is why you need to have fellowship, one with another, properly, in the right way in the Holy Ghost.

Most believers pray in the spirit for five minutes a day on average and they struggle with that. The reason they struggle is because their spirit is not built up. The only way to build a muscle is to use it and use it. One of the things I have learned to do is to read the Bible before and while praying in the spirit. You can get caught up in the realm of the Kingdom by reading the Bible and praying in the spirit. It begins to captivate your mind, reading, 'the Lord is my help', etc. You can begin to quote scriptures, because of your meditating and your speaking forth the Word of God. Praying in tongues is a vital key.

You can pray in tongues in English, you can pray in the tongues of angels and you can pray in the tongues of men (1 Corinthians 13:1). I have seen it all happen in a meeting, and one of the most important things for us to understand is that there is a diversity in tongues. One of the gifts of the spirit is praying in tongues. We have a spirit that prays in tongues and then there is the gift of tongues. That is a totally different thing than praying in tongues. The gift of tongues is an exercising of a gift for a specific purpose.

When you pray in tongues you are exercising your spirit. The Bible says:

"He who speaks in a [strange] tongue edifies and improves himself" (1 Corinthians 14:4 AMP).

That means you. The reason you pray in tongues is to build up your spirit. The word 'edify' means to build up – it means to make strong inside. That is the whole objective of praying in tongues. What I have learned to do is not just to pray in tongues with my mind going, "I wonder what I will be having for breakfast today...? mmm, that dinner smells really nice.. man I am going to have a huge day today, I have got so much I need to do." That is like wiping butter all over the carpet you are walking on. It is actually doing nothing.

The key to praying in tongues is having your mind captivated with the object of your desire, and the way it becomes captivated is to work with the Word. If you have not memorised scripture you go and read it until you can memorise it. I can quote long passages of scripture just because I have read them over and over. When you begin to pray in tongues and you are meditating and mulling over the Word while praying in tongues, in the realm of the spirit, your spirit man starts to savour it and drink it in. Your spirit man is then built up and becomes strong. That takes practice. I was not able to start praying an hour a day in tongues when I first started. If you can do that, well, hallelujah! You are a little bit ahead of me. I went five minutes and then ten minutes. That was a real struggle when I first started praying in tongues. Praying hard in tongues ten minutes a day was exercise enough, like I had just run ten miles! But often it is because we are weak that we cannot do it. It is because our spirit has never had dominion over our soul and our body and made them do what they are supposed to do.

When you pray in tongues it stirs you to have dominion. It stirs your spirit to yearn after God. It stirs who you are, making you into something different than you are and making you into what you are to become. It stirs you up and that is what it is for. It stirs you up, makes you stand, it makes your soul submit and your body conform to the image of the Son of God. You have to do it! No one else can do it for you. You cannot live off this or that conference for the next twenty years, that won't work. All that will ever be is a nice experience. You need to take what you have and work with it. And let me tell you – it is hard work!

When you do not want to pray in tongues and your soul has total control over your spirit, it feels like one big failure! As you pray, and your mind is saying "No, sorry, this isn't working.. oh this is such a pain.. aaahhh, nothing is happening here" and you go on and on and on. You need to say, "Soul, shut up!" because it is just your soul wanting to stay in charge and you need to make it submit. When my soul gets like that I target it and I go into the Gateways of my Soul. I go into my Conscience Gate speaking in tongues and I speak to my conscience "You will submit", into my Mind Gate, "You will bow." I make it do what it is supposed to do. And the only reason I can do that is because I have practised. As you practise the pathway, it becomes familiar and then it is easy. You need to practise.

Another key is speaking the Word of God out loud. You need to take the Word of God and decree it. "Father, thank You that Your Word is a lamp unto my feet and a light unto my path (Psalm 119:105). Thank you, Lord, that Your Word directs my steps, and my steps are ordered by the Word of God (Proverbs 16:9, Psalms 37:23). Thank You, Lord, that I do not stray from the left or the right because You are leading me (Isaiah 30:21). Father, thank You that I hear Your voice and I choose to obey it (John 10:27)." I just take the Word and pray it. You need to take the Word of God and throw it into the spirit world.

God made this statement:

"..the Most High does not dwell in temples made with hands.." (Acts 7:48).

God dwells in the words that you have spoken that create an atmosphere for Him to dwell in. That is why they would offer up praises and do those kinds of things in the temple, because the things you speak create an environment for God's fire to come upon the offering that you create for Him. I do not know about you but I want the glory fire of God to come around my life. I want that glory to come over me. I want it to come and touch my life so that I can touch the world that is around me. Until I have touched the glory in my own life I will never bring the world into being touched by it. You need to experience it in your own life first. It is hard work, but oh, the rewards at the end! I have been in situations where, if I had never built up my spirit, I would never have had victory.

I can remember one day, praying for a woman in our church in the ministry room when it was first set up. I said "I want you to follow after me, 'Father, in the Name of Jesus, (Father in the Name of Jesus) I renounce (I renounce)'..." and then she hissed and her eyes went red and slit like cat's eyes. Now this is a physical human body changing into something that is inside of them, manifesting. It only took me a few seconds to say "Whoa! Rock on! Bring it on!" Why? Because I had built up my spirit with the truth of "Father, I thank you that when I speak, my words confront and destroy every work of the devil. Father it turns them over. Father, when I speak I thank You that men and women are delivered"

"these attesting signs will accompany those who believe: in My name they will drive out demons" (Mark 16:17 AMP).

Now if you do not believe Christians can have devils, you need to perhaps pray. Pastors can have them too. I have had some interesting experiences with pastors!

"Delight yourself also in the Lord, and He will give you the desires and secret petitions of your heart" (Psalm 37:4 AMP).

But you need to meditate on the Word. You need to spend the time cultivating your spirit. You need to spend the time with God, doing some of these things that will grow you, so that when the glory turns up, or when you turn up in the glory, then your body does not get freaked out. Because your spirit man is the candle of the Lord (Proverbs 20:27).

Chapter 8
Eden

I want to talk about something that has been really precious to me and came at the end of a long series of spiritual events that began to happen in my life. It started as I was realising things about the chambers of the heart and the garden of intimacy that you can build with God inside your life. You need to plough the ground of your heart, sow there and plant. I knew that there was a river, and once I had built this garden in my heart, I knew that there was more to this river.

I am going to teach about the way God made things correctly, not the way that we may have often been taught in church. I did not grow up in church. I did things that probably were not very wise. God had a destiny for my life but the devil also had a plan and, unfortunately, from about eight years old I yielded to that other destiny. Then God found me, turned me around and shook me until I said, "I repent! I repent! I repent!"

I never really had any kind of background information or religious doctrine in my mind making me think a certain way that was not actually the truth. When I was growing up in the Baptist Church I would listen to the Words of God being spoken and I relished it because finally I had found something that gave me life and did not steal from me when I thought it was giving me life.

In my first six or seven years with the Lord I became really fascinated with Eden. I am always fascinated with the beginnings of things, so I asked God, "What were You before You was or, before You is, what were You?" I wanted to know what Eden was like. (Since then I have been there and it is really radical.) I began to think around the concept of this garden called Eden that we hear talked about a lot and what it was like there.

One day I was praying about this Garden of Eden when I realised that what I was taught in church is not what my Bible says! I would read the Bible, then I would listen to these guys preaching and I would go back to my Bible and wonder what they were talking about. So I began to ask questions of God. I began to think, "Lord, Adam walked with You in the cool of the day and it says that Adam heard the voice of God walking in the garden. How does a voice have footsteps? How does that work?" (Genesis 3:8; 10) It is a mystery in itself!

When you begin to meditate and revolve these things around your mind, the revelation that is in the Word will captivate your heart and it begins to captivate your imagination. I found myself being caught in awe by some of the statements in the Bible. Before this started to happen I would read through the Bible, just read it and read it. One day the Lord said to me, "Do not read it anymore." I said, "But they say you have to." He said, "But I am telling you not to." I said, "But..." and He said, "But...?" and I said, "But..." and He said, "I will kick your butt if you do not do the 'but' I am telling you to do!" So I said, "Okay!" So, for a year I did not read the Bible. It was probably the best thing that ever happened to me because it made me realise that my source was not just the written Word but also the revelation of what flows in me. Because I could not read it I used to think about it. It suddenly went from just reading information from the outside in to gleaning information from the inside out. So I started to meditate on the gleanings of Genesis. I love Genesis.

After that year I started reading Genesis from chapter one through to the end, and by the time I got to chapter twenty-four I decided to go back to the beginning again. Every time I went back into it I got more revelation out if it because it began to captivate my mind. When no one was looking I would get my Bible out, and then for weeks I would meditate around that one scripture because I had nothing else to hold onto. It is not based on a religious rote. How you get revelation is based on a relationship. What captivates your mind is what releases the power of God on your behalf. When this started it mystified me and when something mystified me I kept on asking God, "Are you going to speak to me?" Eventually God has enough of that! I would spend my 18,500 words (the average amount of words a man can listen to a day) listening to God and that meant I could not listen to my wife!

"Thus the heavens and the earth, and all the host of them, were finished. And on the seventh day God ended His work which He had done, and He rested on the seventh day from all His work which He had done. Then God blessed the seventh day and sanctified it, because in it He rested from all His work which God had created and made. This is the history of the heavens and the earth when they were created, in the day that the Lord God made the earth and the heavens." (Genesis 2:1-4)

Wait a minute. It says "the heavens and the earth", then "the earth and the heavens" – that is interesting.

"..before any plant of the field was in the earth and before any herb of the field had grown. For the Lord God had not caused it to rain on the earth, and there was no man to till the ground.." (Genesis 2:5)

"Before it was in the earth;" that is even more interesting, "and every herb of the field before it grew." Where did it grow before it was in the earth? "And there was not a man to till the ground." So, all this happened before Adam was even on the earth. Where did God cause all those plants to grow first?

"…but a mist went up from the earth and watered the whole face of the ground. And the Lord God formed man of the dust of the ground, and breathed into his nostrils the breath of life; and man became a living being." (Genesis 2:6-7)

"The Lord God planted a garden eastward in Eden…" (Genesis 2:8)

Now, that is really interesting, "...eastward in Eden..." Now, that means that there is Eden and then there is a garden. There is no such thing as 'The Garden of Eden', there is Eden and a garden.

"And out of the ground the Lord God made every tree grow that is pleasant to the sight and good for food. The tree of life was also in the midst of the garden, and the tree of the knowledge of good and evil. Now a river went out of Eden

to water the garden, and from there it parted and became four riverheads.." (Genesis 2:9-10)

So there has got to be two gardens.

"...And from thence it was parted, and became into four heads. The name of the first is Pison: that is it which compasseth the whole land of Havilah, where there is gold; And the gold of that land is good..." (Genesis 2:10-12)

I had believed that the Garden of Eden was a thing I was unable to go and walk in. That was totally wrong doctrine, because there is no such thing as the Garden of Eden. There is a garden in Eden.

God put a garden in Eden, and what would happen is that on the seventh day when God rested He would go into Eden. The closest thing that He could have in relational connection with somebody was when He was off the throne. Eden is God's garden. He put a garden in His garden. It was a place for man to live in His garden.

The Bible says that He caused every herb of the field and tree of the field to grow before it was on the earth (Genesis 2:5). So where did He make them grow first? In Eden. Then after this happened God put Adam in the garden and Adam had access to the earth through the garden. So that means the garden was in the spirit. Then God told Adam and Eve to go and multiply and populate the earth. They then sinned (but she did not bite an apple!).

The reality is that there is a garden that is connected to the heart of God which expresses the pleasure of God. I began to do a study of the Bible just about gardens, how Solomon had a garden and all these men who were kings had a garden. What did they use to do in the garden when they wanted a rest from the throne? They would go into the garden and prune flowers. They would just go and walk among the fragrance of their garden and thoroughly enjoy having time out.

I suddenly began to realise that perhaps on the seventh day God has time out. I had been in Heaven and I knew that Heaven shuts down on the seventh day, which meant that He must go somewhere. I never really understood where He went until this began to click in my brain. I began to realise that when God comes off the throne He goes to walk in His garden called Eden. His main objective for going into His garden, from the point He made Adam, was to go and have a friendship and relationship, to spend time with His son who He had made for Himself to have pleasure in as a Father.

Eden is God's garden. Then there is a garden that God put eastward in Eden, which is called Adam and Eve's garden. Scripture talks about a river which flows from Eden into the garden and from the garden it breaks into four heads and waters the earth. So that is why we have four chambers to our heart, the four heads that flow life around our natural body. Those four heads (before Adam sinned and we had this fallen body) used to flow though the spiritual garden and the spiritual four heads used to water not only the garden but the earth. How did the earth get life except from the river? Where did the river come from? It came out of Adam.

I began to realise that there is a river and that this river has a connection all the way into Eden, through Eden, and right the way to the throne. Revelation talks about the river running out of the throne.

"And he showed me a pure river of water of life, clear as crystal, proceeding from the throne of God and of the Lamb" (Revelation 22:1)

That is the same river that runs through Eden into the garden and from there it waters the earth. How is God going to water the earth today except through us? We are the clouds carrying the rain, full of glory, to water the earth and bring revival.

I realised there was a river and I needed to grow my own garden in my heart, because my heart is the closest thing to that place of God. Whatever goes on in the heart of a person is what they become. The heart is where all the issues of life flow out of.

I began to work on this. First of all I had a garden in my heart I needed to cultivate. I grew this garden in my own heart and life where I would go and celebrate the victories and things that had happened in my life. I have a paddock of daffodils. I love daffodils. But the daffodils that are grown in my own heart garden do not die when you stand on them, they do not break. They bend over, celebrate and shake and then stand up again when you get off them!

I would go and enjoy myself in that garden with the expectation that when I am there God will come walking to meet with me in my garden, because the Bible says He used to go and meet Adam.

So I wanted Him to meet me in my garden. I remember in those days I could never see Him, I just knew He was there. I would feel His presence come into my garden in my heart and I would feel Him there. I can remember one day thinking that this is a pretty one-sided relationship really, He comes to me but I do not go to Him. That began a journey which ended up at an encounter with God in Eden.

Eden is the most amazing place that you could ever imagine. Trees ten times the size of the redwood forests, mountains of gold with glory on them! I began to realise that when God comes off the throne He spends time in His garden. It only says that He came walking in the cool of the day with Adam. So what did He do for the rest of the day? I began to ask, "Father what do You do for the rest of the day? I want to come and share a little bit with You and what You do with the rest of Your day off. If you are going to take a holiday then I would love to come and spend some time with You on holiday." Just like I love going fishing with my friend and spending some time with him.

I began to yearn in my heart, "God I want to spend time with You when You rest. I want to walk with You." I knew the river was the key because when you follow the river it leads through your garden, up this glorious waterfall into Eden, which is His garden. I did not know that you could swim up river, you could float up river, you could fly up river, you could do anything you like up the river. I did not know that, so I figured I would jump into the river and just start walking, because there is no resistance in the river and it is not hard work. In fact, you can just think and you can move, it is just one of those things. So I got into the river and said, "Lord, I am coming." I did not know what to do; I just started moving up the river, "Lord, I am coming!" We get a choice to go, the Bible says:

"Come to Me, all you who labour and are heavy-laden and overburdened, and I will cause you to rest...take my yoke..."(Matthew 11:28-29 AMP).

To come to God you need to make a choice "Lord, I am coming to You". I made that choice that day and I found myself going. Then I saw this waterfall and it was the most amazing thing! I stood there for maybe two or three hours just going "Wow!"

I was thinking, "If I go under there I am going to get pulverised!" There are diamonds, stones and gems that flow out, which have been carved out of Eden. They fall into the river and each one is cut beautifully. I was thinking, "Man, I am not going to go anywhere near that massive fountain of those things!" But there is no resistance, the natural mind is thinking in the natural way. "There is no resistance in the water…but...but...but.." backwards and forwards until I realised that it would not really matter if I died. Who cares?! I could not die in any better place so I went into the fountain. When I got into it I started to float up the waterfall. The more I moved up, the faster I went. When I got up to the top it was like a whole new world had opened up and I was standing on the top, on the very edge, with this great big drop behind me and this water rushing through me, standing there going, "Wow!"

I just fell backwards. You can float and move in the realm of the spirit, there is no gravity. I floated down and it felt really good. So I floated up again. I stood on the edge and I fell off it again. So I just started to play! You can get caught in these little things. The issue is not that you get caught there; the issue is that you are on a journey of discovery to find out what it is really like. So I spent time standing there, diving off, and found that if you do swallow dives you just stay there. Then, when you think, "I will float down", you start to float down. The realm of Heaven is not what we think it is.

It came to the point where I knew I had to go and encounter Jesus. There is a pathway that runs along the river and then there is a bridge. I could see Jesus just looking at the bridge, shaking His head (as if He was thinking, 'it is about time you got here!'). I can remember walking along this pathway and I was fascinated with everything I was seeing. Even the grass was singing! The river was whispering love songs to me, "We love you, welcome!" I was thinking, "I will just sit down here for a minute, Jesus, I will be with You in a minute, You just wait, I am going to enjoy some of this down here….."

Eventually I got up and walked on the path. When you walk on the path it moves, it kind of loves you. I am just describing what happens for me. I am painting a doorway for you. I walked up to the bridge and I saw Jesus. He is interesting. He is so full of love, yet so full of righteousness, judgment, mercy, grace and many things. He looked at me and He said, "I need to carry what you are carrying now because you cannot go in there with this."

I thought I was clean, then I realised on my back was a great big sack of everything that I would try and justify myself with, being in Eden. Then He said, "That is why I died, Ian. It was for this, so that you could come back to the Father. It is My pleasure to carry that for you. You are my friend and I want to carry it for you. I will hold it here for you while you go and talk to the Father. He is waiting for you in the rose garden." I did not know where the rose garden was. I was just in this place going, "Wow! I do not want to go home, in fact I think I will spend eternity here..." And we are actually going to. We are going to be able to spend eternity with God pruning roses and when you prune them they do not die, they just produce life.

I can remember standing on the edge of a field where a path went down and I could smell this fragrance that was coming up out of the valley. To think is to be there, to think is to move. You can walk if you want to but thinking is better, it is quicker. But I also wanted to discover this pathway that is made of gems that shimmer and it is clear. You can see all the way into it. I was thinking about all of this but I wanted to go and meet with God. I was thinking, "Lord, where do I go, where are You?" It is amazing when you listen you can hear His footsteps. I listened and began to shut everything else out and focus on the object of my desire, which was to be with Him. I began to walk down the path. To think was to move, it was like taking one step but taking a twenty metre step. You would fly with each step. It is glorious! It is fantastic!

I went around a corner and there was a rose garden. All I could see was His back. At this stage I had never seen God and I was really petrified, yet I wanted to know Him. The best way to fellowship with a person is shoulder to shoulder, just getting involved with what they are doing. I was terrified of going up to God and saying "Hi! I am Ian." What is He even going to say? "I know....!" But the most amazing thing is that you do not have to say anything. All He wants is just your presence. I can remember going down and standing next to Him, watching this hand that was shimmering.

I was thinking, "Whoa! Look at that, this is my Dad, look at that hand!" He looks different in the garden from the way He does on the throne and different from the way He looks in the dark cloud. He is God; He can do what He likes.

I can remember watching His hand and watching Him prune a rose. When He would prune a rose a new bud would form and then He would prune another one and another new bud would form. I watched the thing fall to the floor and it somehow became one with the floor and then became part of the rose again. How do you explain that? Tell a scientist this is what happened and they will go, "Yeah, right."

That is what happened because there is no death in Heaven. Nothing dies. Everything is alive and stays alive. He was just enjoying doing something that was not "power over the earth!" He was just enjoying doing what He loves doing – walking in His garden, doing little things in His garden. I was just going, "Wow, look at that!" As He moved I did not know what to say, but you do not have to say anything, just being there is reward enough for Him. He wants your friendship and He wants your fellowship.

I had been so fascinated, but I knew that it was time for me to go. I did not want to go but I knew I had to. I said, "Lord, I really enjoyed my time here with You." And He said, "Yeah, Me too." That was it, so I left. I did not turn my back I just kind of backed away, trying to look while thinking, "God, I am going to die if I look at You too much." But when He is in the garden He is not carrying the garment of the authority of the King. He is carrying the personhood of who He is.

I began to walk away and I saw the garment that He carries. It is just amazing! It moves, it is fire and it is life. It falls off and becomes one with the ground and it makes things, just because of who He is.

I backed away and got back to Jesus and Jesus gave me this knowing look and I thought, "You smart alec! You knew what was going to happen and did not say a word! You are supposed to tell me these things!"

Jesus said, "You think so?"

And I said, "Oops! Shut my mouth!"

Jesus is a really good friend and we need to develop a relationship with Him. The Holy Spirit is a really good friend and we need to develop a relationship with Him too. I have talked a lot about the Father, but I have worked on a relationship with Jesus in exactly the same way and I have worked on a relationship with the Holy Spirit in exactly the same way, chasing them. I am a Father freak, there are people who are Jesus freaks and other people who are Holy Spirit freaks. We all have a part of it but you need to know all three, you cannot just relate with one. The church has been missing out a lot because they have not been relating with all three.

I have talked about the Father a lot because many people have never gone anywhere near the Father. You need to know that you can get near Him. A lot of people can talk with Jesus and know the voice of the Holy Ghost, but there is more than that.

I began a journey over a couple of weeks, going back to Eden again. I thought that if I had done it once I was going to do it again. I knew how the human brain thinks and the process, so I practised going into Eden. I would go into Eden and find my path. I would go into that river and I would go up the river and up the fountain. Then I would walk along the stream and go in by the bridge that goes over the stream. Then I would get lost in the arms of the presence of God.

Eden is a place where you can go and walk and enjoy God, not just be with Him there but go and look at what He has done. I can remember thinking, "Man, there are some amazing things here." I went there one day and He was not there. I thought, "Yes!" because I wanted to go and see some other places. I can remember walking down this path and there was a forest that opened up before me and the trees were alive. You walk amongst them and the sound that comes off them caresses your life because they sing of the glory and of His Majesty. They grow like the cedars of Lebanon to exalt Him, their one desire. The creatures that are there are amazing because there is no death in them and their source and food is of another source and another life. Everything is alive there and you and I can enjoy that too.

This would have taken me two and a half or three years to work through. I want to make it real for you. I have painted you a picture, the same way the men of old painted a picture of their vision of the Throne. I have painted you a picture of what Eden is like and you can go and walk with Him. It may take you a while to get there because there may be some things you need to cultivate in your heart first before you can even go there. But I have opened a doorway for you to be able to use if you choose to. If you do not use the door, something else will fill it; it is your choice. You either have an encounter with God or you encounter something else that will resist you encountering God. In my own heart and life I pursued and chased God.

I have done the same with Jesus. Jesus is the most amazing guy. The first time I ever had an encounter with Him I can remember walking along the beach near me and thinking about Jesus. Although I have brothers they have never really been brothers to me. God was on a journey of healing my life, because I wanted to know Jesus as my brother. I am Jesus' brother and I wanted to know Him as a brother. I can remember meditating on all these things walking along the beach one day and, while I was walking, suddenly everything began to change. I realised it was not quite the beach I was walking on before, yet I was still feeling the sand but then the sand changed. I thought, "Man, this is strange."

Then I felt Jesus turn up behind me and I had never met Jesus until this stage, in that form. I was thinking, "Man, if I turn around what is going to happen to me?!" I said, "Well, Lord, I have been yearning after You as my brother, so it cannot be all that bad."

I expected to turn around and see these eyes of fire and lightning and thunder! I turned around and there was a man standing in front of me that looked like the Jesus I used to see when I was about five years old, before the occult occurrences started. I can remember looking at Him thinking, "You are just like a man, but You are more than a man." I began to look at Him and think, "What are You?" He looked at me the same way! Do you know what He said to me:

"What are you?" I went, "You cheeky thing!"

He said, "Yeah, that's right!"

And I went, "Wait a minute. You are the man, You are the resurrected God of the Universe. How can I talk to You like that?!"

He said, "Because I am your brother." I said, "Oh, is that right? Well, my brothers treated me wrong."

And He said, "So? That's not why I am here."

These things happen and you feel like your transistors are being re-wired. Then He started looking at me like this: "What are you going to do about it?!"

I thought, "Well, I only know one thing to do with a brother when they do that." You climb onto them, you wrestle them and you have a rumble!" I thought, "Man! Can I do this?" I was looking at Him, thinking these thoughts.

He said to me, "Why not?" I went, "What did you say?" He replied, "Why not?"

I thought "Right, fine! This is it" So I had a rumble with Jesus on the edge of the water and it ended up with Him throwing me into the water! (You understand, fishermen are pretty strong!) I understand why Jacob got hold of Jesus and tried to pin Him. No wonder God touched His hip; he had his leg wrapped around Him, but then felt "sorry, no more!"

I ended up, after that period, sitting down with Jesus on the beach, on the edge of the shore and He began to talk to me about the pain of my life and how I was not able to relate to Him because of the pain of my relationship with my own brothers. What needed to happen was a restoration in my own soul so that He could become my brother. This is what God is all about. Bringing you back into a relationship. The Holy Ghost is no different, He is amazing.

I hope I have given you some hope beyond your experience with God. God is amazing! Jesus is amazing! The Holy Spirit is amazing! The Father is amazing! The three-in-one are amazing! To see them come together is amazing. To watch what they do when they are together is just amazing! They are always together but they are always separate.

The most important thing for us to understand is that there is a river and that river flows from the Throne and the river flows through Eden into your garden. I have a garden that I can walk in. That garden is connected to the deepest place of intimacy with God, which is Eden. Therefore I can go through the inside of me, my spirit, where God lives inside you and me, because this can transfer us into Eden without any problem. No going through the spirit realm, no doing anything else, your spirit man in Christ transfers you there. No fighting! That is the way it is.

I began to experience a walk with God like this and let me tell you, it never stops and it never ceases to amaze me. Every time I go there I want to stop and look at everything again because it is ever-changing. When you look at the jewels in the river they change shape. The reason they change shape is because they are trying to display your beauty in them. It is just amazing! I really enjoy messing around with the realm of Heaven. You can go on a journey. All of us are supposed to be on a journey. For some of us it is going to be a longer journey than others and that is okay. The issue is not that you have arrived and you have some deep spiritual experience, the issue is that you have started the journey. That is the important thing. It might not be all bells and whistles for you and it might take you three or four years, but I have been at this for twenty-five years now. It does not happen overnight. I have had to learn how it happens and I have been able to teach some of that to you and give you some of the secrets.

I love going into Eden. I love going for a walk and experiencing God. In some of these meetings I have had fifteen, thirty, forty, seventy or eighty people suddenly find themselves in the spirit with me walking on their own journey with God through these realms. I am opening a door of reality for you. God has called me as a door-keeper for some of these things. I open the door by going there. I do not just sit there, it has got to be supernaturally spiritual and naturally spiritual, not a big cloudy thing – this is real!

In one meeting there were about sixty people, and about fifty of them began to feel themselves caught up in the realm of visitation of God that was starting to happen in the meeting through the door that had opened. By the time I was walking down the pathway I knew that others had passed me, running to the presence of God. I was busy talking about what was happening with me and when we all came out of it one of the guys said he wished I would have just shut up and let him have his own experience with God. So if that happens with you, go and enjoy your experience with God. God is omnipotent and omnipresent. We can have fifty relationships with Him all at the same time. Obviously He holds the whole world in the palm of His hand, so He is big enough to have a relationship with all of us separately, all at the same time. That is the most wonderful thing about God.

You need to learn the pathway in and the pathway out. Sometimes the Lord shows you differently and you see things differently when you are going out than when you are coming in. Heaven is most fascinating. There is a portal where these living creatures go. They move like lightning and they bump against things and they have many eyes. I have gone and I have looked at those eyes moving to and fro. The most amazing thing is that they just carry on looking at you and when they look at you, they look right into you and everything is made open to them. That is really scary, but they are alive. I just enjoy it. You need to enjoy Heaven.

ACTIVATION

"Thank You, Lord Jesus. Father, I want to thank You that You are a Spirit and Lord I can relate to You, spirit to spirit. Lord, that I can be entwined in Your arms and Your beauty and get lost in Your magnificence. Father, I thank You that there is a river. Father I thank You that there is a river that flows, that trickles down out of the realm of glory into my life. Father, thank You that in me there is a river that touches the earth. Father, today I come to that river, I draw near that river, to hear it whispering, hear it calling.

Whispering the love songs You put in it. Father, what a wonder to sit down and just watch it flow by. But Father there is more. My pathway that I have worn in the middle of that river to go into it and to feel the rushing of the life of Your presence, like wind blowing through my skin. Lord, I stand in that river. Father, You know the objective of my desire is to see You. Lord, I lift my eyes to Your presence in that far away place. Lord, in that river there are the stones that whisper of Your glory, the diamonds that carry Your beauty and reflect Your magnificence.

Father, to just lie in that river at the bottom and watch the reflection of the glory like fire moving and flickering across the top of it. Father, to move underneath it and to feel the stones' caress.

Father, the blue stones of beauty. But Lord, I hear the fountain. Lord, I hear the river and the roar touching my garden from that waterfall that thunders. Lord, that is where I want to go, to stand under that fountain of pure water, to enjoy it. To go up it Father, because I know where I need to go. Father, I am coming, riding up the wind of that fountain, being blown and drawn by Your love and the expectation of Your beauty. Lord, just to be with You. Lord, the rocks that are in that fountain and the cascading incandescence of the river as they hit those rocks and the road of such beauty and the roar of Your desire.

Lord, for me to come to You today I turn my mind and heart. Lord, I come to stand on the top of the waterfall and to know that I can fall backwards and be caught. Then fall into that river to be tossed to and fro and then to go up to the top and stand on the edge of the waterfall and dive. To know that I can float down, twisting and turning in that river just enjoying myself with Your presence. But knowing You are calling me, Lord, I come. As I stand at the top of that river, I see Jesus. I see You at the bridge. Lord, I am coming.

Lord, You do not mind if I just hang out here and just look. Father, the water that moves with fire, the colours of the rainbow that are woven into it. Lord, I feel the trickle of the moving of Your love for me. Lord, I come on that path that leads to the bridge. I come, Jesus, to be with You again. My brother and my friend, to be with You again. To feel Your embrace and Your love for me. I want to just sit with You for a while, Jesus, just to sit with You. Yes, Lord Jesus, there are things that You can carry. Thank You, Lord.

Thank You that in this place there is no more iniquity, no more transgression of sin, Father. Lord, I can smell the roses, the grass that whispers of Your beauty and Your glory, that speaks of Your love, Lord, that moves in the womb of Your desire. Blown by the Spirits of Heaven, whispering love songs into my ears, Lord. I hear the tinkling as the room begins to rock, Father, the sound of the vibration of the life of Your Kingdom. Father, You call me. Lord, You call me. Lord, You call me! Lord, I come and find You.

Father, You are by the tree. Lord, to hear it sing, to hear and listen to the noises it makes as You touch it, as it changes, it takes on

Your reflection. Such beauty. Lord, just to stand beside you, to feel when You look at me, that is all I need. Lord, I hear the flapping of the eagle's wings. Lord, to hear its cry, the golden eagles roar and encircle the atmosphere around You. Lord, I feel their adoration of Your presence. Just to be with them, to ride the wind current with them, to hear their cries of glory, to be caught up in the whirlwind that they make, twisting and turning like a leaf in autumn. Lord, such beauty. Lord, I see them. Lord, You make these for me. Lord, to watch Your hands touch them, to watch them be formed. Thank You, Lord that You put them in Your garden.

Father, You have changed things since I was here last. All these stones that You have put in place. That altar that you have built Lord, with the gems. Lord, such beauty and a seat to sit on by the tree. Father, thank You that I can sit out with You. Lord, I see the hem of Your garment, moving with flickering light, knowing that Your heart is crying, knowing that You want to love, that You want to be loved. Lord, I am here. Whatever it takes, I am here.

I long to see the creatures watching Lord, their eyes are fixed on You. Father, to see them come to You and watch them love You Lord. Father, You are amazing, just amazing! Such colours and such beauty. Lord, the rose that we pruned together, I see it has grown new flowers. You made indescribable beauty. Father, to hear You, the thunder of the fountain and the river, Lord I am going to be back. Lord I feel Your heart beat and desire for me to stay. Lord, I love You. Lord, I feel Your hand on my shoulder as I walk up the path, the love that flows from that hand. I receive the grace. Father, thank You for the new coat and the new garment. It is something I will wear when I am in the courtroom with You. Lord, I will wear it. Lord, I will keep it hidden with the treasures, the things You have given me in that place and when I come back, Father, I will wear it. Thank You Lord.

Jesus, thank You Lord that You made a way for me to come and be with the Father. Jesus, thank You. Holy Spirit, thank You that You rest with Your wings over my shoulders. To walk back down the path with You, Holy Spirit. To know that You are going to be with me and that this will never leave me. Lord, we share the river just to float in it with You, to watch the wings of Your glory shimmer with the river. To feel Your closeness Holy Spirit. I float, Lord, to the edge and then I take hold of Your wings and hands and fly over the edge, tumbling in Your arms Lord, twisting in Your presence. Holy Spirit, I love You. Thank You Lord, that You come with me and this is a journey we are sharing together. Spirit of Wisdom, thank You for showing me this. Spirit of Understanding, thank You for revealing it and having the patience to teach me. Lord, I will be back. Tomorrow is another day, I will be back. Thank You, Lord, that You are a Spirit. Thank You, Lord, that I am a spirit. Thank You, Lord, I can stay under the edge of the expanse of eternity and know this is Your hand."

This is just the beginning. It is about learning how to come before Him and how to back away from Him. Thank You, Jesus. It is so exciting to see there is enough desire to chase God, to want to get hold of Him. We can choose every day to walk like this. Can you imagine what it would be like to start your day doing this? It kind of sets a different scene and tone for your day. Sometimes it is hard because God will wake you up early and you need to say no to your body and yes to the Holy Spirit. Sometimes He will allow you to sleep, sometimes He will not, but it is exciting, rewarding and it is extremely fulfilling. After all, it is all about Him. He is the source and I would not want to be filled with anyone else.

I would encourage you, if you have any questions, that is okay, take them to the Cross. Go and ask God, you will find out how irrelevant they are when you are with Him! But in it all, start the journey. For some it is going to be a longer journey, for some it is going to be shorter because you have more experience. For some you will have to undo some of the things you have walked with. For some you are going to have to have your transistors re-wired. That is okay. The key is that you are on the pathway and you have started. You have some keys that you can work with, even if nothing happens with you in the spirit, at least you have some practical keys for the areas that you can work with. Start with something.

We will finish in prayer. "Father, I thank You for the offering sown in prayer. Father, I want to give You the glory. I give You everything that has happened as a bouquet of flowers, this is Your Kingdom. Father, I ask that You will protect the seed over the lives of the readers that it would fall on fertile ground that it would grow into trees of height. Father, I ask that our hearts would be captivated with the potential possibility of what can be, in the Name of Jesus. Amen."

Chapter 9
THE RIVER

One of the things that comes out of Heaven is the River of Glory. It is vitally important for us as believers to understand this River. It is important to understand what it means to have the River of Glory flowing, because without the River there is no renewal or refreshing. The Bible talks about the River in Revelation and we will be going into that in this chapter because I want to talk to you about how it has changed my life. So we are going to understand a little bit about the River and what God wanted it to do in the day that Adam ruled the earth, what has been happening to it, and how it is going to come upon the earth again.

The Bible talks about a river that flowed through Eden and then into the garden that God put in Eden.

"And the Lord God planted a garden toward the east, in Eden [delight];... Now a river went out of Eden to water the garden; and from there it divided and became four [river] heads" (Genesis 2:8; 10 AMP).

It parted into four heads and watered the earth. Do you ever wonder why we have four chambers of the heart? The River is very important for us as believers because:

"Out of his belly shall flow rivers of living water" (John 7:38 KJ21).

Our problem is that not many of us have identified with what the River is all about, so I want to talk about that now.

Baptism is one of the basic key foundations that the Bible talks about. The foundations are found in Hebrews 6:

"Therefore, leaving the discussion of the elementary principles of Christ, let's go on to perfection, not laying again the foundation of repentance from dead works and of faith toward God; of the doctrine of baptisms, of laying on of hands, of resurrection of the dead, and of eternal judgment; And this we will do if God permits" (Hebrews 6:1-3).

All these truths are basic foundational truths that every believer needs to know about. Very few churches I have ever been in have actually taught these foundations in a structured process, but we as believers need to get to grips with them and understand what they mean.

If you are a pastor you need to get yourself into the Word of God and study those foundational doctrines of Hebrews 6:1-3. Get some information about them, lay them in your life and lay them in your church's life because the Bible says the church was:

"...built on the foundation of the apostles and prophets" (Ephesians 2:20).

The foundations of the early church were built on these. Unfortunately, much of this truth has been watered down and we have connected other things to it now. But we can still go and get before God and ask Him.

I have identified eight different baptisms that are in the Bible. I know there are more but I want to focus on these because they are the main ones.

1) Baptism into the Cloud of Glory: the 'preparation for relationship'.
2) Baptism of Repentance for the Remission of Sin: the 'preparation for restoration'.
3) Baptism of Water: the 'preparation for a renewed life'.
4) Baptism in the Holy Spirit: the 'preparation for revival'.
5) Baptism of the Holy Spirit and Fire: the 'preparation for renewal and refreshing'.
6) Baptism into His Death: the 'preparation for resurrection'.
7) Baptism of Unity: for the 'preparation of the release of blessing'.
8) Baptism into the Father: to 'identify with the Nature and Character of the Father'.

I have walked my way through all of these baptisms and when I start talking about them I just get caught into the arena of the realm of the Kingdom that is available to us as the sons of God (Galatians 3:26). But because we have never been taught these things we miss out on the relationship we can have. There have been times when I have felt God crying because these things are not taught much in the church. The church usually only teaches two or three of these baptisms but every one of them is vitally important.

1) Baptism into the Cloud of Glory: The Preparation for Relationship

"All were baptised into Moses in the cloud" (1 Corinthians 10:2 KJ21). This is baptism into the Cloud of Glory. It is immersing yourself into that cloud. I want to talk about the baptism into Moses because it is baptism into the marriage celebration, the marriage covenant and the marriage lifestyle with the presence of God. When the glory of God came down onto the mountain, the Bible talks about a cloud that formed over the mountain (Exodus 19:16). In Hebrew the word for 'cloud' or 'covering' is 'huppah'. It was a round cloud that came onto that mountain and sat like a bridal huppah.

The Bible says the mountain shook and that the Israelites were terrified of what they saw (Exodus 19:18; 20:18). It says:

"...all the people saw the thunderings and the lightnings..." (Exodus 20:18 KJ21).

Then God told Moses not to even let them come near the mountain because if they touched it they would die. Barriers were put around it so not even animals could go there, because God had come down and was asking them, "Will you marry Me?"

Moses went into that huppah (or cloud) and the Israelites were terrified by the lightning and thunder that was coming out of the mountain. The Hebrew interpretation of lightning is "glorified fire"; you can see it. You cannot see thunder, but the Bible says all the people saw the thunderings and the lightnings. The Hebrew understanding of thunder is 'glorified voices of fire'.

So when they came to the edge of this mountain they saw glorified fire and glorified voices of fire. It is important to understand that in Hebrew the voices of fire were saying, "Will you marry Me?"

We do not teach the church the baptism into the cloud of Moses that declares, "Will you become My Bride? Will you marry Me?" Moses went up the mountain and got the Ten Commandments. These are the 10 agreements that God has made in the marriage covenant. When God says, "You will have no other gods before Me," He is saying, "Do not put anyone else in front of Me."

A marriage covenant is two-way, so the bride, the bride's parents, the groom and the groom's parents would get together. They would then work out an agreement which was written down. The Ten Commandments are God writing down His side of the agreement. In our day it is our job to write down our side of the agreement in the marriage covenant with the presence of God. When you begin to write down your side of the agreement, this brings you into the baptism of the cloud with Moses.

The issue with the agreement is that when you break any one of those, the other person has the right to divorce you. It gives them the sovereign right to divorce you. It was the only way in Hebrew culture that you could divorce. God says do not commit adultery, but so many of us commit adultery in our hearts with the presence of something else. Yet, God in His love does not divorce us because He wants a bride.

"Will you marry Me?"

This cry has gone on for generation after generation. There was no response from the Israelites on that day when they came out to that mountain where there was cloud, fire, wind and lightning. But something like 1,500 years later on exactly the same day, on the day of Pentecost, it says they were in the upper room together when the wind came and they saw on them cloven tongues of fire (Acts 2:1-4). The tongues of fire were saying, "Will you marry Me?" This time, instead of turning away and saying no, out of their belly came a response of the spirit praying in tongues, "Yes, I will marry You." The baptism in the Holy Spirit seals you into that marriage. This is just one baptism, the baptism into Moses, but they all link into one another like this.

The word baptism means to be immersed into something. The process and spiritual significance of immersing yourself into something is to identify with what you are immersing yourself into. That is why it is vitally important for us to go through some of the foundational studies and relational connections to baptism.

2) Baptism of Repentance for the Remission of Sin: The Preparation for Restoration

In Luke 3 we find the baptism of repentance for the remission of sin:

"And he went into all the country round about the Jordan, preaching a baptism of repentance (of hearty amending of their ways, with abhorrence of past wrongdoing) unto the forgiveness of sin" (Luke 3:3 AMP).

There is a specific baptism that comes on the life of a person where they cannot do anything but confess their sin out before God. It is a supernatural thing where you get in tune with the revelation of your unholy state before the presence of God. You become absolutely aware of the majesty, power and dominion of God and when you are like that all you can do is repent. The word 'remission' means to wipe or cleanse away.

3) The Baptism of Water: The Preparation for a Renewed Life

Acts 1:5 and Acts 10:47 deal with the baptism of water, which is one of the primary doctrines the church teaches:

"For John baptised with water, but not many days from now you shall be baptised with (placed in, introduced into) the Holy Spirit." (Acts 1:5 AMP)

"Can anyone forbid or refuse water for baptising these people, seeing that they have received the Holy Spirit just as we have?" (Acts 10:47 AMP).

Baptism does not mean to be sprinkled, baptism means being immersed in something, totally immersed. You cannot identify with a sprinkling but you can identify with an immersion.

4) Baptism in the Holy Spirit: The Preparation for Revival

Acts 11:16 and Luke 3:16 shows the Baptism in the Holy Spirit:

"Then I recalled the declaration of the Lord, how He said, John indeed baptised with water, but you shall be baptised with (be placed in, introduced into) the Holy Spirit" (Acts 11:16 AMP).

This is where you get endued with the gigawatts of Heaven to be able to do the job of Heaven on the earth. If you are not baptised in the Holy Spirit you need to be or you will be a powerless Christian. The baptism in the Holy Spirit is the enduing or the immersing of yourself into the resurrection power of God to do the work of God on the earth. It turns the switch on for the spiritual volts you get when you are plugged in. Glory to God!

5) The Baptism of the Holy Spirit and With Fire: The Preparation for Renewal and Refreshing

"John answered them all by saying, I baptise you with water; but He Who is mightier than I is coming, the strap of Whose sandals I am not fit to unfasten. He will baptise you with the Holy Spirit and with fire" (Luke 3:16 AMP).

There is a difference between the Baptism of the Holy Spirit and the Baptism of the Holy Spirit and Fire. Fire burns! The Baptism of the Holy Spirit is an enduing of power, and the fire burns and releases the power. There is no power flow if we sin and so the fire burns, purifying us to change our nature. The Baptism of Fire is supposed to change and immerse you into the nature of God. There is a difference between being endued with the power of God and being immersed in the fire of God that changes your nature.

6) The Baptism into His Death: The Preparation for Resurrection

"Are you ignorant of the fact that all of us who have been baptised into Christ Jesus were baptised into His death?" (Romans 6:3 AMP).

This is called the Baptism into His Death. I do not mean the practice done in some churches where they baptise the dead; that is senseless religious practice. What he is talking about is the Baptism into a crucified life. It is being immersed into the reality of the Cross in your life and being baptised into the association with His death, so you can come into the preparation for the fullness of the resurrection (Philippians 3:10-11).

7) Baptism of Unity: The Preparation of the Release of Blessing

"Behold, how good and how pleasant it is; For brethren to dwell together in unity! … For there the Lord commanded the blessing – Life forevermore" (Psalms 133:1; 3).

"For by [means of the personal agency of] one [Holy] Spirit we were all, whether Jews or Greeks, slaves or free, baptised [and by baptism united together] into one body, and all made to drink of one [Holy] Spirit" (1 Corinthians 12:13 AMP).

This is called the Baptism of Unity. It is not a unity of doctrine, but a unity of spirit. This is why I love the scenario where we have different creeds, different races, different churches and different backgrounds, everyone coming together with one desire to be unified in the love of Jesus Christ.

Each of these baptisms has a special significance because each of them is a preparation point for our spiritual life and our encounter and connection with God. Each of them is very significant for us as believers and we need to walk our way through them. If you do not understand them, get your concordance out, get your Bible, get on your face and fast and ask God to show you. That is the only way to do it with some of these things because the church has lost a lot of it.

Each of these baptisms immerses us into the nature and the character of the One who is represented by that baptism. The reason I am teaching you about these baptisms is to help you understand the importance of identification, the process of baptism and what it means to be immersed in something, that when you are immersed in something you identify with the nature of the One you are being immersed in. You identify with the character, the majesty, the power, the dominion and the might of the One that you are being immersed into.

EXPERIENCING THE RIVER

There is a river the Bible talks about in Revelation 22. I got stuck on this scripture and I could not get away from it.

"And he showed me a pure river of water of life, clear as crystal..." (That is important, crystal, that is why we are finding gems) *"proceeding from the throne of God and of the Lamb. In the middle of its street..."* So the river runs like a street, which means you can walk on the water there. Hallelujah Jesus! We can go and practise! *"and on either side of the river, was the tree of life, which bore twelve fruits, each tree yielding its fruit every month. The leaves of the tree were for the healing of the nations. And there*

shall be no more curse, but the throne of God and of the Lamb shall be in it" (Revelation 22:1-3)

Where is the throne of God and of the Lamb? In the River! You need to see this "the Throne of God and of the Lamb will be in it" in the river; in the healing of the nations, in the scrolls that have come from the leaves of the trees giving Life that are beside the water of the River of Life. We have access to the River!

"and His servants shall serve Him" (Revelation 22:3)

Who? The Lamb and God, in the River, that is where you are going to serve God. Is that not amazing!?

"They shall see His face and His Name shall be on their foreheads" (Revelation 22:4); which is a renewed mind.

"There shall be no night there: They need no lamp nor light of the sun, for the Lord God gives them light. And they shall reign forever and ever". (Revelation 22:5)

Who shall reign forever and ever? Those that are in the River. It does not just mean the soaking river and that experience of the soaking place. It means an active participation in the identification of the River. I did not know a lot of this when I was having these experiences. I was speaking at a church in America and I blew their sound system up – $22,000 of sound system – talking about these things!

I had an experience in the spirit with Enoch, who I love. He is one of the most amazing men to talk to. I was talking with him about a whole lot of things and he took me to the River. I had been really fascinated with the River because of my experience in Eden and the garden that is in Eden. I had been in the River, which was a vital key ingredient to the encounter with God that I had in those places. It was the beginning point of everything that happened with me in that realm.

The River is amazing because you can go upstream. Have you ever wondered why people always want to find the source of a river? It is because there is a spiritual significance in it.

"The spiritual is not first, but the natural, and afterwards the spiritual" (1 Corinthians 15:46)

There is a spiritual significance in why we want to find where the spring comes from. I wanted to understand where the spring came from. I have been in the River and I know what it is like and how it falls; what it does and how you can move in it; what it is like to be in it and float in it, see in it, be one with it and have it flow through you. There is no resistance in the River because it is full of life and it goes through you because you are not as you are here. You can breathe in it. Ah, it is wonderful!

The River flows out from where the veil sits, at the edge of the Throne. Because of Who and What God is, He continues to create all the time. The mountain is forever growing because of Who He is. He is forever creating, so it just grows! Shaking and earthquakes often happen, and so diamonds fall off the mountain. So there is a cascade of diamonds coming off the mountain and the oil of the presence of God flowing off the mountain, so you get diamonds and oil mixed together. The Bible talks about the River being as clear as crystal. It is as clear as crystal because there is crystal in it. But you cannot see the crystals until you jump in! There are jewels in the River. You can pick them up and put them in your belly!

8) The Baptism into the Father: To Identify with the Nature and Character of the Father

There is one more baptism I would like to talk to you about; the Baptism into the Father.

I was talking with Enoch on the side of this river. He is amazing! He does not waste words or mince about with what he says, because he has walked with God for so many years.

He said to me, "Don't we have a triune God?" and I said, "Yes, hallelujah! We have a triune God." What do you say when somebody makes a statement like that?

He said, "We have a triune God, great! Tell me who you have identified with?" About now I started to feel like there was a shark chasing me! I said, "Well, I have been baptised in water and I have identified with Christ; and I have been baptised in Holy Spirit and I have identified with Holy Spirit."

He said, "And?" I said, "Well, I have been baptised in the Cloud."

He said, "No, no I am not talking about the experiences. I am talking about the relationships with the people you have been baptised into, because when you get baptised into a person you get baptised into His nature and His character." Then he made this statement to me, "You have identified with Holy Spirit and you have identified with Jesus in the waters of baptism and in the natural world on the earth. What have you done to identify with the Father?"

I came back to the religious, "There is no doctrine about doing anything like that. You show me that in the Bible." He said to me, "Don't you think there is a River in Heaven for a purpose?"

You get these slaps (in the Spirit) when you try and justify yourself! It is the flesh, even in Heaven you still try and justify yourself!

I said, "Yeah, I have been in the River down there in Eden." He said, "No, I am talking about the River here, which flows pure as crystal." He said to me, "You need to immerse yourself in the River, because the River comes straight from Him. The only way you can identify yourself with Him is to immerse yourself in what comes from Him."

I had experience of the River that runs through Eden and by then it is watered down a bit and there are many tributaries of the presence of God that run into it that bring other things into that River, which make it what it is. In the River in Eden all the diamonds are on the bottom and the water runs clear as crystal. It runs clear like water, although it is like oil and like water. My expectation was that it would be the same.

So I said, "Let me at it!" I have been in the River of Life down in Eden. The Bible says it is as pure as crystal when it flows out of the throne. It is pure water when it gets into Eden, but when it comes out of the throne it is crystal. I did not know that and I jumped into it, doing what I call a bomb dive. As I jumped into the River I sank into this honey. I went down into this honey, into this 'quick sand' substance that is flowing out from under the veil of the curtain, where the throne of God is, thinking, "I am going to die, but I can breathe in water." Another thing I was trying to justify myself with. But I had to make the choice to give myself in surrender to God. Baptism of any kind is about absolute surrender.

As I sank in I was breathing pure diamonds and oil into my

nose, my mouth and my body. I stayed there for about half an hour thinking, "Lord, I am identifying with You, I am identifying with Who You are, in the baptism of the River of Glory." I stayed there because I wanted to know what it is to be one with the Father, as Jesus talked about in John 17.

The amazing thing about the river is that it goes straight through you. It does not push you like the water we have here. There is no resistance in Heaven, because everything is alive there. You are alive and because you are as one with it, the River just goes through you. I was sinking, even as it was moving, crashing loudly out of the Throne. I was thinking, "Hallelujah! This is thrilling! I do not know what is going to happen!" I was trying to get into all my past experiences, thinking, "I am in the river of Ezekiel (Chapter 47) and, Father, this is going to be okay." I did not really know what was going on. Nobody had ever taught me about this, but I did not really care, because suddenly I was finding that I was changing on the inside without having to do anything. I was beginning to immerse myself in the very nature of the One who made me. I have taught about the skin of God. The reason there are diamonds and oil that flow as part of the River is because God is Who He is. What sheds off Him is the residue and the residue makes a river. It cannot be controlled, it just flows out under the curtain and then it becomes a raging torrent of His glory to the earth.

When I came out of the River, just like honey sticks to your arm, my skin was covered with oil and diamonds and my skin looked like the skin of God. I was covered with oil and little diamonds all over my body!

Enoch looked at me and he said, "Now you can relate and identify with the Father because you have been in His nature and His character, because His nature and His character are in the River." I did not know what else to do, I just shouted, "Yahoo – Hallelujah! This feels so good – in fact I do not want to go home!" (But I have a job to do, so I had to come home).

In water baptism we get ourselves immersed in the natural environment in water. When you get yourself immersed in water baptism you are immersed in the new nature of Jesus Christ, the new resurrection power and all the doctrinal things. The same is true with the Holy Spirit because you get yourself immersed into the nature and character of the Holy Spirit. So, suddenly I found that inside of me it was so easy to talk with God as a Friend and as a Father. I could talk with Jesus from my past experience with Him. Previously, however, it was kind of hard to relate to God as my Father because I did not have that immersion process accomplished in my life where I had chosen wilfully to go down and be baptised into the River of the glory of God.

THE LEAVES OF THE TREES

The Bible says there is more there than just a River. I had identified with God and I had this experience of being connected and immersed into the nature of the presence and the person of God. There are other things in that scripture regarding the River flowing out. One of them is the trees and how they cast off their leaves and the leaves are for the healing of the nations. I was busy looking at Enoch and looking at these leaves. If these leaves are for the healing of the nations (Rev 22:2) then I wanted some! I was looking at him and sometimes you do not have to say anything, they know the intents of your heart because it shows on the outside when you are in the spirit.

He said, "Go and get some." So I went to get some of these leaves. I picked about eight or nine. They were leaves but they were kind of scrolls and they are alive. They have marks on them. I cannot explain them. All I know is that they are alive, they are like scrolls but they are living, they have power and every word on them makes a doorway for a nation to experience the Glory. The revelation just goes on and on. I came out of the River so happy because "I got me some leaves!" Now my problem was I did not know what to do with them! I am looking at Enoch and he is looking at me. You need to understand, these guys are funny – they have a sense of humour! The Bible says about God that He sits in Heaven and laughs! (Psalms 2:4) When I was looking at Enoch and he was looking at me, God must have been rolling with laughter in the Throne Room behind the curtain!

I said to him, "What do I do with them?" He said, "Put them in your belly."

It got me thinking about the guy in the TV advertisement who has got that foot-long sandwich. He sits down with his mate across the table and you hear this growling stomach. His mate asks, "Would you like a bite of the sandwich?" The guy says, "Yes please." He takes the sandwich and his mouth expands as the entire sandwich disappears into his mouth, leaving a tiny piece on the end of the sandwich for the other guy! My mind went to this picture, trying to take one of these scrolls into my belly!

I said to him, "What do I do with them to get them into my belly?" He said, "You just put them in your belly!"

I said, "What do you mean?" And he said, "Just like you did in the river with the gems that you carried inside of you, you put them in your belly."

I said, "You mean it is that easy? I just.." and as I tried it they just went into my belly.

Some of what I am teaching you now is on those scrolls. They have been unlocked because of the Glory. That is why I look so good, hallelujah! I do not care about being barrel-shaped if I can carry those scrolls! But I could not get the leaves until I had been immersed in the character and nature of the Father who gives the leaves. You cannot bring healing to a nation unless you have been immersed in the nature and character of the One who wants to bring the healing to the nations.

I began to realise that for the last six thousand years that River had been flowing and those leaves had gone somewhere, because the Bible says every month they cast forth their leaves. I began to realise that they must be somewhere.

Then Enoch said, "Come with me." I found myself standing in what some religions call 'Nirvana'. They think it is Heaven, but it is not. It is the most wonderful, beautiful place in the spirit that you could ever imagine. But it is absolutely barren and there is nobody there. The River is stored up like a dam right next to it. The banks of that river are strewn with the leaves for the healing of the nations that have been caught up in there.

Being in that place is amazing because the devil cannot destroy life, although he tries to pervert it and hide it. Being in that place I realised why members of other religions get so sold to the demon spirits that take them there – because of the authority of the place and because there is power in the life of God. The life of God is still in these spiritual realms, the problem is what surrounds it: the demonic enclaving and enslaving of that vicinity. You see, when Jesus was taken up to the exceedingly high mountain on the edge of the atmosphere and shown the kingdoms of this world (Luke 4:5), which world was He shown the kingdoms of? Jesus knew, whoever rules from the spiritual realms has dominion on the earth. Where do you think Adam originally had his dominion from?

I began to realise the tranquillity, peace and glory that was there. But on the outside of it, for about a mile and a half up, was this canopy of the most putrid darkness you could ever imagine. The Bible says the whole of creation is groaning (Romans 8:19-23) and that place is groaning for us to come home.

I then went into the River and it took me down to an everlasting door. The everlasting door was in the atmosphere that is close to the atmosphere of the earth. That everlasting door was now groaning because it has been laid down and cannot be opened. It is now controlled by demon spirits on this side of the atmosphere. There is coming a day when those everlasting doors of Psalms 24:7 are going to stand up again. When those doors open there is going to come a rending in the Heavens and all that which has been stored up is going to be poured out as rain upon the earth. It has been stored up for the last five or six thousand years for you and me today. This is what the Bible talks about, that in our day God is going to give us the rivers and the rain from the Heavens (Ezekiel 34:26; Joel 2:23; Zechariah 10:1).

The rain is going to come out of the Heavens, it is going to hit the earth and it is going to change the nature of the earth again. The first people it is going to change are me and you. Have you ever thought what it would be like walking around with diamond skin? Have you ever thought what people would say? People will look at you and say, "Who is this God that I see in you?" Have you ever wondered what is going to happen with your face? No wonder they will try to kill us. These are the things that need to captivate your heart.

It is all about the River of Glory. God is calling each one of us to immerse ourselves by faith in the River and the stream of life, to identify ourselves with Him as our Father. Most of us have gone through water baptism and most of us have gone through the baptism of the Holy Spirit. What God is looking for now is the identification with Him as the Father, so then we have the Father, the Son and the Holy Spirit, three in one.

ACTIVATION

I am going to jump in the River now and you can come and join me. It is done by faith. I do not care if you do not feel anything; that is immaterial to God. It shows that you are responding to the Word of God which requires you to be identified with Him as your Father. To be identified in His nature, His character, His power, His dominion, His might and His kingdom. I want to look like Him.

It might help you to stand to your feet and thank the Holy Spirit for His presence. When you are ready just close your eyes and start praying in tongues. Do not try to see anything yet. We do not want to look for signs; we want the pursuit of the person of God.

"Father, thank You that Your Word is confirmed with signs and wonders. Thank You, Lord, that Your Kingdom is confirmed because of who You are. Lord, I know what has happened in my life after I went into that secret place by the River which flows from under the veil by Your throne. I know what happened, Lord, when I immersed myself in that River which is like honey and oil and diamonds all mixed together. Lord, as we come up to You today and reach out in faith, I ask in the Name of Jesus that together we would jump into the River of Life and be baptised in Jesus' Name into our identity with our Father. Lord, right now in the Name of Jesus I ask You to release that River. We come by faith and we jump into that River!

Father, I immerse myself into Your character. I immerse myself into Your nature. Lord, I immerse myself into Your life, getting lost in Your power and the dominion of our Father. Lord, today I belong to You. Father, with that glory flowing through me, sinking into the River like warm honey, knowing that You are standing on the other side of the veil watching us as Your children. Father, today I baptise myself into the River of Glory, wilfully by choice and by faith. In Jesus' Name let the fire of the glory of God come over Your house and me. Lord, let the rippling of the thunder and the majesty and the glory that is in that River be imparted to Your people today. Lord, let the fire fall, let the wind blow, let Your thunder roar, let Your glory come!

Father, thank You for the beauty of this place. Thank You for the thunder and lightning that is behind the veil. Father, thank You that You have always seen Your decrees being released because of who You are. Father, I stand in the river in awe of Your beauty, in wonder, in adoration. Father, I drink of the stream of life. I drink of the River of pure water as clear as crystal.

Lord, I come back out of the River and feel the covering of Your presence. Holy Spirit, I know that You are hovering and You are brooding over us, so we can feel Your fire, to feel the rejoicing of Your heart, to know the embrace of the wings of Your presence. Father, thank you that I can come back and keep coming back here. Thank You, Father. We are going to come back soon to be with You in the River again. Hallelujah!"

Chapter 10
The Dark Cloud

"When the priests came out of the holy place, the cloud filled the house of the Lord, so that the priests could not continue ministering because of the cloud; for the glory of the Lord filled the house of the Lord. Then Solomon spoke: "The Lord said He would dwell in the dark cloud."
(1 Kings 8:10-12)

I want to teach on something that has been very dear to my heart. It is a revelation that has built a place of tremendous tenderness and intimacy between God and me. All my Christian life and Christian experience I have wanted to know God as a friend. The only person I could think of whoever did that was Enoch. I knew by heart the little that was written about him and I also read the book of Enoch. It is really radical! The purposeful pursuit of the presence of God needs to be your single desire. Not for a spiritual experience. It is not about having a spiritual experience; it is about your desire to encounter God, which then creates the atmosphere for a spiritual experience. If you chase the experience then you will often get an experience but there will be no long-lasting fruit from it. You need to chase the Person of God.

One of the easiest ways of learning to engage the realm of Heaven is to engage the realm of the Kingdom that is in you. It is the Kingdom that is in you that transitions you and enables you to be seated with Christ in Heavenly places, far above the demonic (Ephesians 1:20-21; 2:6). It is an instant transition; you do not have to go through any realm or layers. So, one minute I am here engaging this Kingdom, the next minute I am in the realm of Heaven engaging and thoroughly enjoying the realm of Heaven. Then I can step back through the realm of Heaven bringing all the glory with me. Guess what happens to darkness when light comes in? The greatest truth that is hidden is that darkness cannot penetrate light. You, being a child of light, walk in the light and you will have fellowship, one with another (1 John 1:7). Where does your fellowship happen when you walk in the light? -In Heaven; and you experience the reality of love on the earth. Fellowship in Heaven creates love on the earth because you are bonded one to another.

This teaching is something very dear to me. It came out of an experience that was a death in my life, but then it produced life around me. One of the things I have learned is that whenever something happens around your life, it happens for a purpose. For me, a circumstance happened, some time ago, where there was tremendous injustice. I came to terms with the reality of the injustice through being able to be in the spirit, being able to go and see what had happened in a meeting and know what was said there, which is sometimes a blessing and sometimes not! That is part of the life of being in the spirit. Through the pain of injustice, after having to get to grips with what to do with all this, I can remember standing before the Lord. He said to me, "My Son stood before Pilate and did not say anything. Are you prepared to die?" I said, "Yes Lord." I did not know it would take a year of going to the Cross 140 times a day!

Every day, day after day, knowing who those people were, I had to love them at the Cross. The Cross is the pinnacle of all spiritual experience. It is a springboard that leads you into spiritual encounter. Through some of the things I experienced in that place and that time I began to realise that my pain was supposed to be a springboard to drive me into intimacy with God. So, instead of going into my pain and all the rubbish that goes with it, I realised that if I could hit my pain and use it as a springboard to drive me to

God, then I could retrain my thinking and my desires. So I would look forward to the time when the pain would come because it was my springboard to engage God. But I had to go to the Cross and I had to die at the Cross, to the injustice and all the feelings related to the injustice. I had to nail it all to the Cross.

It took me about six months to realise that God would keep on doing this, year after year, unless I realised my pain was supposed to be this springboard. Pain is supposed to be under our feet. Instead it was sitting over my head. I would be walking around work and these angry thoughts would start going around my mind. We are all subject to sin. I began to realise that when these feelings started I could hit the Cross and use it as a springboard to drive me towards God as a friend and a Father, because He is my source of rescue. The Bible says:

"I will lift up my eyes to the hills – from whence comes my help? My help comes from the LORD, Who made heaven and earth. He will not allow your foot to be moved." (Psalms 121:1-3)

Verse 5 continues to talk about what God is to you and me:

"...The LORD is your keeper" (Psalms 121:5).

He will keep me in this place. He will bring me to a place of encounter with His presence. If I knew the encounter I was going to come into I would have died willingly, knowing what was there. But there are times when God does things because He wants to check the integrity of your heart, whether you are willing to die where no one sees, where no one is going to reward you and pat you on the back except Him. You see, it is all about Him.

Through that time I began to realise that there was more. God wanted to bring me into something more. So for about ten or eleven months I began to be aware that when I would use this pain as a springboard I would go into the realm of Heaven and begin to experience this 'terror'. I always thought that fear was associated with demons because God did not make fear. Well, yes He did actually because:

"It is a fearful thing to fall into the hands of the living God" (Hebrews 10:31).

So I began to become aware that there were things happening that I had no knowledge of. I had never heard anybody talk about this. I had inklings that we were able to meet with God, but no one had ever said, "Ian, I have talked with God face to face". But the Bible said Moses did (Exodus 33:11) and:

"Blessed are the pure in heart, for they shall see God." (Matthew 5:8).

The Bible says you are going to see Him. I had all these scriptures going round in my brain as I was going through this process, because I wanted to know God. My desire in life is I want to know God. I want to know Him. I want to be able to sit with Him as a mate and talk with Him about what He is doing and for Him to talk to me about what I am doing. God is as interested in you and what you are doing in Heaven as you are about Him. Did you know that? Jesus said:

"he who believes in Me, the works that I do he will do also; and greater works than these he will do" (John 14:12)

The Bible says that. Do you agree with the Word? Okay, did God create a universe? The purposeful pursuit of God has our brains skidding around corners! The purposeful pursuit of God should be your desire. I began to become aware that there was more to the person of God than I had ever experienced. These five things need to be taught in the church:

1) The realm of God; His dominion; His influence; His power; and His authority
2) The place of God and where He does His business
3) The function of God and what He does in Heaven
4) The role of God and how He does it
5) The person of God and who He is

Nowhere did I hear people talking about the person of God and who He is. I got so hungry, I wanted to know God. So everywhere the Bible said "God", I would start to read. I got the concordance out and there are about 490 or more scriptures where it says "God – Elohim/Yahweh" and I began to read the scriptures, one after the other, trying to get to know God. I wanted to know God as my Father. I have a right as a son to get to know Him as a Father.

I came across an interesting scripture which talks about the treasures of darkness:

"I will give you the treasures of darkness and hidden riches of secret places,

that you may know that I, the LORD, Who call you by your name, am the God of Israel" (Isaiah 45:3).

I began to ponder these treasures of darkness and to think, "God, what on earth is this treasure of darkness that Your Bible talks about there?" Little scriptures like that populate your brain and you read the Bible and think "Whoa! What is going on there?" So I began to hold it in my heart.

"They were all baptised into Moses in the cloud and in the sea" (1 Corinthians 10:2 NIV).

It is talking about Israel, how they met with God at Mount Sinai and about the darkness that was around Mount Sinai and the cloud that was there. Suddenly the treasure of darkness started to look like it might be the cloud of darkness, where the presence of the glory of God is.

There is a difference between demonic darkness and a veil of darkness. I began to go through the Bible for the word 'darkness'. There are about six or seven different meanings in the Greek and Hebrew that mean darkness and it actually does not mean dark, it means something totally different. Suddenly I realised that the terror I was feeling when I saw this darkness actually was not terror of the demonic. It was an awareness of my absolute impurity. It is a terrifying thing to fall into the hands of God because when you stand in His presence all that you are is made absolutely open and plain to be seen.

God is a Person. He is not just an ultimate power source for you and me. It is important for us to connect with God on the basis of friendship, not on a need basis. God Himself has a need, did you know that? God has one need – the need for someone to love Him. I do not know what I would do without my family, because they nurture me as a father. How do they do that? They just love me. In all my hobnailed boots and the nakedness of my soul, they love me. If that is what it is like in the natural, how much more in the spirit? God has a yearning for us to experience Him and to love on Him. So, I had all these thoughts going around in my brain and I suddenly had all these scriptures going on too.

Seeing and being part of the realm of God, the place of God, the function of God and the role of God is wonderful and they will change your life – but for me, I found it still was not enough. I knew there was more to Him than the God that I saw on the throne in majesty and burning fire, with the angels and the things that go on there, because on the seventh day Heaven shuts down. I began to think, "God gets off His throne on the seventh day, because it says He rests and He does not have to do anything". I know because I have been to Heaven. So I wanted to know what He did and what He was like. I started to ask the question, "Father, what are you like when You get off the throne?" When I am at work, I have government in my work place. I am different from how I am at home, although I am the same person. I carry something different. When I am in church teaching I carry something different. Then when I go home I can be open with my kids and I am a family man, I can enjoy life. I wanted that 'enjoying life' thing. It is great to know the authority in church, to know the power around you, but it does not bring you into relationship that allows you to know about someone. It does not allow you to know who they are.

So I began to meditate around all these things. It is important to understand, when a door opens in the realm of the spirit for us and God begins to quicken us, if you do not work with the door that God has given you until it comes to fruition, you will lose it and something else will stand in that door – and usually it is a demon. So when a door has been opened in the spirit for you, with knowledge that is starting to come and a yearning and a desire, you need to keep on that path until you find its fruit. I understand that, because I have seen what happens when you do not keep the door open. So I began to chase God. I did not know how to do it, all I knew was Enoch walked with God.

I began to ask in my heart, "God, who are you?" I asked a question which I now know the answer to, "What were You before You were? You know, when you lived in the 'was' before the 'is'? What 'was' You?" The Bible says, the God:

"who is and who was and who is to come" (Revelation 1:4).

I now understand the process and how it all works. "But God, what 'was' You? I want to know what You were. I want to know You. I want a relationship with You beyond just having an ultimate power source. I want to know You, I want to know who You are".

"And this is eternal life, that they may know You, the only true God, and Jesus Christ whom You have sent" (John 17:3)

It does not just say you may know Jesus Christ. Unfortunately, the church has got stuck there. The scripture says to know God and Jesus, who are two distinct persons. But they are in such unity that they are One, because each One's desire is bound up with the other, just like you have a body, a soul and a spirit. You are one but you actually have three different functions inside you. It is the same with the Godhead. We are made just like Him – you are made in the image of God. The issue is to know Him.

"the pure in heart…shall see God" (Matthew 5:8)

So how do I become pure in heart? The Blood of Jesus is the only way. I can remember having an encounter with the Pillar of Fire in my room over a seven day period. At first the Pillar of Fire was there for about fifteen seconds, but then I said, "Lord, You need to go, I cannot handle this anymore". Then it went on and I was able to handle it for a longer period of time because the more familiar you become with it the longer you can stay in His presence. The more you are changed into the image of the One that is there, His image, you do not get consumed by the fire. When fire burns it does not consume something; it actually changes the nature of it. What is displayed as flame is the gases that are coming out of that changing nature. So the more you draw near to the fire and the glory of God the more that nature changes your nature and conforms you to the fire. What comes off your life is the dross being burned. God is changing our nature. The Bible says:

"Many will say to Me in that day, 'Lord, Lord, have we not prophesied in Your name, cast out demons in Your name, and done many wonders in Your name?'" (Matthew 7:22).

I found myself standing in front of the Pillar of Fire in my bedroom and a sword would come out of the fire and go across me. I found myself saying, "But Lord I have prophesied in Your Name" and the sword came back across me; "But Lord I have fed the poor in Your Name" and the sword swung across me again; "But Lord.." I got to the stage where I had no more 'buts' left to justify myself being in the presence of God. The only thing that makes you pure in heart is the Blood of Jesus Christ. Out of this flame came a Lamb and stood in front of the flame and the Lord said to me, "The only way you can come into My glory is by the Blood of the Lamb. Now come". I put my hand into that flame and my arm went totally transparent. Then I pulled it out and it became my flesh again. I would put it in and think, "Wow! Glory! Look at this" because I want to know Him. The only way you can know Him is to hang around Him, understanding fire, the terror that happens there and the desire to know Him.

John the Apostle makes an amazing statement. He says, this God:

"the One who was from the beginning. We have seen Him with our own eyes, heard Him with our own ears, and touched Him with our own hands" (1 John 1:1 VOICE).

In that scripture there is a woven truth: not only can I hear Him, which the church is very efficient at doing, but I can see Him. Not only can I see Him, but my hands can handle Him too. Another translation puts it like this:

"I myself have seen him with my own eyes and listened to him speak. I have touched him with my own hands" (1 John 1:1 TLB).

So that means I have a legal right to go and touch my Father. My family would not be very impressed if I did not touch them. When I come home my son comes running out and we have a hug. I am not afraid of showing affection to them and they are not afraid of showing affection with me. How much more should we be like that with God? How do you show someone affection? You do not sit on the throne at the other side of the room and have them stand twenty-five miles away worshipping you. The way you show them affection is you walk up to them, you embrace them, you be with them, you hang around them, you sit with them and care for the things they care for.

"The God of our Lord Jesus Christ, the Father of glory, may give to you the spirit of wisdom and revelation in the knowledge of Him, the eyes of your understanding being enlightened; that you may know what is the hope of His calling". (Ephesians 1:17-18)

It is not about your calling, it is about His calling. His calling is that you would be a son or daughter of His, a spirit child before the Lord; His child. He wants you to know His calling for you. His calling is that you would know Him; that you would be with Him; that you would experience Him; that you would understand Him; that you would talk with Him, not just have Him talk to you.

The church has been taught how to listen to Him and they are very proficient at hearing the voice of God, but they are not so good at standing before God talking to Him. That is because they have never been taught that you can go to Heaven and talk with Him.

There are two key issues that flow like a vein of gold through all the scriptures:
(1) I can know the Father, and (2) I can talk with Him and see Him, not only while He is on the throne but also off the throne.

"For now we see through a glass, darkly, but then face to face" (1 Corinthians 13:12).

"Lord, what is this darkly stuff? If I see now darkly, then face to face, what is this darkly thing?" There is obviously some progression through 'darkly' to 'face to face'. Would you agree? In Genesis 15 it says:

"As the sun was going down [setting], Abram fell into a deep sleep. While he was asleep, a very terrible [or frightening] darkness came" (Genesis 15:12 EXB).

In all my Christian experience darkness had always been associated with demon spirits. This comes from the doctrinal belief that when Jesus died and it got dark – that the darkness was demonic. I wonder if it was demonic or if we just believed it was? The Bible does not say, but it does talk about the darkness that descended:

"It was now about the sixth hour (midday), and darkness enveloped the whole land and earth until the ninth hour (about three o'clock in the afternoon), While the sun's light faded or was darkened" (Luke 23:44-45 AMP).

I wonder if it was God coming to stand and watch over His Son? Deuteronomy 5 says:

"And when you heard the voice out of the midst of the darkness, while the mountain was burning with fire, you came near me, all the heads of your tribes and your elders; And you said, Behold, the Lord our God has shown us His glory and His greatness, and we have heard His voice out of the midst of the fire; we have this day seen that God speaks with man and man still lives" (Deuteronomy 5:23-24 AMP).

So wherever there is this 'darkly' and 'dark', there is God; and wherever God is, you can talk with Him. So why does the Bible refer to the voice out of the midst of darkness?

"Then Solomon said, The Lord said that He would dwell in the thick darkness" (1 Kings 8:12 and 2 Chronicles 6:1 AMP).

"For God made my heart weak, And the Almighty terrifies me; Because I was not cut off from the presence of darkness, And He did not hide deep darkness from my face" (Job 23:16-17)

"Clouds and darkness are round about Him [as at Sinai]; righteousness and justice are the foundation of His throne" (Psalm 97:2 AMP).

So clouds and darkness are about Him. I wonder what He is like in the cloud? I wonder what He looks like? If people can speak to Him in the cloud, that means He is not on the throne. That means I have access to be near Him when He is off the throne. Why the darkness when He comes off the throne? A veil is an amazing thing. It covers the full reality of the person so you cannot see – thus, you see darkly. The cloud is a veil that surrounds the very Person of God, not just when He sits on the throne with governmental authority, but as our Father, with absolute power, absolute purity and absolute dominion – we have a right to speak to Him face to face.

My journey with the springboard came with all these scriptures and my meditating around them, trying to get to grips with this darkness and horror that I felt under this coming veil. When I got into the Bible and looked up the word 'horror', I found that it means 'absolutely in terror'. Not just being afraid, but in terror. I began to become aware that every time I would springboard into this place that the horror and the terror would grow. I began to hate going there, but was so fascinated and so yearning to know Him that I would go anyway. The most amazing thing is that you not only become aware of yourself but you become aware of the yearning of God in that cloud. On the day of the fall:

"the Lord God called to Adam and said to him, 'Where are you?' (Genesis 3:9).

God was not on His throne when He said that, He was walking in Eden. When God finishes on the seventh day He has one purpose – that is to see who is coming to draw near Him. He wants a relationship with us.

There are three common threads that run through all these scriptures:

1. Every single one of these people had a deep personal encounter with the Person of God.
2. There is darkness all around Him as a veil, as a cloud.
3. They are all connected with the dread or horror or awareness of His absolute holiness and absolute power.

The Greek and Hebrew use six different words which are translated 'darkness'. They all have similar elements: It is thick; it always covers around the Person of God (not His realm); all of the words express an attitude of surrender by the one that encounters it.

In Psalm 97:2 the word 'darkness' means to dread or to be afraid, to fear or to shake terribly.

"The Lord said that He would dwell in the thick darkness" (1 Kings 8:12 AMP).

The throne of God, where He displays what He is, is only part of who He is. At Jesus' transfiguration it says:

"While he was saying these things, a cloud came and covered [overshadowed] them, and they became afraid as the cloud covered them [they entered the cloud]" (Luke 9:34 EXB).

I have been meditating around these scriptures and I have been thinking, "God, I wonder what will happen if I go into that cloud? I wonder what it is going to be like to actually be able to draw near to You and maybe even say hello?!"

I do not know anybody who has taught this anywhere. As I am thinking, the religious spirit gets in there saying, "You know, all the believers say if you see God you will die". Well, actually, that is what you are supposed to do anyway so I thought, "I have absolutely nothing to lose! If I physically die I cannot die in any better place!" But my greatest fear was going through the cloud, because of the horror and the terror and the shaking. That is the scary part. Here is the most amazing thing – the scary part is all this side of the cloud. Because, once you go into it, you become transfigured into His image. So I am busy thinking "Do I go in? Don't I go in? Do I go in?"

It is amazing how the flesh wants to stay alive! I had my legal will written, as I started thinking, "If I die, what are my kids going to think? What am I thinking anyway? If I die, He is going to take care of them, isn't He? That is what He says." You need to go to the Cross with all these things. There is no other way but the Cross.

The Bible talks about the priest who would go in when the cloud of God would descend over the Holy of Holies. The priest would go in, get the incense and swing it around. Then he would stick his hand through the veil and swing the incense around (the veil was twelve inches thick! Did you know that?), hoping there would be enough smoke, that when he got inside, he would not die. They used to tie these little bells on the end of His garment so they could hear him moving around. They knew that if there was not any noise the guy was dead – a crisp, lying on a floor somewhere. They also used to tie a rope to his leg so that if he fell down they could pull him out because they were afraid of going inside (Leviticus 16:2).

Because I knew this I was thinking, "Lord, this darkness is a veil, what am I going to do? Stick my hand in there and swing some incense around? What am I going to do?" It is amazing how religious doctrine tries to stop us relating one on one with God. I would go through this religious process: "Father, I take the Blood of Jesus and apply it to my life". It is great to do that but God is more interested in you than even the Blood. He wants you because when you are with Him you are already sanctified by His presence, but the Blood helps you get there. It makes you righteous. It enables you to become pure, because when you are pure you can see God.

So I began to go through this process of praying, "Lord, I take the Blood of Jesus and I apply it to my life, but...Oh God, I just want You." It began to turn from a doing of all these things, to "Lord I just want You, Lord, I just want You, I want Your presence, I want to know You, I want to see You, I want to talk with You." For weeks the burning desire to talk with Him would be inside me. Then suddenly, my pain was gone. I woke up one morning and all the clamour of all that pain of the injustice had gone because I had turned from my sinful nature to the realm of God. It had gone! I was feeling, "Yahoo! I'm free!" Now that I was healed I had no springboard to bounce from and I started thinking "Oh no! I am going to have to go there, to actually make a choice myself to go there".

You have to choose, you have to make a choice to go into the presence of God. No one else can make the decision for you. A springboard enables you to find the pathway but then you need to choose to go along the pathway.

"He who dwells in the secret place of the Most High shall abide under the shadow of the Almighty" (Psalms 91:1).

The clouds and the darkness are His secret place. The word 'secret place' can be translated 'cloud' and 'darkness', and 'shadow' can mean 'cloud' and 'darkness'. I made a choice that day, "Whatever happens Lord, the next time I am in the spirit, standing on that hill where your darkness is, I am going to walk into it".

You can pray in tongues all you want and think that you are going to be ready, but when you stand there and the cloud is standing in front of you!

"It is a terrible [dreadful; terrifying] thing to fall into the hands of the living God" (Hebrews 10:31 EXB).

But it is also the most wonderful, blissful experience. That is the other side of the coin, you choose what you desire. So I chose that day "Lord, when I stand there, I am going to come into that cloud". You can understand I literally wet my pants! And that is ok, the Bible is full of men of God who did that and if it is good enough for them, it is good enough for me. That is what washing machines are for, thank You Jesus!

So, I can remember making a choice that day to go into the cloud of darkness and the horror and the terror and the absolute awareness of my sin, my nature and everything I am not supposed to be. I am a spirit being, I am just in this body that is a representation. When I made a choice to walk through that cloud, all the fight was all on this side of the veil. I stepped into the dark cloud and when I came through it, on the other side, there was this absolute total tranquillity and peace that is beyond human words to describe. I was standing in a canopy about seven metres wide. I had all my religious beliefs like "You can't see the face of God because you will die", so I had my eyes turned away. But man – I really wanted to look! And I stood there. What do you say? I went there with a list of all these things I wanted to ask but when I was there, how irrelevant they all were!

I can remember standing there thinking, "What am I doing here? This is the God of the universe..I can see His feet" Let me tell you something: God is not what you think! I kind of looked and then thought, "I am still alive" Then I heard this drip, drip, drip, drip, drip as tears were falling down by His feet. He said to me, "It has been a long time since anybody has been here, son."

I was a mess. I backed out and I was a mess for quite some time. Yet there was the desire, wanting to go back. For the simple reason He was crying – that was reason enough to make me go through that cloud and face the pain. So, it took me about a week. Often, when my wife and kids would go away I would be praying in tongues, saying "Lord, this is my time now. Every night I am going to come into your presence, I am going to go into the spirit and meet with You like that."

What began to happen was I got more and more bold with all the questions I had. I had not received answers yet, but that was immaterial because when you are there they are immaterial anyway. I do not just make small talk with my children like, "Hi son, how are you? Great weather we are having." If that was how my son spoke to me every day I would slap him! He speaks to me and engages me face to face. In the same way I was feeling, "Lord, I want to see You, I have a right to see You." So, gradually I began to lift my eyes. Let me tell you what God's skin is like – if you could get a mat of diamonds of about five or six carats each, weave them all together like skin, put the colours of the rainbow in it, make it go blue-white, burning and rippling with fire and flickering with light, then you have an idea of what His skin is like!

Nobody ever told me that this is what I am going to look like. The Bible says that we will be conformed into His image (Romans 8:29), so what He looks like is already living in me and I am going to become like that. Hallelujah! I wonder why they covered Moses' face?

I wanted to speak to God face to face. I wanted to see Him smile at me. If I die, I die. I cannot die in any better place. I love being here and I am happy to spend the rest of eternity here. I do not care. I made a choice, "God, I am going to speak to You and I am going to look on You." I chose that day to lift my eyes slowly and when I looked at Him a number of things happened.

Firstly, I almost got swallowed up into the eternity that is in God. The eyes are the window of the soul; that is what the Bible says (Matthew 6:22). God is eternal and eternity dwells in Him. Eternity is in His eyes because He is eternity. I found myself getting sucked into this vortex of absolute wonder and glory, into the Person of God – which is what we are supposed to do anyway. Then I started putting the brakes on, feeling "this is too much!" Just that alone took me about three weeks to try and get some understanding on – and it still fries my brain! And that is okay.

What stopped me going into His eyes was the fascination of what was happening with the outside of His body. His eyes stayed the same, that fascinated me, but there was a transition of what was happening to His body. His face was changing between the face of a man, a lion, an ox, an eagle, a lion, a man, an ox, a man...I spoke with Him as a man speaks face to face with his child – and I am still alive today.

That has totally changed my life. What made Satan ridicule God was His vulnerability with Adam and Eve, because when He played with them He was like a child with them. That is what Satan mocked because He saw God with all this power and authority but with absolute vulnerability. So when God is like that with you, He makes Himself absolutely vulnerable with you. I am a person who loves touching things. You are allowed to touch as a family, isn't that true? Well, God is my Father. Aren't I allowed to touch Him?

I can remember reaching out and feeling "Man, I am going to get fried here! But who cares, because I am in the most wonderful place anyway." And I can remember reaching out and touching, and I expected to get blown out of the water – out of the cloud, onto the earth, flat on my back, with my hand fried. But what I found when I touched Him was my yearning and my love for Him went through me into Him. This is because His desire is to be loved by His family.

I touched Him and it was like the most warm, fuzzy feeling of comfort, just in the touch. I have no words to describe it. Then the love of God came through that touch back to me and that is what laid me on the floor. It was the absolute abandonment of God towards me, as a child that dared to come into His presence.

God is calling all of us to come into His presence. Not just to His throne, but to the Person. You see, God is a Person. He is not just our ultimate power source. He is a Person who wants a relationship with you and me. He wants to be able to talk to you face to face. He wants to be able to express Himself to you and talk with you. I love going into the realm of the Kingdom and spending time just watching what happens around the throne. Just watching is the most amazing thing you can experience. I am trying to make this real for you. I am a normal person. I do not consider myself super-spiritual. All I have done is pursue God, and that is all I have done. When I chase God, people call me super-spiritual. Does that mean that they are naturally carnal then? That is the reality. They mock the very thing that they want, because they know that there is a price to be paid to get it. Now you and I can reach out and touch God and it will change you. It will change the way you do things. It will change the way you think. It will change your life.

No one ever told me I am going to look like my Father. No one ever told me what my Father was like. The Bible is quite clear about the semblance of what He is like, because there are angels around Him and they take on His image because of the power of who He is. God is our Dad and we have His seed in us and that seed is going to make us look like Him. You can have skin that is going to look like diamonds matted together, moving with fire, full of glory and light blue, full of light and flickering with power.

You can have a face that turns from lion to ox, to eagle, to man (Revelation 4:7, Ezekiel 1:10) I wonder why they covered Moses' face? Was it just because of the glory or was it that his face was doing the same thing? I have not spent forty days with God, I have spent about half an hour; that was enough. Forty days and you would take on the image of the Father. Remember, the fire changes whatever it touches. It changes that nature into its image.

When Moses had his face covered, it was not just because of the glory, it was the revealing of the glory, the revealing of the glories of the faces of God. What they were terrified of was the changes in His image. They were not afraid of the light, they were terrified of the revealing of that light, hallelujah!

We need to spend time just worshipping Him. I love the exercise of just worshipping God. I know that God wants to touch your life. It is all about you encountering God and pursuing God, so that you can speak with Him. Then you will get some more secrets and some things that will help to bring you to a place where you can meet with Him. I am not saying it is going to happen for you today, but you need to set your heart and you need to make the choice to go down the pathway. The reward of dying is absolute life! That is the good part about it.

Let us chase God. It is about you pursing God and chasing Him. If you find it hard just spend some time praying in tongues or listening to music, or words of life – just begin to engage God.

ACTIVATION

"Holy Spirit, we come as your sons and Your daughters. Father, Your Word says You have given us free access to You. Father, You have given us access, according to who You are, into Your presence. Your Word says that we can come boldly before You, into Your throne room. Father, I want more than just Your throne. I want Your presence. I want to know You – the only true God and Your Son Jesus Christ. I want to know You Father. I want to see Your beauty and gaze at Your majesty. Father, I know that there is terror and there is absolute awareness of You and the nature of the body that I live in.

But Father, there is another nature. That nature is You who lives in me. It is that nature that I turn to today. Lord, it is Your nature that allows me to come into Your presence. Lord, it is Your nature that I turn to today. Lord, I come, Lord, like Enoch, like Moses, like Abraham, like John, like Paul, Lord, who my eyes have seen, my ears have heard and my hands have handled.

Lord, I come, in my nakedness and my vulnerability as You say I can. Lord, in Your Bible it says that You wait, looking for the son to come. It says that You ran towards him, that You covered him with Your garment (Luke 15:20-22). Lord, today I come."

Chapter 11
THE COURTROOM OF GOD

How to access the courtroom of God is a vitally important ingredient that we need to understand as believers. Ezekiel 1 talks about the throne that moves and comes down. It is on four wheels, which are four cherubs that carry the movable ark. This throne is like the throne that is in Heaven, but it is different from the one that is called a Judgment Throne. The reason it is not in Heaven but only comes into the spiritual realms is because the devil cannot get into Heaven. This throne comes down from Heaven and judgments happen before it.

I want to lay a scriptural foundation for this. Let's start in Zechariah:

"Then he showed me Joshua the high priest standing before the Angel of the LORD, and Satan standing at his right hand to oppose him" (Zechariah 3:1).

Here is Joshua, the high priest, standing before the angel of the Lord, and Satan is standing right next to him. The reason Satan is there is to resist Joshua standing before the Lord and Joshua's petition. So Satan is not actually resisting Joshua, he is resisting what Joshua is doing there. So you have a scripture that paints a picture of something that goes on in the spirit world.

In 2 Chronicles there is another scene in the courtroom, where

God says "Who will go and do this?" And a spirit comes before the court.

"Then Micaiah said, 'Therefore hear the word of the LORD: I saw the LORD sitting on His throne, and all the host of heaven standing on His right hand and His left.' And the LORD said, 'Who will persuade Ahab king of Israel to go up, that he may fall at Ramoth Gilead?' So one spoke in this manner, and another spoke in that manner. Then a spirit came forward and stood before the LORD, and said, 'I will persuade him.' The LORD said to him, 'In what way?' So he said, 'I will go out and be a lying spirit in the mouth of all his prophets.' And the LORD said, 'You shall persuade him and also prevail; go out and do so'" (2 Chronicles 18:18-21).

A picture is painted here of what the courtroom looks like. It begins with the throne, and the host of heaven on the left hand side and on the right hand side. Now, you can see that devils have access to this arena. So it is not the Throne Room of Heaven, because devils cannot go into the Throne Room of Heaven, which is the realm of the dominion of God.

In Job we read:

"Now there was a day when the sons of God came to present themselves before the LORD, and Satan also came among them. And the LORD said to Satan, 'From where do you come?' So Satan answered the LORD and said "From going to and fro on the earth, and from walking back and forth on it" (Job 1:6-7).

The devil can walk to and fro on the earth and up and down in it, so what is he talking about? From the earth into the spiritual realms. So Satan came to present himself. It says "and Satan came also amongst them." Now it is amazing that the people that were around just accepted his role of being there. I do not know about you, but I would have given him a beating! What kind of right does he have to come next to me when I present myself before the Lord? Well, in this context he has every right; because the spirit world works on laws – laws that govern the realm of the spirit.

We find the scene repeated in Job 2:

"There was a day when the sons of God came to present themselves before the LORD, and Satan came also among them to present himself before the LORD" (Job 2:1).

In the first scene it says Satan only came amongst the sons of

God (Job 1:6). Now in Job 2 it says he came there to present himself before the Lord. What an arrogant cheek! But the reason he can present himself is because nothing was done with him in the first instance.

"And the Lord said to Satan..." (Job 2:2).

I tell you I get really mad when God has to speak to the devil! Because we should speak to him; where should we speak to him? Under our feet, that is where he belongs! He has no right in the court. The only reason he is there is because no one has done anything with him in the first place!

"Then the LORD said to Satan, 'Have you considered My servant Job, that there is none like him on the earth, a blameless and upright man, one who fears God and shuns evil? And still he holds fast to his integrity, although you incited Me against him, to destroy him without cause.' So Satan answered the LORD and said, 'Skin for skin! Yes, all that a man has he will give for his life'" (Job 2:3-4).

What the devil wants there is permission to go and do something, and the courtroom is a place where permission is granted. This is really important. If you can get to grips with some of these things, you can do something about the issues that go on around your life.

The courtroom is very important. It is where all judgments and decrees are made by the presence of God. The devil has a right to come into the courtroom because we do not go into the courtroom and do our business with God. Now, in the courtroom is where all the activity of right and wrong occurs. It is where permission is granted to do wrong and where permission is refused from doing wrong. What this means is that, if I came in like Job or like Joshua to stand before the Lord and the devil comes in, he has a right to counter-petition my petition before the Lord. Here is the problem. The devil has been turning up in the courtroom but not many believers have been turning up in the courtroom. He makes his petition and there is no one that stands and says to him, "No, this is the way it is going to be."

The courtroom is a 'fixed' courtroom. God who sits on the throne is our Father, and Jesus, who is the executor of the Will of God, is our brother. All who stand around Him are from the realm of glory. Now, who do you think is going to win in the courtroom?

Do you think the devil is going to win? Or do you think it will be the court that has been fixed by God that is going to win on our behalf? The reason we do not win is because we do not often turn up at the courtroom.

In Luke, the devil comes to make a petition:

"And the Lord said, 'Simon, Simon! Indeed, Satan has asked for you, that he may sift you as wheat. But I have prayed for you, that your faith should not fail; and when you have returned to Me, strengthen your brethren.' But he said to Him, 'Lord, I am ready to go with You, both to prison and to death.' Then He said, 'I tell you, Peter, the rooster shall not crow this day before you will deny three times that you know Me'" (Luke 22:31-34).

Where did Jesus see this? How did Jesus know that the devil had desired to sift Peter as wheat? In the courtroom. Jesus knew about the courtroom. He knew how to go into the courtroom and he knew how to counter-petition the devil's desire. I guarantee you, the devil's desire was to destroy Peter and make him die, not to help him to overcome. You see, you can change things by going into the courtroom. You have a legal mandated right from God to present yourself in the courtroom. It is amazing what happens in the courtroom. What God wants us to do is to understand there is a legal process that goes on of petition and counter-petition. That is what intercession is supposed to be; petition and counter-petition.

I have wrestled with demon spirits in the courtroom. Not physically, not fighting with them, but with petition: "No! The Bible says it is by the Blood. The Bible says I am redeemed by the Blood." Now, who is going to win? If I was not standing there in the courtroom to present myself before the Lord and the devil came there whispering – what has God got to work with? Nothing. What God wants us to understand is that there is a courtroom. There is a Throne of Judgment and we have a right to come and make our petition before that courtroom to destroy the works of the enemy and change what the devil is doing. It happens in the courtroom. We can change what the devil is doing and we change it by being in the courtroom.

Jesus changed what would happen to Simon Peter's life and he changed that in the courtroom. He changed it, firstly, because He was the Son of God. You and I are sons of God. Secondly, He knew about the courtroom. He went there, experienced it and did something about what was going on. I have not been in the courtroom yet when Jesus comes and makes petition, although the Bible says that He stands and makes petition for us day and night before the Lord. I have not seen Jesus speaking for me yet but I know this: all He has to do is stand there and sigh and Satan just goes backwards and crawls out of the courtroom. If that happens with Jesus, and we are little Jesuses, how much more does God want to release to the church today? You see, it happens in the courtroom.

I want to go back into Zechariah 3 again. I want to do this part because the Old Testament tells us how to come into the courtroom. It is a simple process, it is not hard:

"Then he showed me Joshua the high priest standing before the Angel of the Lord, and Satan standing at his right hand to oppose him. And the Lord said to Satan, 'The Lord rebuke you, Satan! The Lord who has chosen Jerusalem rebuke you! Is this not a brand plucked from the fire?' Now Joshua was clothed with filthy garments, and was standing before the Angel. Then He answered and spoke to those who stood before Him, saying, 'Take away the filthy garments from him.' And to him He said, 'See, I have removed your iniquity from you, and I will clothe you with rich robes.' And I said, 'Let them put a clean turban on his head.' So they put a clean turban on his head, and they put the clothes on him. And the Angel of the Lord stood by." (Zechariah 3:1-5).

When we turn up in the courtroom, God kind of tricks the devil because when we turn up, he has to turn up too. The devil does not have a choice. It says that Joshua came and stood there, and the devil stood there resisting. You see, every time you turn up in the courtroom the devil has to stand up and come into the courtroom. And here is the greatest thing I like about it: when we turn up in our filthy garments and the devil rubs his hands and thinks, "Ha ha, I've got 'em." Then the first thing God does in the courtroom is to say, "New garments!" This is why we win in the courtroom. It is because of the new garments. Then it says He put a fair mitre (which is a crown) upon his head. When you wear a crown it is a symbol of the invested authority in your life as a prince of God. So when you come into the courtroom, you may turn up filthy.

That is God's disguise for you. He wants the devil to turn up there too. You know why? Because He loves beating up on him! You have got to love the things that God loves, and I love beating up on the devil. Where do you do it? In the courtroom. It is great! You get there and thump him. Then you can start to make your petition and when he starts to speak you put your foot on his neck and you squeeze! You need to understand this is the fun part of being a believer! This is the kind of thing that happens in the courtroom. The moment you turn up, God endues you with a garment. The garment is called the Garment of Righteousness. That is what Adam lost, except his whole body was righteous. So when we turn up in court God begins to give rights back to His children.

"My little children, these things I write to you, so that you may not sin. And if anyone sins, we have an Advocate with the Father, Jesus Christ the righteous. And He Himself is the propitiation for our sins, and not for ours only but also for the whole world" (1 John 2:1-2).

When we sin we have an advocate. An advocate means someone who takes our case before a courtroom. The moment we sin the devil turns up in the courtroom because he accuses us before the Father day and night. That is what the Bible says. But if we sin we have an advocate Jesus Christ, the righteous. So Jesus is standing there as our advocate waiting.

In Hebrews 3:1, it shows us what God is waiting to see happen. It says that Jesus is the High Priest of our confession. The word confession comes from a Greek word 'homologia' which means to confess the same thing. The moment you speak confession of your sin, Jesus confesses that sin before the Father and it is under the Blood and the devil has got no further right to accuse you. Then Jesus has some fun with the devil because He can stand on the devil on our behalf!

Now, one shall put a thousand to flight, two shall put ten thousand to flight. When you turn up in the courtroom you have Jesus, the High Priest of your confession standing there. When you are speaking to God, Jesus is saying the same thing in agreement – the Blood has cleansed you. If we confess your sins,

He is faithful and just to forgive us our sins and cleanse us from all unrighteousness (1 John 1:9). The Blood of Jesus Christ cleanses us from all sin (1 John 1:7). This is what Jesus has done. He took the sin of the whole world on Himself and made an open show of the devil, triumphing over him. He totally and absolutely spoilt every principality and power (Isaiah 53:6; 1 Peter 2:24; Colossians 2:15).

Hebrews 7:25 says Jesus makes intercession. Read Hebrews 7, 8 and 9 from the aspect of the role Jesus plays in the courtroom and you will get a much clearer idea of what He does with your confession. You get a much clearer idea of what He does when He is in that courtroom and even how He prayed for Simon.

I love going into the courtroom. I love going there, because we win! We win in the courtroom. You do not win when you are on the earth. Too many intercessors have been caught and trapped on the earth trying to eventually go to Heaven instead of realising they can go to Heaven immediately, do transactions and win! We win, hallelujah!

Revelation 12:11 says they overcome him by three things. Firstly, by the 'Blood of the Lamb'. The only way you are going to defeat and overcome is by the Blood of the Lamb. You have to take that blood and apply it to your life. The only way you are going to experience the realm of the Kingdom is by that Blood, because it is only the Blood that gives you the right standing in that realm. It is the Blood that makes you righteous.

The second is by the 'word of their testimony'. Now, my testimony is not that I have sinned; my testimony is that I have overcome by the Blood. My testimony is not that I am struggling in my life; my testimony is that I have the victory because Jesus has given it to me. I just have not caught up with that revelation yet. I might be struggling, but that is not what God is interested in. He is interested in your focus. What you look at you are going to become, because you turn into the very thing you gaze at. Can you see why it is important to see God? Because you change into the image of the things you look at. The Bible says "think about things which are holy, acceptable and pure" (Philippians 4:8). The word 'think' means to dwell on in your mind and captivate your imagination. It is not just looking with your eyes. We have taken this in the natural for too long. It is about a spirit realm encounter. What God is looking for is the reality of Heaven in your life.

So we have the Blood and the word of their testimony. Thirdly, it says they "loved not their lives to death". The "death" there means the cross. It does not mean you physically die. What a waste of time if you are going to be transformed by the Blood and transfigured because of the testimony of Christ in your life and He takes you home. He does not want to take you home once you become a son of God, He wants to display you to the world (Out the door goes the rapture theory! Sorry if you believe in that).

What He is looking for is your death on the cross in correlation with Christ's resurrection from the Cross. As you die, your sin becomes one with Him on the cross and, in that death, we identify. Jesus is looking for the reality of the resurrection life and you can only have resurrection life if you experience the cross. You need to chase God. There is no way around it. Three things: the Blood, the testimony (and we have talked about what you confess with your mouth) and the cross. All these things come out of Revelation 12:11.

So, how do I get into the courtroom? Very easily, as we see in Psalm 100. I love this Psalm, I learned so much from it.

"Make a joyful shout to the LORD, all you lands! Serve the LORD with gladness; Come before His presence with singing. Know that the LORD, He is God; It is He who has made us, and not we ourselves; We are His people and the sheep of His pasture." (Which is in Eden). "Enter into His gates with thanksgiving, And into His courts with praise. Be thankful to Him, and bless His name. For the LORD is good; His mercy is everlasting, And His truth endures to all generations" (Psalms 100:1-5).

There are three things there. The first is to "make a joyful noise." You need to make a choice to make a joyful noise. In verse 2 it says "come before His presence with singing." With many churches that is where it stops. We have a nice sing-song time, we come before His presence and God says, "Hello, why are you here?" Then we carry on with our service! You come before the Lord with singing and that is all it is – just getting us to a place where we can come before the Lord, not Him before us.

I just want to clarify something. I have said that instead of God always coming down, it is time for us to go up. God will still come down in His grace and His mercy. But there is a higher level – that is where you go up.

The second point is that we get into His gate with thanksgiving. Not our gate, His gate. When the Bible talks about God's gate it is the entry into the realm of the courtroom of God. When you come into a gate you come in expressing and expecting victory. There is no other reason why a king would come in through a gate into another city unless it is to conquer it. Usually they would carry their spoils of victory through the gates as a procession to show the people that they have won. They take all the spoils of war.

The devil does the same thing when the sons of God fall. He steals their trophy and their crown. He then takes it into the catacombs of the earth, before the demonic spirit world, as a procession and shows his victory over the church again. Those days are coming to an end. The reason they are coming to an end is because the courtroom is becoming known.

When we come out of the courtroom we come out with victory. The only reason you go into the courtroom is because you win; there is no other reason. God wants you there to make intercession, pray and do business. So we come before Him with singing, we enter His gates with thanksgiving and into His courts with praise. That is the third element. The way you enter this courtroom of God is with praise. When the Bible talks about praise there, it means with a strong, loud, persistent, rejoicing shout, clapping, celebrating and jumping and making the greatest noise that you can make!

The reason the Word says that is because praise releases the realm of Heaven to move on your behalf. This is the very thing you need to practise, because what I want to happen is for us to go in and out of the courtroom. If you learn that, you can chose to go in there any time you like. You can choose to go into the courtroom and you can choose to come out of the courtroom. You can choose to go in and do some business and you can choose to come out of it. Often I like standing by the door to the courtroom to watch what devils go in and listen; "Oh I do not like that one". Slap! "Next one!" You see, whoever has the gate has the authority of what goes in and comes out, isn't that true? So you need to learn about the gate of God.

The gate of God is the entry to the courtroom and you can stand there and have dominion over the gate. If you do not stand there, something else will! And it could say, "Oh, I think I will let that devil in, or I will let this one in. These sons of God do not know what they are doing. I will stand in their way and make them feel like they are sinners who cannot come before God!" So the devils go right on through! This is how the devil wins against us. He condemns us and accuses us and we believe him. We feel condemned and accused and we do not go to the courts, not realising that if we did, God would point to us and say "New garments," just like that!

I love going to the courtroom. I love it because you can bring any aspect of your life, any aspect of the life of another, a city or a region before the courtroom of God. You can slap the devil around a bit, kick him out and decree what needs to happen. You do not stand here in the natural on earth and pray, you do it in the spirit, in the courtroom, before the living God. This courtroom is where judgment is decreed, where judgment is released and where the elders sit and bring judgment to decree that the righteous rule will prevail. The courtroom is also where the angels of God are released on assignment to see it come to pass on the earth. It is done in the courtroom, not on the earth. As intercessors we spend so much time praying down here and it has been good, but we have not always had the victory. We have to learn another way. This is another way to pray.

ACTIVATION

The judgment of God came on the wall of Jericho (Joshua 6:20). That wall still stands, did you know that? The wall is still solid, what happened is it sank into the ground. Their walking around that wall of Jericho shattered the structure of the earth underneath, which was like limestone, and then when they shouted and stamped their feet it shattered that layer and the whole wall sank into the ground. That is why the Bible says every man could go straight every which way. When there is a really high wall you cannot go straight over it.

The wall sank, excavations have been done and it still exists today! But it is in the ground. God will make everything bow the knee with a shout of triumph. When we shout like this it activates the spirit world for victory. It activates the realm of Heaven to bring victory on the earth for the sons of the living God. So we are going to go into the courtroom and to shout! The way of entry is by shouting. If you are not used to doing this, hallelujah!

I want you to clap and shout and keep it sustained for at least two minutes. For most people, you will last about thirty seconds, so we are going to exercise your spirit and make you last two minutes. I want you to work on doing it. If you are in a group, work on joining in, one with another. Remember we talked about how I link with this gate (person), we link with this gate, we link with this gate and we have an exponential increase of the glory and the praises of God. When you shout I want you to express yourself with gratitude, with thanksgiving and celebration. The reason you are celebrating is because when you turn up there you have the victory! Then after two minutes what I am going to get you to do is take an issue and an area of your life and we are going to take that issue into the courtroom. We are going to pray over it, shout over it, decree victory over it and the devil's defeat – so they will not want to come out again! So we will practise going in and out. I want you to put everything that is inside of you into this. I want you to take your spirit and put it into the atmosphere behind your praise as an offering to the presence of God for two minutes. Go ahead and shout!

Didn't that feel good? Now I want you to take an area of your life that you have wrestled with. I want you to go to court, inside your mind, and I want you to come before the presence of God shouting and decreeing into this realm. Decree the victory of the presence of the Lord by the Blood, by the word of your testimony and by choosing to die to that area of your life. That is how we are going to overcome. I want you to begin to do the same thing and to hold it for 1 minute. 1 minute is not long, we have just done it for two minutes. I want you to hold it for one minute, then decree a victory in the courtroom of the living God over the chosen area of your life.

This will totally change the atmosphere in the room. This kind of thing affects a city and a nation. I want you to do this for your nation. You see, this is not just about you, your ministry, your pastors and your churches – this is about your nation. I want you to go into the courtroom for your nation. I want you to hold your nation before the living God in prayer like this, decreeing the presence of God over the nation, decreeing the victory of God over every spiritual force, every wicked thing that has sought devices into your nation. Just begin to decree the victory of God into it. So we are going to do the same thing for one minute. Cry out with victory for the nation! Let the spirit world hear. The Bible says in the high places of God, God sends surprise attacks against the enemy that he did not see coming (2 Chronicles 20:22). This is what we are doing today, Hallelujah!

"Father, we love our nation. Lord, You have given us a land, and today, Father, it belongs to the seed of the righteous. Amen."

I suggest you practise some of this. Just get in and practise again with two or three other people. Practise in your own personal life. Practise this process. It is just another key of entering the realm of the Kingdom. You see, what we have done, whether you feel it or not, is entered the realm of the spirit. We come before the courtroom of God with a cry of praise that lifts the ability of Jesus to be able to act on some of the issues in our personal lives and nation. Remember I said first in Jerusalem, then in Samaria. You must practise in your own life first. Achieve victories in your own life. Then you can take other people there. Amen.

Chapter 12
The Seven Spirits of God

The Seven Spirits of God are not the Holy Spirit. They are sentient beings designed to train us, mandate us and equip us to become sons of God. They testify to the covenant of adoption. They testify to every covenant. Every time God moves the Seven Spirits of God move. That is what the colours of the rainbow around people are. They always testify to a covenant. If you do not have the Seven Spirits functioning around your life then you will literally be a powerless Christian.

I have had interesting conflicts with people who have religious mind sets and who cannot believe that there are powerful spiritual beings in Heaven other than God. Because of the religious teachings that they have had, the perceptions and way they see things are from an old mind set and they really struggle when they are presented with something new.

The first time I engaged one of the Seven Spirits of God was an amazing day because it changed my life. This is some years ago now that I began to form a relationship with these sentient beings, these beings are like men and women, who look like God but are not God. First I want to go through some scriptural foundations for you.

"Now I say that the heir, as long as he is a child, does not differ at all from a slave, though he is master of all, but is under guardians and stewards until the time appointed by the father" (Galatians 4:1-2).

I became very interested with regard to who these tutors and governors were. A tutor means someone who trains you. A governor means someone who teaches you how to rule or who rules over you until you can rule. I used to get really frustrated because I knew that there was more about the arena around Heaven's throne than I had experienced.

"And if you are Christ's, then you are Abraham's seed, and heirs according to the promise." (Galatians 3:29)

If we are an heir to a promise then we need to be trained to become a joint heir in Christ. To be an heir of a promise does not mean you are going to automatically inherit the promise, it just means you are an heir to it. We have to go through a process to inherit the promise.

When Jesus was baptised in water, the Father came over Him and said "This is My beloved Son, in whom I am well pleased" (Matthew 3:17). The Father was testifying to his desired relationship with the Son. Then when Jesus was transfigured God said, "This is My beloved Son, in whom I am well pleased. Hear Him!" (Matthew 17:5). One was a statement of potential, the other was a statement of maturity. As an heir I have huge potential to come to maturity, but I need to be trained to be brought to maturity.

"And there shall come forth a Shoot out of the stock of Jesse [David's father], and a Branch out of his roots shall grow and bear fruit. And the Spirit of the Lord shall rest upon Him-the Spirit of wisdom and understanding, the Spirit of counsel and might, the Spirit of knowledge and of the reverential and obedient fear of the Lord-And shall make Him of quick understanding, and His delight shall be in the reverential and obedient fear of the Lord. And He shall not judge by the sight of His eyes, neither decide by the hearing of His ears; But with righteousness and justice shall He judge the poor" (Isaiah 11:1-4 AMP).

Jesus was not talking about the Holy Spirit when He said:

"The Spirit of the LORD is upon Me, Because He has anointed Me To preach the gospel to the poor; He has sent Me to heal the broken-hearted, To proclaim liberty to the captives And recovery of sight to the blind, To set at liberty those who are oppressed" (Luke 4:18)

When He said "The Spirit of the Lord is upon Me," He was talking about the mandate of the full expression of that tutorage training in His life, now being fully expressed through Him. All the Seven Spirits of God were fully expressed in Christ.

Jesus' expressed government in its fullness as the Spirit of the Lord is the centre of the Seven Spirits and is about government, with all the other Seven Spirits being associated with that government. In Hebrew thinking: 'a + b + c = d = c + b + a'. So in the menorah you have the Spirit of the Lord in the centre, then the Spirit of Wisdom, the Spirit of Understanding, the Spirit of Counsel, the Spirit of Might, the Spirit of Knowledge and then the Spirit of the Fear of the Lord. It is amazing because the Spirit of Wisdom, Understanding and Counsel are predominantly feminine in appearance. The Spirit of Might, Knowledge and the Fear of the Lord are predominantly male in their appearance. The centre one, the Spirit of the Lord, has both male and female appearance. Each one of them is symbolised by a colour of the rainbow. Often when people see colours in the spirit it is the manifestation of one of the Seven Spirits of God around them wanting to reveal the person's mandate and the place they are supposed to move in.

"And from the throne proceeded lightnings, thunderings, and voices. Seven lamps of fire were burning before the throne, which are the seven Spirits of God" (Revelation 4:5).

When the Bible talks about the Seven Spirits of God it is talking about the person not the position. There are Seven Spirits of God. They are not God, as the Bible says very clearly they burn before the throne. The Father is seated on the throne, Jesus is seated on the throne, the Holy Spirit is seated on the throne. Those seven are the full expression of everything that goes on from the throne. So who is the Holy Spirit? The Holy Spirit is God; and God sits on the throne. If the Seven Spirits are before the throne then there must be seven individual beings that he is talking about.

Some people say "Well, the Spirit of the Lord is the Holy Spirit". If that is the case there are not Seven Spirits of God, there are six Spirits of God. God's number is not six! The Seven Spirits of God follow the instructions given by God to teach us about His Kingdom, His will, His purpose and how to express these into the world around us.

"Having seven horns and seven eyes, which are the seven Spirits of God sent out into all the earth" (Revelation 5:6).

Seven Spirits are sent out into all the earth – not the Holy Spirit. The reason they are sent out is to see who is ready to be trained as a son. They are the eyes of the Lamb of God that move to and fro over the whole earth looking to approve a son in a matter (2 Chronicles 16:9). When something is 'sent out' it is given a purpose, a mandate, an authority to do a job. You and I are called the sent out ones of the Father. That means I have a spirit in me. The purpose of the Seven Spirits of God is to empower you and me to establish the Kingdom and to express it as heirs of God to the world around us that needs Him.

So who and what are the Seven Spirits of God, these tutors and governors that God has put over us that are part of our covenant of adoption? The covenant of adoption is a very interesting thing when you understand the depth of it. When a king wanted to have a son and did not have a son of his own, he would adopt one. He would bring him into the court room and the judge would have a parchment with the testimony of the child's birth and everything that he had ever done, everything that had ever been recorded, where he lived, who his mum and dad were, etc. That would be on one parchment, and on another parchment he would have a blank page. The judge would then say to the king, "What is your son's name?" The king would say "So and so" and the judge would write that new name on the new parchment.

Then he would say "Who testifies to this adoption?" And then seven men would come into the court room and would sign the document paper as the ones that would train the boy to become a fully-fledged son. They were the tutors that the Father had given responsibility in his kingdom to train people to take responsibility as sons. They would sign the new parchment. In those days they did not have acid in their ink so they could take a rag and wipe the original parchment clean. The Roman judge would take a damp rag and the old parchment would be wiped clean so that no record would remain of the person's previous life. The son then came under the tutorage of the seven that signed the new parchment and said "We will train him."

After they had completed their task of tutoring they would present the son to the father saying "I cannot train him anymore, he knows everything I need him to." Then the father would pick him up and train his son about the kingdom and what he is doing himself.

Vitally, the parchment had to be made clean. That is why the Blood of Jesus is so important. That is why it is important to walk through your life with the Blood. Jesus wants the parchment clean so that you can come into the inheritance of your new name. You are adopted into the seed of Jesse (Romans 11:17-24), you are grafted into the vine, Jesus Christ (John 15:1-9), but your adoption cannot come into force until you have cleansed the old parchment. Once you have cleansed the old record away you can then come under the tutorage of the Seven Spirits of God, who signed your adoption document and said "We will train him." Once completed, they will present you to the Father, saying "We cannot train him anymore, he knows everything we need him to." Then the Father will pick you up and train you himself.

"The Revelation of Jesus Christ, which God gave Him to show His servants—things which must shortly take place. And He sent and signified it by His angel to His servant John, who bore witness to the word of God, and to the testimony of Jesus Christ, to all things that he saw.." (Revelation 1:1-2).

Notice that the Bible says, things that he "saw", not things that he heard. I do not know how much more I can emphasise this issue of seeing and not hearing.

"Blessed is he who reads and those who hear the words of this prophecy, and keep those things which are written in it; for the time is near. John, to the seven churches which are in Asia: Grace to you and peace from Him who is and who was and who is to come, and from the seven Spirits who are before His throne, and from Jesus Christ, the faithful witness, the first born from the dead, and the ruler over the kings of the earth" (Revelation 1:3-5).

John would not have brought greetings to the churches from the Seven Spirits of God unless there was a relational connection. So he brings greetings from the Father, Son and Holy Spirit, then he says 'and' which means they are included in the greeting "from the Seven Spirits of God which are before the throne". This means that there is some relationship that has to be developed for them to bring a greeting to the face of the earth out of Heaven. It must be important then to develop a relationship if there are going to be greetings out of Heaven.

People have asked me, "Are these Seven Spirits of God omnipresent?" No they are not, but there is a classroom that is omnipresent. You can go to the classroom any time you like with as many people as are on the face of the earth. Usually when I go to the classroom, there have only been two or three other people. That is why there are not many mature sons of God on the face of the earth yet. The greatest problem is that people do not visit the classroom.

I can remember going to the classroom one day and seeing these pillars of glory, the colours that burn around the throne, kind of moving around and I looked at them and thought, "What on earth are these?" This pillar of cloud, this blue thing turns to me and says "Hi!" When you see things in the spirit you might see them at a distance, but when they say 'hi' they are present and they are bigger than you think! The Spirit of Might has shoulders like two pillars, a waist as skinny as I am and he just stands there, and he is! I have experienced him turning up twice on the face of the earth when I have been praying. When the Spirit of Might turns up and stands there, every demon in Hell backs off! They back off because if they come near, they know someone is going to die! Now if he looks like that and you get trained and mentored by him, what are you going to look like to the spirit world?

Just imagine looking like all seven at the same time! John saw it:

"His feet glowed like burnished (bright) bronze as it is refined in a furnace, and His voice was like the sound of many waters. In His right hand He held seven stars, and from His mouth there came forth a sharp two-edged sword, and His face was like the sun shining in full power at midday" (Revelation 1:15-16 AMP).

He had a picture of what we look like. John turned and saw Jesus, but who is likened unto the son of man? Let's go a bit deeper. God has called us to be kings who sit on a throne. We all agree with that doctrine? In Ezekiel 1, we find Ezekiel looking in the spirit and he sees a cloud enfolding in itself and he sees one like the Son of Man sitting on the throne. Have you ever wondered what you look like to the spirit world when you sit on your throne? I challenge you to read it and read it in a new light. That is me sitting there when I turn up as a fully-fledged son in the realm of the spirit. That is what I look like. That is how I am perceived in the spirit world. When I move in the galaxies that is what I look like.

Here is a testimony of someone that has seen me in the spirit:

> "I was in my house with a friend and we were up in the spirit realm and my friend said to me, "Shall I call for Ian to come and join us?" and I'm like, "Whatever, dude!" I mean – my mind was fried anyway! My friend just called for Ian to come through and I just started hearing this roaring coming and my friend fell on his back and started laughing going, "Here he comes, dudes! Here he comes! Are you ready?!" And all I know was it was like – 'Whoa!' – a couple of hundred feet tall like a cocoon of light. It took probably two or three minutes to come rolling through and there was this sound like a roaring steam train or hurricane for two or three minutes rolling through my house! We sat in the heavens looking down at the earth and this thing just comes rolling through. And all my friend could say was, "He's big, isn't he, dudes?! He's big! He's my big brother! He's big isn't he!" So from that moment on I realised how big this guy was in the spirit world and I realised there's no devils want to play around with him. Ian, there's a lot of authority, a lot of glory so we honour you, man."

I am just me, hallelujah! I am a guy who lives on the earth, has a family, runs a business and enjoys racing cars – but I also live in another world! I do not want you to get your eyes on me and say this is all about Ian. This is a testimony to a life that I have lived with the person of God. It is a testimony of what I have desired that God has now manifested. It is manifested because I have given myself to the Kingdom and to be revealed in the arena of the Kingdom that God has destined me to be a king in. We have been given a throne and, let me tell you, when you begin to occupy your throne everything changes, but you cannot get on your throne unless you have been taught. The Seven Spirits of God teach you how to govern from a throne.

The first time I met my friend Jason, we met in the spirit and were doing a whole lot of activities. Later I met him in the natural and it was so funny. He shouted "Ian, buddy!" All these pastors were looking at me thinking "Who is this guy?!" I said to Jason one day as we were walking around, "Listen, I want to make a living covenant with you because you need people to stand with you. Here is my mountain, whatever is in my mountain I open up, you can have whatever you need out of that mountain." And Jason has been very faithful in gleaning what he has needed out of it, so it is awesome. I have a fantastic relationship with him, he is a good young man.

The Seven Spirits of God

Spirit of Knowledge
Spirit of Counsel
Spirit of Wisdom
Spirit of The Lord
Spirit of Understanding
Spirit of Might
Spirit of the Fear of The Lord

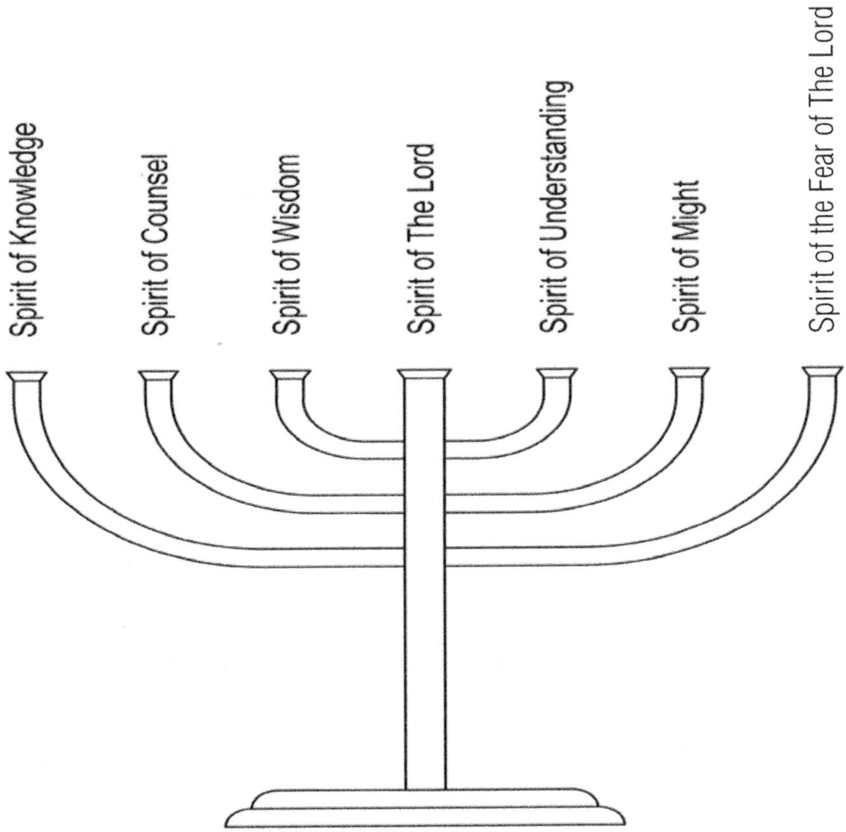

Each pair of the Seven Spirits of God (Isaiah 11:2) forms an arc over the centre branch, making a rainbow.

The Seven Spirits of God are:

The Spirit of the Lord: Mandates Us For Position

The Spirit of the Lord is the centre candlestick in the menorah and holds the whole arena of the Seven Spirits together. The Spirit of the Lord is about positional dominion and mandates us for position. It teaches us and enables us to experience and see the reality of the dimensions of the Kingdom; about the throne room, about power, authority, dominion, sonship, rulership, transfiguration, translation and trans-relocation. The Spirit of the Lord teaches us about bringing divine order and divine government out of justice from Heaven and how to assert it on the face of the earth. The Spirit of the Lord is about anything to do with the glory realm of God and how to exercise dominion on the face of the earth.

The Spirit of Wisdom: Equips Us for Position

Solomon is a prime example of the Spirit of Wisdom fully manifested on the face of the earth. The Spirit of Wisdom equips us for position and produces prosperity and delight towards God. It teaches us how to judge and how to bring justice. It teaches us how to exercise these things as sons from the throne that we have been given to rule in. It teaches us how to bring divine order and authority into the spirit realm and how to bring divine justice out of it. It teaches us what to do in the realm of rulership as a son. The Spirit of Wisdom releases contentment and joy, not only for you but for all those that are around you.

The Spirit of Understanding: Authorises Us for Position

The Spirit of Understanding teaches us where and how to access the realm of God. It teaches us how to use what we have at the right time. It helps us to decipher revelation and visions. The Spirit of Understanding teaches us how to perceive and how to teach and inform others about the realm of the Kingdom. It teaches us how to rule in the realms of God as a son.

The Spirit of Counsel: Prepares Us for Position

The Spirit of Counsel teaches us which ways to rule as a son and how to access the counsels of God – how to consult with them, how to resolve issues and bring the advice of God to those around us out of the realm of the spirit. It teaches us how to commune with God and gain His advice. It instructs us in the function of the different council chambers of God, about the role of the royal advisers to Him, about the Holy Spirit and about the Son. It teaches us about the triune God and their role in our lives today.

The Spirit of Might: Reveals Us for Position

The Spirit of Might teaches us how to exercise the supernatural realm of God to reveal the power of God, the dominion of God and how to exercise it in the World, in the earth and in the spirit realm around us. It teaches us about the Council Chamber of War and the secrets of how to war in the spirit realm in the heavenlies. The Spirit of Might teaches us about the heavenly places of God and how we are seated there (Ephesians 2:6). It instructs us about our seats of rulership and the governmental arenas that we operate in as a king and how to do the works of the Kingdom.

The Spirit of Knowledge: Empowers Us for Position

The Spirit of Knowledge teaches us how to access the knowledge of God and how to apply that knowledge of God to the world around us. It enables us to become aware of our place to rule as a son of God and what to do with what we know. It enables us to gain access to knowledge about the supernatural realms of God, how they operate and how they function. The Spirit of Knowledge also teaches us how to retain what we see and to process and store the information until it becomes permanent in us. It teaches us how to meditate and receive divine insight and revelation into circumstances through visions, visitations and dreams, and to bring God's will to bear on the face of the earth.

The Spirit of the Fear of the Lord: Brings Us into Accountability for Position

This fear is not being afraid but rather an understanding of the awe, wonder, majesty, might and dominion of the person of God. The Spirit of the Fear of the Lord is all about and around the person of God, and teaches us about the realms of holiness, intimacy, worship, reverence and righteousness. The Spirit of the Fear of the Lord teaches us how to access and bring divine order and its application to the world around us.

COLOURS OF THE SEVEN SPIRITS OF GOD

Each of the Seven Spirits of God is related to the seven colours of the rainbow: red, orange, yellow, green, blue, indigo and violet.

The Spirit of the Lord is red and mandates us for position.

The Spirit of Wisdom is orange and equips us for position.

The Spirit of Understanding is yellow and authorises us for position.

The Spirit of Counsel is green and prepares us for position.

The Spirit of Might is blue and reveals us for position.

The Spirit of Knowledge is indigo and empowers us for position.

The Spirit of the Fear of the Lord is violet (purple) and brings accountability for position.

That is why when the Spirit of the Fear of the Lord comes around you, you see people in a purple robe. It is to do with the honour of their presence and the person of the presence of God. He will cloak you in a garment that has majesty in it.

All Seven Spirits of God are very functional in their relationship with God, how they do what they do and what they train us in. Each of them is very important. The primary purpose of the Seven Spirits of God is to teach and instruct us in things pertaining to the realms of the Kingdom and to present us to the courts of the King in His mountain as mature, mandated sons of God. Once this happens the King can then release us to reveal His Kingdom in every strata and sphere He has set up.

There is going to come a day very soon when people will come to you to admire God seen in you. We will be known as the shining ones. God says we are going to shine. If you were to take the seven colours of the rainbow and put them on a plaque and spin them round at 2,800 revolutions per minute (rpm) the plaque would go white. The only way that you are going to shine is if you are fully mandated by the Seven Spirits of God and the colours are thoroughly mixed in your life. You are then going to turn white.

The rainbow colours are: red, orange, yellow, green, blue, indigo and violet. They are the major colours that need to be around our life.

In the demonic world, if you were to take what they call the 'tertiary' or 'intermediate' colours, which are an off-red, an off-blue, an off-yellow and an off-green and so on, you mix them in the same proportions and spin them together at 2,800 rpm, it would turn black.

So the only way we can get into harmony is to engage the Seven Spirits of God, not the chaos and disharmony that we have been born into.

Out of our lives comes a fragrance, a song and a colour. If you do not have the Seven Spirits of God operating around your life, being mandated and tutored by them, you will not have any colour in you and the spirit world will see that. If you try to go into spiritual warfare without their mandate you are going to end up in trouble. That is how so many people are hurt, because they have never been trained to do the work of God by the Seven Spirits of God. We have been trying to do it with our own strength by the knowledge of man and not the wisdom of God.

I am just going to address something here briefly. A thing that frustrates me is the way the Church has turned into darkness, and the way that we have become so pre-occupied with the demonic world. You need to know and understand the demonic but you do not need to be pre-occupied with it. I would rather be pre-occupied with the angelic arena. It is good to understand that there are demonic things that have happened in each nation, but if that is all you are seeing then that is all you are going to get. What you should be looking for is: Where do the angels of the Lord move in the nation? Where do they stand? What do I need to do to activate them and to motivate them to be released to do their work in the nation? When you can classify the angelic arena the same way as you can classify the demonic arena then you might find we start to win a lot more; hallelujah Father!

EFFECTS OF THE SEVEN SPIRITS OF GOD

When the Seven Spirits of God are functioning around our lives they seal us; the Bible says God is going to seal us. When the Seven Spirits of God are functional around our lives they seal us for position. You cannot be a king unless you have been sealed with the ring of the Father, which has the mandate of the Seven Spirits of God on it saying 'mature son'. I want my throne; I do not want anybody else to have it.

Jesus learned how to operate in, function in and reveal the characteristic traits and nature of all these Seven Spirits of God. That is why when Jesus went up into the mountain He was transfigured, because by then He was a mature son and He had the capacity to then be revealed in white. That is also why He was glorified on that mountain, because He had the mandate of all the Seven Spirits of God fully manifested in Him, being fully revealed as a son. When you are fully revealed as a son you can communicate properly with the cloud of witnesses because you look just like them. In fact, you become one of them, even though you are present here. That is why in the first resurrection you are going to live forever, because you are going to be just like them.

The purpose of all these Seven Spirits of God is to manifest in the earth the nature of the Kingdom in the person of God.

ACCESSING THE SEVEN SPIRITS OF GOD

How do we access these Seven Spirits? The first way is inside our spirit man where we willingly choose to give ourselves to be tutored by these seven, individually and then as a corporate body.

I can remember when I first started on this journey I did not even know the Seven Spirits of God existed. All I knew was there would be this thing called the Spirit of Knowledge and he wanted to teach me. I would be praying every day "Father, by faith I submit myself to the Spirit of Knowledge, to be trained by him, to be tutored by him, to be instructed by him. I give myself, my life and my spirit man to be tutored by the Spirit of Knowledge in the name of Jesus, that out of that knowledge would come the knowledge of God upon my life."

For about six months that is almost all I prayed. In the mornings

I would get up and pray "Father, I thank you that I am under the tutorage of the Spirit of Knowledge. Father I thank you that the Spirit of Knowledge walks with me. Father, wherever I go he goes and wherever he goes, I can go! He shows to me the things out of the Kingdom and reveals to me things that come out of the realm of Heaven. He enables me – giving me understanding." And all of a sudden I realised there was a Spirit of Understanding! Because when I said, "Lord I give myself to the Spirit of Understanding," I saw him. You see, I did not have all the theology I have just given you. I had to find it and uncover it. I work out of revelation because I am a son and I want revelation. Revelation must come first for me, not my head knowledge; Hallelujah Jesus!

ACTIVATION

Let's pray: "Father, I want to thank You that You have given us the capacity as Your sons to be mandated and to become all that You have desired us to be in the nations. Father, everything that You have written and spoken about was to reveal us as fully-fledged, mandated, empowered and equipped sons. Father, You have given us a full capacity to retain everything of Your Kingdom. In each of us dwells the full capacity of the Godhead to be fully manifested on the earth as it is in Heaven. Father, I ask in Jesus Name, that You would open the door for the tutorage of the Seven Spirits of God around our lives, that they would become real, as we submit to their government and their governance in our lives. Father, I ask that You would raise up a mature body of people that would take the earth back out of the hands of the enemy in the Name of Jesus. Amen."

Chapter 13
The DNA of God

One of the most important things the enemy has kept hidden from us in our walk with God is our identity – who we are, what we actually carry and the reality of what is inside of us as sons of God.

I grew up in my early church years with communion being a celebration of Jesus' death. It was a time to be sorrowful and remember what He did. We need to do that, and there is a point in celebrating His death. However, if that is all it is for us, then something is wrong – when Jesus does something He does not just do one thing, He does the complete work.

I want to pull some scriptures out for you and discuss the DNA of God and what it means to you and me today. Later in this chapter I will discuss how we can take hold of the DNA of God in communion and why there is more to communion than just celebrating Jesus' death.

The Lord gave me a Word about sanctifying ourselves. I do not think there is any better way to sanctify ourselves than by acknowledging what Jesus has done for us to give us a way into the arena of the Kingdom of God. I want to address this issue of DNA because it is very important that you understand what it means to carry the DNA of God and the problems we have as human beings with the DNA that we currently carry.

Science has found two strands of DNA, showing that human DNA has a record of what you are going to be like – what your soul is going to be and the way your body is going to be displayed. DNA indicates very clearly what colour eyes you are going to have, what kind of nose you are going to have, and how bald you are going to be or not going to be. It is a record of what you are going to be like. That record goes right back to Adam when he fell.

There is a protein called laminin, which is the foundational building block that holds every molecule in the human body together. It has three strands to it and it is shaped like a cross. Even the human body is trying to tell the scientists that there is a way to become something different than what we currently are.

In a well researched program called the Genome Project, the scientists started to prove that the actual DNA of a human can be programmed by languages and frequency. The Hebrew language is not just a language to be spoken but a felt language that goes right down into the very core of our DNA and has the capacity to regenerate the defects within it. This has now been proven by Russian researchers. The English language is 180 degrees opposite to the Hebrew language vibrationally, mathematically and directionally and actually creates chaos in the DNA strand when spoken. I just find this stuff interesting.

Because there are a group of crazy freaks like me who know that there is something wrong with the two-stranded cord of the DNA in our genes. God does not usually work with two, unless it is to form an arc over something. When we were born we had a body, a soul and a spirit. In Genesis 1, God formed man out of the dust of the earth, breathed His Spirit into him and man became a living soul.

"For there are three that bear witness in heaven: the Father, the Word, and the Holy Spirit; and these three are one. And there are three that bear witness on earth: the Spirit, the water, and the Blood; and these three agree as one." (1 John 5:7-8)

Right there I had the secret about why we only see two strands of the cord in the DNA. Humans are only seeing the natural world, they do not know that there is another strand. Scientists are discovering that there is something that holds all the genes together. There is a white light and they cannot figure out how it has got into the middle of the DNA! The white light has got its own programme. It seems that it is a little different when people are believers than when they are not believers. The white strain in believers seems to link everything together better than in unbelievers.

One day I asked some questions: "I wonder if our DNA strand is different. I wonder if God's DNA is three strands – body, soul and spirit? I wonder if there is a whole strand that the cameras and the scientists cannot explain and it is hidden inside there because the natural cannot see the spirit world?" (Some cameras are starting to be able to see the glory, now that the veil is getting thin).

My personal belief is that when Adam sinned, what had been three became two. Two thirds numerically is 0.666, which is called the mark of the flesh or the mark of the beast (Revelation 13:17-18).

When you were born in the natural world you had a scroll written that testified to what you were going to be like. This scroll is on your DNA. It is a record made from twenty-three chromosomes from your mother and twenty-three chromosomes from your father. You have a record made from the testimony of their lives, brought together to make you. So you are made in the record of your parents.

"Then the word of the LORD came to me, saying: "Before I formed you in the womb I knew you; Before you were born I sanctified you; I ordained you a prophet to the nations" (Jeremiah 1:4-5).

God is saying to Jeremiah, before you were on the earth you were a spirit being. Before you were on the earth I knew you. I knew everything there was about your life as a spirit being and as a supernatural being. I have plans for you that I formed from the foundation of the earth (Jeremiah 29:11). I have works for you to do Jeremiah. God has a scroll in Heaven with a threefold strand of DNA, a record of what you were before you were on the earth.

"A three-stranded cord is not easily broken" (Ecclesiastes 4:12 CJB).

But a two-fold cord can quite easily be snapped. Now that is interesting! We wonder why people get broken by the demonic world. It is because they are only living out of a two-fold cord.

"We know that whoever is born of God does not sin" (1 John 5:18).

As a believer, are you born of God? Because the Bible says that you have the capacity not to sin on this earth!

The reason we sin is because of the record of the two-stranded DNA back through to Adam. But what happens if my DNA changes when I am born of God as a believer in Christ? I am now a different being and the strand of God is in my life – the capacity inside of me to not sin any longer. That is what the Bible is saying; he that is born of God sins not. But then it says:

"We know that whosoever is born of God sins not; but he that is begotten of God keeps himself, and that wicked one touches him not" (1 John 5:18 KJ2000)

Why? Because corruption cannot access the incorrupt. The word 'begotten' means carrying the record of the DNA. The enemy does not touch the one that is born of the record of the DNA of God. So who is going to win the fight? Why do we get so bashed around by the enemy? It is because we are living out of the wrong DNA, the wrong scroll, the wrong record of our lives and the wrong testimony that keeps us bound as human beings!

I am not just a human being. I am a spirit being that has a soul and lives in a physical body. I am not fully conformed to my spirit being yet, but I am working on it. The Bible says that if I am born of God then I am not going to sin, which means that there is an incorruptible nature now living inside of me.

There are three things that need to happen in our lives:

First, we are born as a human being.

Second, when we get born again we become a spirit being, but there is a step further. There are some places in the Bible where God works in twos: when you need someone to testify with you while you are on the earth (John 8:17), where two agree when asking God for something in prayer (Matthew 18:19) and where Jesus sent them out two by two (Mark 6:7). But God usually works in threes: Father, Son, Holy Spirit (Matthew 28:19), body, soul, spirit (1 Thessalonians 5:23).

Becoming a living being is the third step. When you are a living being you no longer rely on this world, its theories, its laws and its nature. You live out of something totally different. I am chasing that with everything that is inside of me because I live in this physical world but it is not my reality.

We have a governmental authority structure set up over us as human beings. "For there are three that bear witness in heaven: the Father, the Word, and the Holy Spirit; and these three are one" (1 John 5:7).

"That they all may be one, as You, Father, are in Me, and I in You; that they also may be one in Us" (John 17:21).

What an amazing statement. I am one with God!

"But he who is joined to the Lord is one spirit with Him" (1 Corinthians 6:17).

One spirit, not one human being! The devil hates this Word because it releases the glory of the Kingdom and the reality of Heaven to you and me as believers on the earth today.

"And there are three that bear witness on earth: the Spirit, the water, and the blood; and these three agree as one" (1 John 5:8).

So when it is in Heaven, they are one and when it is on earth, they agree in one. Looking at each of these:

Firstly, your spirit knows the record of your DNA that was created before you were in the earth (Ephesians 1:4-5; 2:10, Romans 8:29). Your spirit holds a record of that DNA. When you are born again your spirit becomes alive and quickened by the presence of God. That capacity to enable the DNA strand of God to work in your life is then given again to you, to change you back into heavenly beings; the capacity is there.

The next one that testifies is water. What a weird substance to testify to DNA! Do you know that your body is over fifty percent water? Whatever goes on in your spirit, water is a carrier of it. Every single trace element can be carried in water, so the water of your body carries the record into your body.

You have the capacity as a spirit being to speak to the water of your body. You can release the record of the DNA of God into the water of your body so that your body can become that one which is begotten of God, who does not sin any longer.

The last one is the Blood. Every time something undesirable happens in my family I have been saying, "Heaps of Blood – it is all under the Blood of Jesus" because the Blood bears record to the DNA.

COMMUNION

I am pulling these strands of truth together now and you can then take communion as you read the activation at the end of this chapter.

Communion is about the death of Jesus Christ and why He died on the cross. There have been many people who have been offended by what it really means to have communion, so we have a little celebration around it. We mention His death, but very little is mentioned about His resurrection! There is nothing mentioned about the life of eternity that is after the Blood. It is like the Blood is the end product. No! The Blood is the doorway that leads you to an end product. It leads you somewhere, it does not stop there! But we have taught the Church to stop there in our religious theology. The Blood to me is the beginning, not the end.

"I am the living bread which came down from heaven" (John 6:51).

Jesus had a different DNA do you know why? It is because He had a different Father who was not on the earth. Jesus coming into us enables us to carry the same DNA that He carried. We were born again in the realm of the Kingdom, here on the earth. We carry the same record in us as Jesus did, so there is no excuse for any of us.

"If anyone eats of this bread, he will live forever" (John 6:51).

I am going to live forever, hallelujah! So why should I die in my physical body (Genesis 5:24, 2 Kings 2:11, Hebrews 11:5)?

"And the bread that I shall give is My flesh which I shall give for the life of the world." (Oops! Isn't that a bit occultish?) *The Jews therefore quarrelled among themselves, saying, "How can this Man give us His flesh to eat?" Then Jesus said to them, "Most assuredly, I say to you, unless you eat the flesh of the Son of Man and drink His blood, you have no life in you"* (John 6:51-53).

You have no life in you! Why? Because there is no record of the DNA!

"Whoever eats My flesh and drinks My blood has eternal life" (John 6:54)

He is talking about eternal life there, which is different from living forever. Living forever addresses the body, eternal life addresses the spirit.

"And I will raise him up at the last day. For My flesh is food indeed, and My blood is drink indeed" (John 6:54-55).

With just a nip and a sip once a month, we miss it!

"He who eats My flesh and drinks My blood abides in Me, and I in him" (John 6:56).

Jesus is saying, "When you drink My Blood and eat My Body, I am living in you! So it is more than just being born again – my spirit has come alive and the moment I start to eat, He comes into me.

"As the living Father sent Me, and I live because of the Father, so he who feeds on Me will live because of Me. This is the bread which came down from heaven—not as your fathers ate the manna, and are dead. He who eats this bread will live forever" (John 6:57-58).

This means that if I take the Body and the Blood of Jesus, and Jesus lives by the Father, I live by Jesus and I am going to live by the power of the Father. Jesus is now talking about the record that the Father put in Mary's body, so that the record could be given to you and me. He is talking about His power and who He is on the throne, so that we can become the enthroned ones.

The Blood holds the record of the resonance of who God was in Christ. When overshadowing Mary, He put His own DNA into Mary's body. The Blood holds the record of the DNA that gives your spirit an anchor of the resonance – the sound vibration to bring your body, your spirit and your soul into divine order. That is the Blood! It is not a two-stranded cord. It is amazing – a human being is a three-fold being. A person who is not born again has two parts of their creation operating: their body and their soul. Their spirit is in darkness so they are a two thirds being, or 0.666 of a whole being. So we are busy looking for a man and it is already right in front of us.

As for the Body, Jesus said, "If you eat my Body you will live forever." The Body of Jesus is the record of the power of the resurrection, the life that can flow from that Body. The record of His Body gives your spirit something to release in your body.

You take on the image of the record that you eat when you take communion. When you take the Body of Jesus Christ you eat the record of the resurrection power. It gives your spirit the resonance and the anchor to come into the fullness of the expression of the resurrected Christ. Now, that changes the way you take communion! That is why the metamorphosing process of a human being, like the caterpillar, has to be spun in a cocoon of glory – so that the DNA can be disseminated. A record of a new DNA is then put in place so that you can take on the form of that new DNA. It is all done by taking communion!

When the Bible says you are going to live forever, it is not talking about when you die and your spirit being lives forever. It is talking about the present tense: you living forever. The key is that you need to believe it. All I have done is showed you scripture. I have just told you the reason for taking communion is not only to celebrate Jesus death and resurrection, but to give you something that your spirit man can get hold of, to graft in, to become like. Communion gives your spirit an anchor to form the first nucleus inside of you, a record for the brooding tent of God to overshadow.

Everybody says, "God, come down" and He comes down, but He has already given His record to us. All He wants to do is vibrate over His record in us to call the light that is in the middle of it into fullness. God wants to sit over the top of this record to change us and to make us into something different.

THE TWO TREES IN THE GARDEN

"And on the next day, when they had come from Bethany, he was hungry: And seeing a fig tree afar off having leaves, he came, if perhaps he might find anything thereon: and when he came to it, he found nothing but leaves; for the time of figs was not yet. And Jesus **answered** *and said unto it, No man eat fruit of you hereafter forever. And his disciples heard it... And when evening was come, he went out of the city. And in the morning, as they passed by, they saw the fig tree dried up from the roots. And Peter calling to remembrance said unto him, Teacher, behold, the fig tree which you cursed is withered away."* (Mark 11:12-14; 19-21. KJ2000)

The most amazing thing is that the tree did not speak to Him, and yet Jesus answered the tree! Jesus did not curse the fig tree.

Peter's interpretation of what happened was a curse, but Jesus spoke to it.

Whenever you find something in the Bible, do not just read it as a story. There is a reason Jesus spoke to the fig tree. There is a biblical key called "The Principle of First Mention." When you are looking for keys in the Bible, always go back to its first mention. The first time fig leaves are mentioned is in the Garden when Adam and Eve had sinned:

"Then the eyes of both of them were opened, and they knew that they were naked; and they sewed fig leaves together and made themselves coverings" (Genesis 3:7).

So now we have Jesus, thousands of years later, coming down to Jerusalem and there is a fig tree. The Bible very pointedly says there were leaves on the fig tree but there was no fruit. Jesus did not curse the fig tree. I do not find anywhere in the Bible that says Jesus cursed anything. He spoke to something and commanded it to happen and it did. He had the dominion of God in Him and He was able to do that, the same way as we can! Do you realise you can speak to trees and make them die?!

"Death and life are in the power of the tongue, and they who indulge in it shall eat the fruit of it for death or life" (Proverbs 18:21 AMP)

Jesus is addressing the very core nature of the covering that we, as human beings, have had over our lives. He did this because when Adam sinned, what was in Adam before he sinned changed into something different, which then had to be covered. Jesus spoke to the very root of the problem that is in the DNA of man. It is called the false covering. He is saying to it, "No man will eat fruit from you any longer, that thing will not be your covering any more. No longer will you be able to draw on that DNA, on the power of that thing that has given you life, because I have spoken to the root and it is going to die." That puts a bit of a different light on this scripture does it not?

"So Jesus answered and said to them, 'Have faith in God. For assuredly, I say to you, whoever says to this mountain, 'Be removed and be cast into the sea,' and does not doubt in his heart, but believes that those things he says will be done, he will have whatever he says. Therefore I say to you, whatever things you ask when you pray, believe that you receive them, and you will have them. And

whenever you stand praying, if you have anything against anyone, forgive him, that your Father in heaven may also forgive you your trespasses. But if you do not forgive, neither will your Father in heaven forgive your trespasses'" (Mark 11:22-26).

So, Jesus goes from speaking to a fig tree to suddenly speaking to a mountain. Very often, a mountain in the Bible can represent the government of God. A mountain can also symbolise a resting place of the thrones of God, the house of God or the establishing of a government. So Jesus was teaching that if you would say to this mountain – this government that has ruled over your lives as a human being:

"You will no longer rule over me, but you will be cast and removed into the sea," and when you pray you do not doubt, you will have whatsoever you say. But the key is that you need to desire to be free from it! Jesus said, "...whatever things you ask when you pray, believe that you receive them, and you will have them" (Mark 11:24).

When Jesus said "whoever says to this mountain, 'Be removed and be cast into the sea,' and does not doubt in his heart, but believes that those things he says will be done, he will have whatever he says" (Mark 11:23), He was talking about the mountain of sin that lives over your life.

But when Jesus said, "if you have faith as a mustard seed, you will say to this mountain, 'Move from here to there,' and it will move; and nothing will be impossible for you" (Matthew 17:20), He was not talking about the mountain of sin. He was talking about the mountain of transfiguration. He is saying that when you and I take communion we have the capacity to speak to the resurrection power that Jesus was glorified in and command that mountain to come here. We have the capacity to shift the resurrection power out of Heaven and to bring it here. Jesus has given us that capacity and the record of what to do when we take communion.

Here in the Word you have Jesus talking about the DNA that Adam had to cover himself. When Adam was in the garden, he was not a body with a soul and a spirit in the middle. He was a spirit, with a soul and then a body in the middle of his spirit. We are made in the image of God.

"God is a Spirit (a spiritual Being) and those who worship Him must

worship Him in spirit and in truth (reality)" (John 4:24 AMP).

We are made in the image of God and God is a spirit, therefore we are a spirit. The problem is we have been taught how to be a human being, not how to be a spirit being.

When you take the fullness of the human being, spirit, soul and body as Adam was in the garden, your spirit will be on the outside again, your soul will be in there – in the covering of your spirit and your body will be in the middle. Then you will be able to go into the realm of the spirit and partake in the unseen arena, not be subject to it any longer! They can try to lock you in prison and you will walk through the door! When they try to put something around your hand it will keep falling off because your body does not have any solidity to it that they can touch! These are the things that I dream about and it is all in the Word. Hallelujah Father!

The first human cell that is formed starts reproducing itself into other cells around it and then that original cell implodes and goes into the centre of that little cluster of nuclei. The moment it hits the centre it becomes the human heart and it starts to beat. God is going to reverse that process with us so that our spirit man comes out from the centre of the nuclei of the body and soul, and begins to encase the outside again. That record is found in the Body and Blood of Jesus Christ.

"The Lord God planted a garden eastward in Eden...The tree of life was also in the midst of the garden, and the tree of the knowledge of good and evil" (Genesis 2:8-9).

When we are born as a human being, what is represented in our DNA is the nature of the components of the 'tree of the knowledge of good and evil' (Genesis 2:17). Your DNA has a full record of what your parents' parents' parents' parents did – all the way back to Adam. Your DNA is conditioned to respond, and to make you respond, in a certain way and fashion to an outside stimulant. Thus you will stay in that condition and you will pass that condition onto your children. That is not the plan of God. God's plan was that you would walk in and fulfil His mandate for your life and the works that He ordained for you to do before the foundation of the earth; that is His desire. This plan is not connected to a two-stranded DNA cord, it is connected to the three-stranded DNA cord found in the Body and Blood of Jesus Christ. You need to make a conscious choice to disconnect from the fruit of the tree of the knowledge of good and evil.

It is all about us being trees (Psalms 1:3). You need to let the life out so it can speak to the very volume of your soul and body. Let the life say, "No longer am I going to glean and eat from you tree of the knowledge of good and evil; no longer are you going to be a fruit in my life; I have a different record in my spirit that is going to grow me into something different."

"After driving them out, He stationed winged guardians at the east end of the garden of Eden and set up a sword of flames which alertly turned back and forth to guard the way to the tree of life" (Genesis 3:24 VOICE).

God put cherubim and a flaming sword that turned every which way. It was not one cherub with a sword moving around. The Bible says very clearly it was guardians or cherubim, plural, with a flaming sword. So you have two cherubim, which is dealing with the two-stranded DNA that we exist in. Then you have the middle strand, which is the third strand of God's DNA. This is the light of His glory that sits in believers, who then have the capacity to pass through that sword to eat of the way of the Tree of Life. This is to live eternally – the way of the Tree of Life means to live forever.

The record to enable you and me to live eternally is in there, past the two cherubim and the sword, to the Tree of Life. It is the way into eternity. The way back into the arena of the realm of Heaven is through the Body and the Blood of Jesus. Jesus' Body was transfigured on the mountain (Matthew 17:1-2) to give us a testimony. This means that when I take His Body and brood over it I will have in me the capacity to take on the same image.

"To him who overcomes I will give to eat from the tree of life, which is in the midst of the Paradise of God" (Revelation 2:7).

How are you going to overcome unless you get hold of the reality of living as a different being? Living in the place where the sword cannot touch you, because it is already in you. This is not formed with the knowledge of man through doctrinal understanding; it is formed through experience and revelation of the unfolding wisdom of God from His Word. God wants us to change.

RAPTURE THEORY, ETERNAL LIFE AND LIVING FOREVER

"These things He said in the synagogue as He taught in Capernaum. Therefore many of His disciples, when they heard this, said, 'This is a hard saying; who can understand it?' When Jesus knew in Himself that His disciples complained about this, He said to them, 'Does this offend you? What then if you should see the Son of Man ascend where He was before? It is the Spirit who gives life; the flesh profits nothing. The words that I speak to you are spirit, and they are life. But there are some of you who do not believe.' For Jesus knew from the beginning who they were who did not believe, and who would betray Him. And He said, 'Therefore I have said to you that no one can come to Me unless it has been granted to him by My Father.' From that time many of His disciples went back and walked with Him no more" (John 6:59-66).

It is interesting that His disciples "went back and walked with Him no more" in John 6:66! If you do not have the record of the DNA of God in you, what do you represent? You represent two thirds, which is 0.666. If you represent that record then you will no longer walk with God.

There is so much garbage being said about the mark of the beast. A lot of it is based on what I call the 'sky bus' rapture theory, and is not about the Kingdom. It is a kingdom of fear because it is not about the returning power of the sons of God. You do not find anyone who teaches the rapture theory talking about the resurrection in the life of every believer, or of the glory of the Son of God. I do not find the manifestation of the Kingdom in their lives: the power to raise the dead today and for us to live forever in that glory. I do not hear them talking about the coming glory. When darkness rises, the glory must come in a greater measure (Isaiah 60:1-2). I do not see them talking about the coming glory, all the rapture theory does is create a generation of fearful people – a people who will not sow into the future with their words to make their children believe that there is a hope for them to live for today.

All rapture theory says is, "I am waiting to go somewhere; I am going to be taken out of this mess; it is such a mess and I cannot change it." In fact God's Word says clearly we are going to change it. But in the last forty years there has been a generation of people growing up who are hopeless. The young people today are hopeless because we have not sown hope into their spirits, for them to get hold of, that there is something better waiting for them than what they currently have. It is one of the most demonic things I have ever seen in my life!

I have started sowing into my children, saying: "There is a resurrection coming that you are going to be part of. There is a power that is going to be unleashed out of Heaven and you are going to see it with your own eyes! Even if I am 195 years old, I am going to see it as well! In fact, I am going to live forever, so I am going to be standing right there with you. When you get glorified, I am going to get glorified." I do not want them to get taken away. I want them to overcome. I do not see in the Bible anywhere "those who get taken away get the reward in Heaven".

"To him who overcomes I will give to eat from the tree of life, which is in the midst of the Paradise of God" (Revelation 2:7).

"He who overcomes, I will make him a pillar in the temple of My God" (Revelation 3:12).

To them that overcome! Overcoming does not mean flying away. It means living in the resurrection power of the glory of the Lord today on the face of the earth!

This is a controversial thing to say, but I am fed up with this religious nonsense that has been fed to the Church – it is not the Kingdom. The Kingdom is about giving you a hope to live for, for tomorrow and giving you a hope to die for, for tomorrow. Can you imagine what it is going to be like to be in a body that shines?! That makes me live my life here with a prize worthy to be paid for.

The mark of the beast is a very interesting thing. The Bible says we receive a mark on the outside. Well, I am going to receive a new name and a mark on the inside of my forehead! You can have yours if you want it, all you have to do is ask, go there and get it, because He says:

"I will write on them the name of my God and the name of the city of my God, the new Jerusalem...I will also write on them my new name" (Revelation 3:12 EXB).

Where do we get it? In Heaven!

The mark of the beast will be received by many who in these last days are going to stop following Jesus. They are going to become the ones who try to destroy you because they can see the truth in what you have. But I do not talk about end time issues too much because I would really rather teach people how to live today.

When Jesus talked about us eating His Flesh and drinking His Blood (John 6:54), the reason many people were offended (John 6:66) was because they knew the occult practices of human and animal sacrifice. They knew what it was to eat and drink blood and they knew what happened when people did it. Blood is the highest form of covenant, because you are eating the DNA and everything that is connected to it. That is the key – when there is a blood sacrifice you are not just drinking the blood, you are drinking everything that is connected to it. So when you take communion, you are eating, drinking and taking in everything that is connected to it! The Blood carries the record of the DNA.

"The life of the flesh is in the blood" (Leviticus 17:11).

There is life in the record of the DNA, but it is the body that produces the record; one is the carrier of life, the other one produces the record of it.

THE HEAVENS BELONG TO THE HIGHEST BIDDER

We have a brother in Africa who is a tall black guy and I have never seen anyone who is as much of a soldier in all my life. He has planted three churches in the occult capital of the world! In this country they lose many people in a three month period in human sacrifice when all the witches, warlocks and new age people go there. The rivers run red with blood. He has planted three churches in the middle of his country and got right in the face of the enemy. I have never seen anybody with grunt like that in my life! He has been attacked by werewolves and vampires. He has even got marks on his arms where vampires have come for him, missed and hit his arms! God has really been doing some work over there.

One of the things this brother would say in some of his conferences is that the heavens belong to the highest bidder. An example of that in scripture is when the king came and asked if he was going to win the war:

"While the harp [lyre] was being played, the LORD gave Elisha power [hand of the LORD came upon him]. Then Elisha said, "The LORD

says…he will also hand Moab over to you. You will destroy every strong, walled [fortified] city… When the Moabites came to the camp of Israel, the Israelites came out and fought them until they ran away. Then the Israelites went on into [invaded] the land, killing [slaughtering] the Moabites… When the king of Moab saw that the battle was too much for him… the king of Moab took his oldest son, who would have been king after him, and offered [sacrificed] him as a burnt offering on the wall. So there was great anger against the Israelites, who [or Alarmed at this, the Israelites] left and went back to their own land" (2 Kings 3:15-16; 18-19; 24; 26-27 EXB).

Did they have a right word from God? Yes they did, but the problem was, instead of laying out a sacrifice and giving an offering to the Lord, they went to war. So, because the demonic world knows about sacrifices, when the king of Moab offered his sacrifice, which was higher than just a 'thank You' from the Children of Israel, there was no sacrifice given to God to work with. So the war went against them.

This is what has been happening in the Church. The Church has been taking communion once a month. The result is not much trading in the heavens. Not much trading for the arena of the Kingdom and trading into the Kingdom to release the realm of heaven on the face of the earth. There have been times when I have been on the Sea of Glass (Revelation 4:6; 15:2), when I have been the only one standing there for days and days. It is a distressing thing when you can see how much potential could be unleashed – particularly with regard to the Body and Blood of Christ and what it means for us to trade with them in the heavens.

"Buy pure gold from me, gold purified by fire—only then will you truly be rich...purchase from me white garments, clean and pure, so you won't be naked and ashamed; and... medicine from me to heal your eyes and give you back your sight" (Revelation 3:18 TLB).

How do you buy gold from God? With the Blood of Jesus; that is what you do – you go onto the Sea of Glass, you take communion and you offer yourself and the Blood He has given you, as a supreme sacrifice to receive out of Heaven the fullness of the Kingdom. You buy it on the Sea of Glass – you trade. The chief trader is Melchizedek, he is the guy who looks after all the treasury rooms and receives all the treasure.

I remember one of the first times I ended up on the trading floor of Heaven – I did not really know what it was all about. I can remember sitting on the Sea of Glass and I sank into it.
The Lord asked me, "What can I trade with?" I said, "Well, I do not know, whatever You need You can trade with." He said, "No, no, no – what is in you that I can trade with?"

I thought, "What is in me? Flip, what do I say is in me?! What do I have in me to trade with? If God wants to purchase something with my life, what is there that I have to give? My will… my time… my desire… my money?" I said, "Lord, these are all the things I am trading with."

When I sank into the trading floor, all that was left were two or three gem stones – out of all of my life! When I came back out of the trading floor, the Lord just looked at me. I said, "Lord, I just do not know what to do?"

He said, "Why did you spend time in Heaven picking things up? You go into the River of Glory and you put diamonds and gold out of Heaven in your belly – what are you doing with that? Don't you think I gave it to you to trade with it?"

I remembered that when I went into the spirit, back into my mountain, I had filled my belly with the things I had taken out of the river, the scrolls and the things I had taken out of the dragons' bellies. So I took the whole lot onto the trading floor.

I can remember the Lord smiled and said, "Yes, it is about time you remembered all the things you overcame to get the treasure." It is the very things in our lives that we have overcome that are the precious things to God – but the highest form of trading is blood. The demonic world knows that and this is why there is so much human sacrifice.

In the USA people go missing all the time to human sacrifice, they just go missing. In my nation (New Zealand) a baby went missing and they found her dead. It is sacrificial activity that is going on because the demons know that they need blood for power. Jesus has given us the ultimate power in His Blood. Blood is power.

"For the life of the flesh is in the blood, and I have given it to you upon the altar to make atonement for your souls; for it is the blood that makes atonement for the soul" (Leviticus 17:11).

If there is power in life, then blood is power. Jesus has given us His Blood to take into the realm of the heavens and trade with, to receive out of the realm of the Kingdom.

THE RECORD OF THE DNA OF GOD IN COMMUNION

It is very important to understand that when God came down and brooded over Mary, He put His own DNA into Mary's womb. God took a record of His own DNA, and out of His and her DNA, He formed a child inside her womb. This is significant – in that DNA there is a record and a copy of God. Jesus went through His life and then got hung on the Cross. Before He was hung on the Cross He met with His disciples and started to talk about His Body and His Blood. We know scientifically now what He was talking about. However, most people throughout history have not known the truth – that the Father had begotten a copy of His DNA. Now, when we take the DNA in communion, that record goes into us! Then our spirit and body will have a record to be able to brood over, so that this record can begin to be reproduced in our own bodies. So it means that what I have is the capacity to become a God-like being.

Jesus is saying that you take communion and you eat His Body as a symbol – there is no such thing as transubstantiation, where communion becomes the Body and Blood of Christ and you chew part of His Body and drink His Blood in the natural. That is not what it is about. Communion is a symbol to recognise the power of the resurrection that is behind it.

When Jesus says in John 6:56 (VOICE) *"I will abide in you"*, He is not talking about the physical state that He was born in and the natural body He is living in. He is talking about the resurrected state, as He says *"and I will raise him up at the last day"*. (John 6:54). The last day is after His death. Jesus was talking about the resurrected body that He is in now. When you take this symbol of the bread here on earth, you receive the resurrection power from Him in Heaven. You take it by faith so that it can come inside of you. There is a record by faith that is released because you receive Him by faith.

"The Jews therefore quarrelled among themselves, saying, "How can this Man give us His flesh to eat?" (John 6:52).

You need to understand that the Jews knew all about human sacrifices because they had experience with a god called Baal. They used to sacrifice their children to the god Baal. Their first born would be sacrificed to Baal to give them power, protection and provision. Now Jesus is saying, "Here is my Body; I am going to be sacrificed for you; and not only am I going to be sacrificed for you, but you are going to have to eat My Body". Can you see why they got offended? They did not want anything to do with the occult world, but they were not hearing what Jesus was saying.

So here we have the record and the ability to produce the realm of the Kingdom of Heaven in you and make you a differently-stranded DNA creature by communion. So communion immediately takes on a whole different meaning for me now because when I take communion I am celebrating by drinking the Blood of Jesus Christ by faith. It is the record of His DNA. Jesus wants you to get hold of that record in your life.

For you to take on a bug, you need to ingest it, so that it goes inside your body, gets into your blood stream and starts to reproduce itself. So we have a virus called 'The DNA of God' living in the Blood that we drink at communion. It is a virus called, 'Becoming a son or daughter of the Kingdom – becoming a spirit being again'. Becoming what God originally designed me to be is like a virus in the Blood! I am freely drinking that virus, knowing that it is going to come and impact my life, because I am taking it in faith.

"But without faith it is impossible to please Him" (Hebrews 11:6).

So I take communion now with full understanding. That is why the Bible says:

"Let a man [thoroughly] examine himself, and [only when he has done] so should he eat of the bread and drink of the cup. For anyone who eats and drinks without discriminating and recognising with due appreciation that [it is Christ's] body, eats and drinks a sentence (a verdict of judgment) upon himself" (1 Corinthians 11:28-30 AMP).

The reason they do not judge correctly is because they do not realise what they are eating, not realising that it is a beginning of a whole new experience in life! Communion is what sanctifies you – it is what sets you apart. It is what makes you something different from what you are today. Communion is that strand that enables you not to sin any longer – the Body of Christ and carrying its record.

When I eat that little bit of bread, by faith I hold it in the realm of the spirit, saying, "See this – as I take this, that record is beginning to get imprinted into my system and that is what is going to change me. No works, no things I can do for God to give me brownie points! But a little piece of bread is going to enable me to overcome." One little piece of bread and that is all it takes. Just take communion once to begin the changing process. That is why Jesus said:

"*'Take, eat; this is My body which is broken for you; do this in remembrance of Me.' In the same manner He also took the cup after supper, saying, 'This cup is the new covenant in My blood. This do, as often as you drink it, in remembrance of Me'*" (1 Corinthians 11:24-25).

The word 'remembrance' comes from the Greek word 'record'; do this in the record of what I am and what I have done. Take communion in that record.

For some time now I have been taking communion every day, at least once a day, mostly two or three times a day. I go to work and I cannot wait until morning tea, praying in tongues with the bread in my mouth. Once I ate a whole loaf of bread! Why? Because I wanted to – it tasted good! I want more of this record in my life, hallelujah! I am trading on the resurrection power and the DNA on the Sea of Glass because I want to be like Him and I want to live forever. If the heavens belong to the highest bidder, I want to do it until it becomes a reality in my life, to out-bid every other thing that is crying out!

When you take communion, if it has previously been 'a nip and a sip' for you, then I hope this is going to change your theology from this time forward. I want you to take it with full knowledge of what you are doing as a spirit being – you do not do this just as a human being: you do it by faith as a spirit being. God has called you to be a spirit being. I am made in the image of God, so I am called to be a spirit being.

God has given us a mandate on His DNA. His DNA says, "You have the capacity inside of you to never sin again!" Communion is the capacity to do just that, but it depends on how much you work on it and how much you yield to it. It is called a cross and without the cross and the Blood there is no life in the spirit. The cross is not the end. The cross is the doorway to the start of spirituality. You need to have the reality of the cross in your life. You need to experience what it means to hang your life on the cross by getting offended. There is no greater way to deal with issues in your life than to get offended by someone and nail it to the cross until the offence says, "I give up!"

The potential that is in the Body and the Blood of Jesus Christ is put in communion so that it can reproduce itself inside of you when you understand it by faith. The idea is to give you a record so the record can reproduce itself inside of you. So, as you brood over what you take, that resonance brings divine order to your spirit. Then your spirit brings divine order to your soul and your soul brings divine order to your body until your spirit man comes to the outside again – like Adam was in that day. It is all found in taking communion.

Eternal life here (John 6:51-58) does not just mean that when I die I am going to live for eternity, it means that I have the capacity to live for eternity while I am alive. The Body and Blood of Jesus Christ give me the capacity to live in the full reality of the future today. I do not have to wait to die!

So when I take communion, not only am I taking eternal life and not only do I have the capacity to live forever, but it actually gives me the capacity to be in Him and Him in me.

Usually when scripture refers to something three times, it is important – Jesus is saying, take note of this. Jesus tells us three times in one chapter (John 6:51, 54 and 58), if you eat His Body and drink His Blood, you are going to live forever!

"These things He said in the synagogue as He taught in Capernaum. Therefore many of His disciples, when they heard this, said, "This is a hard saying; who can understand it?" When Jesus knew in Himself that His disciples complained about this, He said to them, "Does this offend you?" (John 6:59-61). Well, of course it did because Jesus was saying He was going to be their sacrifice! They really believed in a religious system of self-rescue. I think most of the Church does today. Jesus also says,

"Does this offend you? Then what will you think if you see me, the Messiah, return to heaven again?" (John 6:61-62 TLB).

This was a slap to the Jewish religious system because they did not want to acknowledge Him. So what is Jesus talking about there? Well, if I am in Jesus and I am eating His Body and drinking His Blood, where do you think I am going to go? Whatever happened to Jesus is going to happen to me. So that means that I too am going to ascend to the Father, which means I will never have to die!

Divine order from chaos – that is what the Blood does. The Blood of Jesus brings divine order into the chaos of your DNA, your DNA that is a double helix shape instead of being the perfect strand of the presence of God. God wants to give us perfection. The Bible says I am perfected in Christ (Hebrews 10:14). The way we come into perfection is by taking the Body and the Blood of Jesus; then I live out of perfection and then I become perfection. It is really joyful! It is something to celebrate and say, Thank You Jesus, hallelujah!

So we are going to take communion together, but I do not want you to take it in your normal way of celebrating His death. I want you to take it with the understanding that today you are taking the record of the reason He died; so that you can live forever. You are taking the record of the Blood that has the three-stranded cord DNA in it. Even if it is only grape juice, when something is activated by faith it releases the potential possibility for that reality to become your own.

ACTIVATION

Please get some bread and wine/juice for yourself.

"Whoever eats My flesh and drinks My blood has eternal life, and I will raise him up at the last day...He who eats My flesh and drinks My blood abides in Me, and I in him. As the living Father sent Me, and I live because of the Father, so he who feeds on Me will live because of Me" (John 6:54, 56-57).

Angels know about communion, and when we start to take it and believe what Jesus has done, they rejoice because they are waiting for us to take our place. They come into meetings where this kind of activity happens because they rejoice that a son is finally starting to do something that has been provided for them.

"Father, today we lift the cup. Lord Jesus, Your Word says that this is Your Blood. You shed Your Blood and You gave it. Today I ask that this would change to Your Blood by faith because Your Blood carries all the potential of all that there is in the Godhead. Even as the Godhead are One in their strands singularly and testify that they are One, all that record is in the Blood. Lord, when I drink this Blood, my body and my soul and spirit have the capacity to reproduce this Blood with the DNA that it carries, to make me into something different. Father, Your Word says, "Until Christ is formed in you" (Galatians 4:19).

Lord, today as a corporate body of people, we come into agreement and testify that this cup is Your Blood; that we are in You and when we drink this we become one with Your presence. With full knowledge of the DNA and the full desire to become one with Your presence Lord, we drink today in the Name of Jesus. Father, release Your glory on the cup today, hallelujah! Father, thank You for the power of the Blood. Thank You for the record of the dominion and the rulership in that Blood – for the DNA of the record that is in that Blood to change us, and make each of us into something different. Lord, that it would sanctify us and make us holy in Your presence.

Father, today we take this little piece of bread. According to Your Word and Jesus' decree, this is Your Body, the carrier of that record that testifies to the capacity for us to be conformed into Your image. Father, today by faith we take hold of this bread and say this is the Body of Jesus Christ – the remembrance of the resurrection power and glory and of what He did to make a way for us to become spirit beings again. It has the record to enable us and quicken us to become what we have been called to be on the earth. Father, we eat it today by faith with full knowledge that it makes us one with You, one with Your desire, one with Your will, one with Your scroll, one with the testimony of what You have written. It is all in Your Body and we eat it today in the Name of Jesus."

I want to think about one more thing that is connected with communion, and that is which scroll you are feeding from? I wrote earlier about your having two scrolls, two records: one made by your mum and dad as a human being, the other scroll made by God as a spirit being. What I want you to do inside your mind and your heart is to repent of connecting and drawing from the scroll of the knowledge of your being, as a human being. I want you to begin to repent of drawing on that knowledge to fulfil your life. To repent of drawing on the wisdom and the foundation of that human record, enabling it and giving it a power to operate in your life. I want you just to begin to do that today.

Father, today we begin to draw to the place of repentance before Your presence. Father, we confess our sin of drawing on the old record of the old nature of the human being that we have in our bodies, of enabling that record and giving it power to function in our lives. Father, today we come boldly before You and we repent and ask You to forgive us for never realising that there is a higher calling, that there is a different scroll written for us to have.

Father, today we disconnect the umbilical cord of the supply of that scroll in our lives. Father, we disconnect in the Name of Jesus. We disconnect that umbilical cord, we break its power, we break its power – we break its power today! Father, we take that source of supply and connect it to the record of the scroll that You have for our lives. We connect it into what we should have been at the beginning, Father, we connect to it today in Jesus' Name."

Chapter 14
Crowns

We are living in the days that are shortening. We must get to grips with who we are as the sons and heirs of the Kingdom of Heaven. We must get to grips with the fact that we are able to go into Heaven and we are able to experience Heaven today.

Whatever you look like in the spirit is how the demonic spirit world sees you. Whatever you carry of the Kingdom is what you represent when you are in the spirit realm. Some of the vital things we need to carry as believers are the crowns that God has given us. Crowns are very important because a crown speaks of a realm of authority. Whenever a king would wear his crown he would have that dominion over his realm. He usually only wore his crown when he was out amongst the people or when he was sitting on his throne. The reason he wore that crown is because it represented the land he had authority over.

As believers we have crowns and the Bible is very clear about these crowns. I want to teach about this because, for many of us, some of our crowns are in the trophy room of the devil and we are going to get them back!

Crowns are important to us as believers, particularly when we come before the throne. Revelation tells us that:

"the twenty-four elders bow down before the One who sits on the throne, and they worship him who lives forever and ever. They put their crowns down [cast/

lay their crowns] before the throne" (Revelation 4:10 EXB).

I do not want to turn up in Heaven and have no crown to throw before Him as an offering. The crown is the very thing He has given you to wear to display Him, so when you lose a crown it is important to go back and pick up your crown.

So what is the objective of carrying a crown? It is the provision of the relevant anointing or mandate that the crown represents. A crown mandates us to do a job and enables us to have rulership over the circumstances that are arrayed against us. These crowns are a means of identifying who you are in the spirit. This identification releases the government of God around your life and the power of God around you into the atmosphere. It is a recognition – the spirit world knows what you look like.

In Jerusalem when the seven sons of Sceva tried to cast demons out of a man, seven guys with one man, they said:

"We exorcise you by the Jesus whom Paul preaches." And the evil spirit answered and said, "Jesus I know, and Paul I know; but who are you?" Then the man in whom the evil spirit was leaped on them, overpowered them, and prevailed against them, so that they fled out of that house naked and wounded" (Acts 19:13, 15-16).

That is about where the Church is at when confronting the enemy: "Jesus I know, Paul I know but who are you?! You do not go into the glory, who are you?" Most of the church is running away from demons naked.

Being able to see in the spirit is really neat because you can see what people are carrying on their lives. Many of us only have two or three crowns. Oh Jesus, I want more of the realm of Heaven than I have today!

A crown is symbolic of the representative of a realm of government. Without a crown there is no symbol of that recognition. You can be going down the street and see a police car with a flashing light at the side of the road. Usually most of us gasp to ourselves quietly and take our foot off the accelerator! It is because of who they are and what they carry that we do this. If you feel guilty about something, or you have done something wrong, when you go past a policeman you will feel it. They do not even have to look at you, they may not even know that you are there, but what they carry on their body and on their car perpetrates something in the spirit world.

You and I are no different in the realm of the spirit, we carry the government of Heaven and whenever we arrive, the devil gasps! But the devil has made the church think that we are the kitten and he is the lion. Then God tells us to "roar!" But we go "meow!" The devil has made us think that he is the lion, but the Bible says the lion is the Lion of the tribe of Judah, who is Jesus. I belong to that pride of the Lion of the tribe of Judah, so that means I am a lion too! The devil has made us believe that we are the animals in the field and he is the lion who goes around hunting us. He hunts those who are lonely, isolated, weak or injured because they are easy prey. That is why we need to have fellowship one with another. That is why we need to be knitted into a body of people and that is why we need to exercise the realm of dominion so that we stay strong and healthy.

I was born in Africa in the middle of the jungle of Swaziland. When a lion comes into view all the other animals are happy if they can see it. The moment a lion disappears somebody is in trouble! The animals will always keep an eye on the lion and the moment the lion disappears the other animals get jittery because something is going to happen. When a lion is hunting it does not put its mouth into the air to roar, (it does that in the night watch and in the cool of the day.) When it is hunting and on the prowl for meat, it puts its mouth to the ground and it roars into the ground. Then the ground erupts all around the animals so they do not know where the point of attack is coming from.

When we roar, we put our face against the realm of the spirit. We roar into the ground of the realm of the spirit and the enemy does not know where the attack is coming from. That is why God can send an ambush against him – a surprise attack, because the enemy gets so confused! First that which is in the natural, then that which is spiritual (1 Corinthians 15:46). When a lion roars like that the animals suddenly scatter and this is also what happens in the spirit. But we have believed that the devil is the lion so when he roars the church scatters! This should not be so, but we have learned this because it has been our experience and we do not know enough about the realm of the Kingdom. We have never been there and seen how the Kingdom really works, so God is trying to unlock some of these things for us now. Crowns are very symbolic, particularly of the pride that you belong to. They represent who you are and the spirit world sees them. When you are in the spirit world you have them on your head. The devils know how much authority you have by which crowns you are wearing. It is very clear.

Unless you hold what God has given you through prayer, worship and encounters with God, the crowns will be removed from your life by the hand of man through circumstances in the natural as well as in the spirit.

A crown can be removed by the hand of man, so who do you think is going to knock our crowns off our heads? Man. Why do you think Jesus used some very strong words against the Pharisees and the religious leaders of His day? What was He doing? He was addressing the crowns that they were wearing. He spoke to them very clearly:

"Woe to you, scribes and Pharisees, hypocrites!...Whitewashed tombs... full of dead men's bones and all uncleanness...brood of vipers!" (Matthew 23:27, 33).

Jesus spoke about the crown of death that they carried – religious pride. I hate it! There are times when I find I am being religious too. It is okay, you just need to repent and pick your crown up again because it has been lost.

If the devil can orchestrate circumstances around your life where the hand of man can remove your crown, then he will. You need to hold onto your crown:

"hold fast what you have, so that no one may rob you and deprive you of your crown" (Revelation 3:11 AMP).

It is the carnal and natural man in the lives of others that will try and remove that crown through natural circumstances around you, to shut down your spirit life. It could come through accusation, through guilt, through shame, through the sin of another against your life, through trespass or our own sin or iniquity that we carry – anything that can give the devil a handle for somebody to come beside you and knock one of your crowns off. When the crown falls off your head, the devil picks it up and takes it down into the trophy room and shows all the other devils his victory. I do not know about you, but that makes me really angry!

There are two places that crowns can be removed. One is by sin and the other by the hand of man. Both result in a loss of rulership. With the loss of the crown comes a loss of that relevant flow of the anointing of the life of the Kingdom. Sin is your own choices, your own desires, your own issues and the things that you have not responded to in God. The hand of man is the choices of others and the behaviour of others against you, often against your will and against your choices. Both are subject to circumstances and often the right responses are the remedies that will prevent your crown being stolen. When somebody rejects you, you can lose a crown if you choose to receive the rejection. If somebody speaks destructive words to you, you can lose a crown if you choose to receive their words. You will receive their words or their rejection if your soul is broken. If your soul is broken then you will not want to wear the crown anyway, so you are going to hide it from the spirit world.

So, how do I recognise where I have lost a crown or that it has been removed from my life? It is quite simple really. I cannot do something I used to do. I used to spend hours praying in tongues, focused on the realm of the Kingdom. It is great to be like that for a season. One day it was like a switch was turned off and it was so hard just to pray for 20 minutes a day in the spirit. I wondered what was going on! Then the Lord told me that I knew about this crowns teaching and was not doing the very thing I had taught others to do. So I had to go back.

You deal with a crown being knocked off your life by going back to the last place you experienced that element of the Kingdom, or the last time that experience was happening to you – when it stopped. Where abuse or that kind of experience has happened, often many of these crowns are knocked off your head at the same time. Then something will happen and you will feel like you do not want to go on living any more. The reason that happens is because the crowns have been removed from your life and there is no more covering and displaying of that manifestation, because it is the manifestation that keeps you going.

When we are working with these crowns like this it is very important to see that they can be removed from our lives. This can happen by man through natural circumstances or by the spirit world through supernatural circumstances. Some of us were in Asia in a room once, busy praying and talking, when I became aware that there was something spiritual outside and around the room that should not have been there. When the occult world wants to shut something down the enemy will send assignments. God has given us dominion over these assignments. It is the Crown of Righteousness that gives us dominion because corruption cannot touch righteousness.

So, I was sitting inside the room with righteous anger growing and by this stage I was considering whether I would confront this thing or not. As my resolve strengthened I said, "Father in the Name of Jesus I bind this spirit that has been on assignment." Then in the house, further down the passage from us, came this howling sound! You can make two choices in response to that, you can either shrink in fear or you can rise in your spirit. In about twenty seconds I had raised my spirit man, taking authority over the evil spirit in Jesus Name. It was as though somebody had flicked a switch and turned the howling noise off.

So let's look at some of these crowns.

THE CROWN OF RIGHTEOUSNESS

"Finally, there is laid up for me the crown of righteousness, which the Lord, the righteous Judge, will give to me on that Day, and not to me only but also to all who have loved His appearing" (2 Timothy 4:8).

This crown is received at salvation and is the base of all other layers because without righteousness nothing can sit firmly on your life. Righteousness basically means 'As though I had never sinned'. The cross and salvation in our lives releases righteousness, *"... the blessedness of the man to whom God imputes righteousness"* (Romans 4:6).

God is looking for a release of the glory, but to have righteousness you need to carry a Crown of Righteousness. Righteousness can be destroyed by a willful choice to sin. Many of us struggle with the arena of sin in our lives and so often we do not have a Crown of Righteousness on our lives because of the sin nature we are struggling with. That is why we need to go into the courtroom, because that is where God puts a new garment on us and a new crown (or mitre) on our head (Zechariah 3:5). The moment you go back into the courtroom you get your Crown of Righteousness back again. This is woven into the Word but, unless you see it, there is no reality of revelation for it. If you do not have the Crown of Righteousness on your life at all, it means that you have committed apostasy and turned your back on God.

THE CROWN OF LIFE

"Blessed is the man who endures temptation; for when he has been approved, he will receive the Crown of Life which the Lord has promised to those who love Him" (James 1:12).

This is the crown that is received through the trials of life and our dealings with temptations, coming to a place of expressive abandonment and love of Jesus Christ as we experience victory over our sin. When we experience victory over the struggles in life, we begin to rejoice a little bit. Too many of us are walking around like sour persimmons, going to the unsaved to say, "Come along to church with me, come and let's suck some lemons every Sunday!" If there is no joy, there is no strength because the joy of the Lord is your strength (Nehemiah 8:10). That is why there is so little power in the church, because there is not much joy.

Drawing on the government of the Crown of Life releases inside of me the life of God. This then releases the life of God into the realm of the spirit through me, coming from my spirit, through my soul and into my body. My body will come alive because it is full of life. That is how I can teach for twelve or fourteen hours in a day – because of the Crown of Life.

You must exercise the crowns. Just wearing a crown is great, but when you exercise it, the crown becomes a weapon of war in your hand and establishes a realm of government around you.

THE CROWN OF GLORY

"When the Chief Shepherd appears, you will receive the Crown of Glory that does not fade away" (1 Peter 5:4).

When the Christ in you begins to manifest around you, and you manifest God in the world around you as a king, then the Crown of Glory is manifested and revealed to the spirit world. Every time we manifest God to the world around us this crown is displayed for the world to see. I love the Crown of Glory because throughout my whole life I want to be around the glory. The crown you wear displays the manifestation of the relationship you have with the God of glory. If you do not have a relationship with God do not expect it to be displayed. I want the realm of glory to be manifest!

Once when I had a meeting in Asia, I said to the other people that there is a whirlwind of fire that is going to come, and when it touches down the glory is going to come. I thought it would manifest in one of our meetings, but it did not happen.

Later we were in another meeting where a particular brother happened to get up and preach and it came down with spiritual impact and it was glorious! That is a displaying of the Crown of Glory as a manifestation of the supernatural world of God on the earth. Unless you carry the Crown of Glory you will not manifest the supernatural world of God. We must carry these crowns in our lives.

THE INCORRUPTIBLE CROWN

"And every man that strives for self control is temperate in all things. Now they do it to obtain a corruptible crown; but we an incorruptible" (1 Corinthians 9:25 KJ2000).

This crown is represented by our personal yieldedness to the life of God, doing His will and the personal pursuit of His presence, because unless you go into His presence you will still remain corruptible.

You go into His presence to get clean. It is only areas that are unclean that can become corrupt. When something is clean and pure then it cannot be corrupted. When something is unrighteous it can be corrupted. When it is holy and righteous it cannot be corrupted. That is why you go into His presence to become righteous. You do not stand here in the natural and try to earn brownie points to make yourself feel righteous; you go into His presence and become righteous, because righteousness is given to you. Then you manifest it here and you deal with your mess.

The only thing the Bible talks about as incorruptible is God, all that He is and all that He has. The more we spend time there in that atmosphere of incorruption, the more we are going to put on incorruption. We struggle with sin because our body is in corruption because of the corruption in the nature that Adam gave us. We were endowed with it when he sinned with Satan. When crowns are removed from our lives, when we willfully choose to sin and do not come into the presence of God, often we do not have the Crown of Life. We know there is supposed to be a flow of life, but how do we receive it? We only receive it by wearing the Crown of Life. There is a life flow of the Kingdom that is in that crown. It will flow out of your life when you are in the spirit. Wherever it goes it will bring life.

THE CROWN OF THE ANOINTING OIL

"Neither shall he go out of the sanctuary, nor profane the sanctuary of his God; for the crown of the anointing oil of his God is upon him: I am the LORD" (Leviticus 21:12 KJ2000).

This crown is given in the places that we encounter the presence of God in a deeply relational way and it is maintained by our daily connection with God. Every time you express this relationship and you bring the Kingdom, the crown is magnified in your life. The demons hate the Crown of the Anointing Oil because it speaks of their burning! They cannot stand it because when we show up with that anointing they wonder, "Who is going to get burned today? Who is going to have their little beady brain stuck into the Cross with a nail between the eyes?" Hallelujah!

How many of us want the anointing? I know I do. Not only do I want that anointing for what is around me but also for my own life. I want to be anointed by God. When you are anointed by God there is a crown with that anointing and the spirit world respects that crown when you are under that anointing. That crown is visible to the spirit world. It sees that Crown of the Anointing Oil on your life and the spirit world knows that when you pray things are going to happen because you are wearing that crown.

Many believers wear the Crown of the Anointing Oil because they hunger for the anointing. Remember, there is more than just the anointing. There is a whole stack of other crowns you need to go after in your life, to pursue and keep on your life.

THE CROWN OF REJOICING

"For what is our hope, or joy, or crown of rejoicing? Is it not even you in the presence of our Lord Jesus Christ at His coming?" (1 Thessalonians 2:19).

"Rejoicing" means to have an overflow of joy with the ability to express it. The implication behind it includes shouts and expressions of joy. When you are in the spirit and that crown is on your head, you will have unsaved people come to you and say, "Man, what are you on?" They feel the tangible reality in the natural world of the rejoicing.

I was a manager in a health and fitness complex in New Zealand. My manager and the management team I worked for knew I was born again and that I did these types of conferences and teachings. They were always saying how wired I was all the time and asking me how I did what I did! I did things in 7 hours that it would take somebody else thirty-five hours to do. Hallelujah!

This crown is carried by the fruit of your life. If you do not rejoice, do not expect to carry this crown. The demonic world looks at you and wonders how much joy you have. They look for the crown. If you have not got this crown, it means you are busy sucking sour persimmons, which means you are becoming religious! If you do not have any joy, you have a problem – you have a major religious, demonised problem! You need to have joy. The joy of the Lord is your strength (Nehemiah 8:10). He gives you joy for mourning, He turns your ashes into joy (Isaiah 61:3). You need to have joy!

There are times when I do not feel joy, I stand in front of my mirror saying, "Joy come forth, ha ha ha!" Sometimes you just have to do something stupid. If I find I am not rejoicing I go and get a really funny, crazy movie out and I watch it until I laugh! Once I start laughing, I turn it off and carry on laughing, just because it feels good to laugh! You need to get some joy in your bones! The Crown of Rejoicing is carried by the fruit of your life, represented by your daily encounter and connection with God.

THE SERVANT KING CROWN

The last crown that Jesus is going to place upon our heads is the Servant King Crown, the interlocking crown, the fair mitre that is set upon our head when we go into Heaven.

God wants us to learn how to be kings. Unless you are carrying your crowns you will never become a king. A king wears crowns. The enemy sees what crowns you carry. He knows the measure of your government by the crowns that you carry in the spirit. He hates the crowns of the governmental arena of the Kingdom. He hates them and wants them off your life. The devil does not like you carrying them. Not only can you carry them and devils can see them but you can trade with them in Heaven. That is why the Bible says the elders cast their crowns down before the Lord, trading before God on the Sea of Glass for government:

"The twenty-four elders fall down before Him who sits on the throne and worship Him who lives forever and ever, and cast their crowns before the throne, saying: 'You are worthy, O Lord, To receive glory and honour and power; For You created all things, And by Your will they exist and were created.'" (Revelation 4:10-11).

A crown is a symbol of a representative of a realm of government. A king does not exist outside of his crown. If you were to sit on your throne without your crown on, you would not have any government. That is why when a king sits on his throne, he has a crown on his head and a sceptre in his hand. This is because a crown is representing the principality or dominion that you rule over with all that government brings. The sceptre is the power to bring judgment from that arena of government. God never judges to death. God only judges towards righteousness; but where there is a remaining in the chaos of unrighteousness the result is death. He judges to truth, to life and to righteousness and out of that He brings justice. Justice is not judging bad things and trying to make bad things right. Justice is judging and bringing life, where there has been bad and good things, because they are all suffering underneath the crown of death.

Without a crown there is no symbol of the recognition of the government of the realm of the spirit that you and I are supposed to walk in. When you come along in the realm of the spirit, the first things the demons will look for are your crowns. Do you have any crowns on? Because if you do not you are in a bit of a mess.

Are you covered with garments? (Exodus 28:3, Revelation 3:5). If not, you are in a mess.

Do you have a sceptre? (Genesis 49:10, Psalms 110:2, Hebrews 1:8).

Do you have the ring with the power of eternity around your life? (Haggai 2:23, Luke 15:22).

Do you have the governmental stones inside your life?

Are they embedded in the breast plate you carry in your spirit man? (Exodus 28:15-21, Ephesians 6:14).

Are you a living stone? (1 Peter 2:5).

Is your new name on the living stone? (Revelation 2:17).

Are you a pillar? (Revelation 3:12).

Is the new name of Jerusalem written on your life yet?

If not, why not?

If you are not carrying your mantle then your back is exposed (1 Samuel 28:14, 1 Kings 19:13).

Are you armoured? (Ephesians 6:13-18). The spirit world looks at what you carry.

Do you have the seven colours of the Seven Spirits of God manifesting through your life – so you look white to them? If you do not, you have a problem, because you are still a little baby, which means they can toy with you like a mouse.

The wrestling that goes on between the two kingdoms is all about positional power and authority, about government and dominion. It is God who puts you in His Kingdom and it is the flesh that wants you in the other kingdom. Unless you hold onto what God has given to you, you may lose it.

Almost everyone has crowns missing from their life, some people more than others because they have allowed the hand of man and circumstances to remove them from their life. We must all go back in our lives and pick our crowns up so each of us can understand the arena that God wants us to walk in. This enables you to become a king, to rule again and have something to trade with when you come before the presence of God.

It is a waste of time coming before the Throne of God unless you have a crown on your head. That is why so many of us cannot get there – because we do not have the crowns we need to go before the Throne of God. You can go into His presence, but to go into His throne is a totally different thing. The Throne of God is all about government. If you do not go in there with government on your life then you are in trouble! If there is no government, that means there is judgment, because you are not holding rank.

BAD CROWNS

There are some bad crowns. The first one is found in 1 Corinthians 9:25. It is called the 'Corruptible Crown'. This is known as the crown of your own efforts. Another one is found in Isaiah 28:1, the 'Crown of Pride'. Another one is found in John 19:2 which is the 'Crown of Thorns' which Jesus wore to carry every single corruptible, broken piece of crown. That is why Jesus had a crown of thorns put on His head – to give us the power to pick up our crowns again.

You need to see this is why Jesus died. That is why He had the thorns put on his head willingly. He had that crown stuck on his head and they mocked him, King of Kings and Lord of Lords. Oh boy! They did not know half the truth! Jesus had to identify with us, not only to be mocked by the Romans for the kingly realm that He walks in, but also to be identified with the destructive Crown of Sin that we carry in our lives.

You can have bad crowns you wear by your choices. You can choose to have a Crown of Thorns on your head as well. You can choose to have a Crown of Pride on your head. You can choose those crowns and you can wear them. Jesus took away the identity of the Crown of Sin that we carry by our actions, then He identifies us with the Crown of the Pride of the Lion of Judah. This is what Jesus has done – Hallelujah! Thank You Lord that You made a way for me to have my crowns back, because you carried all the filthy sin on the Cross!

Each of these crowns makes a statement to the spirit world about who you are and I love it! It is how we look when we carry a crown. If you do not carry a crown you might feel, "Well I have had a bad day today." Most of the church comes in on a Sunday with an attitude of, "I've had a bad week, pastor. Please make it feel better today." We are supposed to come into church with, "Yeah! Hallelujah! I have got something to give into the atmosphere from who I am – I am a son of the King." This changes the way you come into church. You enter His gates with thanksgiving. Do not expect to come into His gates and have everyone else let you become a spiritual vampire of their joy! There are times when I am at the back of my church praying and I see these demons come in on the lives of people with attitudes like, "I'm hungry – feed me!" Thirty year old Christians are still having their nappies changed by the pastor every week! But mature Christians are supposed to be grown up.

HOW I LOST A CROWN

I am going to describe a circumstance in my life that you may be able to relate to. It was a period in my life where I had been experiencing quite a lot of spiritual growth. Through that period of time I became aware of the spiritual authority that God had given me. All I ever did was fight. Show me a devil and I was at it! Take me into the realm of the Kingdom Father, and I will do whatever. If I get bored I will just look for a fight because I enjoyed fighting! I am made as a soldier. Then, through natural circumstances, suddenly it was like a switch had been turned off and the joy of fighting was just not there any longer. I used to enjoy it, but it felt like I just could not get back to that place. Have you ever experienced that? Many of us have this problem.

This is how it happened – I can remember coming into contact with a senior person and he said to me one day, "Ian, you are such a soldier, you will never build anything being a soldier." He said to me, "You need to be more like Solomon. Solomon spent time waiting on God. Solomon built the temple. You will never build a temple if you always fight." I spent the next two years in hell trying to be a Solomon! I began to pray and I would have this thing challenging me in the spirit, like a menacing growl! But the most amazing part was that I had lost something, the joy of fighting. About two years later I said, "Lord, this is just a load of dunghill! I have spent two years of my life trying to be tender and soft. I have too many muscles to be like that; but I am learning how to be a bride – Hallelujah Jesus!" So I began the process of going back into that whole two years and trying to figure out what had happened to me.

It takes a soldier to conquer and lay the foundation for a castle to be built on. Once you have taken the land, then you can retire from being a soldier and build the castle. I noticed that is what David did. I would read through the scriptures about what David did and think that what I did in response to the advice from church was a load of nonsense! I had spent two years of my life trying to be nice and soft. There is a place where you can be soft and tender, even as a soldier before the presence of the Lord, but that is right in His face. Out of intimacy with His glory in His presence you can become soft with His presence. But there is no softness with the devil, there is no softness with the demonic world – the kingdom that is 'in' darkness. It is not a kingdom 'of' darkness. Satan did not make that kingdom, God did. The devil just filled it; it is all part of the one Kingdom, just filled with something else.

"[The Father] has delivered and drawn us to Himself out of the control and the dominion of darkness and has transferred us into the kingdom of the Son of His love" (Colossians 1:13 AMP).

I can remember going back in the spirit. I thought I would just walk back on the timeline of my life and the book of my life and just try to figure out what happened. If it has happened for me then it has happened for hundreds of believers and if I can find that answer to the problem then I have a key that can mandate believers to get back on track again. So I spent some time going through my life, looking through the two years trying to figure it out and I always stopped at this time when the senior person spoke to me. Just before it in the timeline I could feel the glory – I would then come to this situation of what was being spoken to me and immediately afterwards I would feel the loss. I had lost something from my life. The Lord gave me a scripture:

"Behold, I am coming quickly! Hold fast what you have, that no one may take your crown" (Revelation 3:11).

I got mad; I had spent two years without my crown, trying to carry somebody else's rubbish. Somebody had removed my crown.

I went back to that moment and because I had got the revelation I was able to stand back and watch. What I saw happen was these words came out like a hand and swiped my head, knocking off my head the crown that the Father had given me to carry.

I went back and repented of allowing that crown to be removed from my life. I picked it up out of the realm of the spirit again, put it on my head and brought it back two years down the line with me. So I did not have to try to recover those two years because they were covered by the restoration of bringing it back to the present. Now I feel I have grown two years without having to walk the pathway, because those words had no mandated right to remove my crown. That is why Haggai 2:9 (KJ21) says, "The glory of this latter house shall be greater than of the former" if you understand the principle of being outside of time. God took me on a journey to speak to me about the crowns I had lost in my life and what I needed to do to pick them up again. I am going to share this process with you and then we are going to activate it and pick some crowns up again.

RESTORATION OF CROWNS

How do I recognise that the crowns have been removed? Simply, by looking at what I do not have today that I used to have yesterday. What am I missing? I guarantee you that you will find elements missing as you go back through your pathway of life. You will find yourself thinking, "I used to pray there and now I don't any more, hmm... I wonder what happened?" Or, "I used to lay hands on the sick. I was not afraid to tell people Jesus loves them". Or you can feel your heart pounding and Jesus saying to you, "Tell them, they are waiting to hear." And you are thinking, "No, no, no!" The moment you say, "No" Apollyon says, "I receive your offering thank you very much." You are trading on Apollyon's floor and your crown falls off your life. It sits on the floor and there is no glory. All of us have lost our crowns, one of them, two of them, three of them, eight of them. It does not really matter that you have lost them, but now that you understand you have lost them, you can go and do something about it.

You need to recognise the place where you lost them. When

I walked back into my life I recognised I did not have things I used to have. I would spend time praying in tongues, engaging my spirit, walking back in time, into my memories in the realm of the spirit to begin to see what I had lost. I would walk down the timeline and then I would begin to feel the presence that would come around my life at certain times. I would go into that moment and look at what happened around my life. Most of us have very clear memories of when our crowns have been removed, because they are spiritual and your spirit man gets impacted with grief because it feels it's uncovering. You need to ask Holy Spirit to give you revelation if you do not know where a crown was removed. More often than not it is removed by the hand of man. That is why Revelation 3:11 says, "lest any man take your crown". You are a man as well and you can remove your own crown by yielding to something, just as I chose to yield to the words of another man.

You need to repent for allowing your crowns to be taken away from you by another person. You need to go back in the timeline, pick them up and restore them upon your head. When you have done that, you need to reaffirm by prayer that the restoration has happened: "Father, I thank You that I now have my Incorruptible Crown back on my head. My Crown of glory sits back on my head. Father, I thank you that I have received it back out of the realm of the spirit, from where I lost it, and I have got it back on my life in the Name of Jesus!" Then you need to rebuild the expectation of them around your life. Go into corporate encounters with people. Go into individual encounters in your own life. The crowns are symbols of rulership. You and I need to realise that we have sinned when we have allowed our crowns to be removed from our lives. So regardless of who has removed our crowns, you and I have sinned by allowing this.

"The crown has fallen from our head. Woe to us, for we have sinned!" (Lamentations 5:16).

It is pretty straight forward.

Often I find that a person who has been molested, or had something done to them outside of their will, has had their crowns removed. Regardless of what has happened, you need to take responsibility for this sin. You cannot be connected with that record any longer. You need to deal with that record and confess it as your own.

Nehemiah did not commit the sin of the whole of his generation before him but he still took responsibility for it. You need to take responsibility for your own messy situation. Once you own it, you can deal with it. Until then it is always shifting blame – it is called unholy transference!

So what is the process of restoring the crowns that you have lost?

1) You need to recognise the place that you lost it. You do this by memory recall, thinking what it was like back then. "Yes, I had it then, what happened?" Was there a circumstance that occurred that allowed this to be removed from my life?

2) You must go back and spend time praying in the spirit, drawing on the memory, with two things in mind: what it was like to wear it and what it was like to lose it. This helps you to recognise the price you paid in losing your crown.

I would be busy praying in tongues and drawing on the record of the memory of what happened in that circumstance. Often it is emotional pain, pain that is related directly to you as a person, or pain against your personhood that will remove a crown. So I will go back to that specific circumstance and pray into it.

3) Repent! You are the one that has lost your crown, so you need to own that fact so you can repent of losing it. You are the one that is the problem – not God, not the circumstances around you. Regardless of the circumstances, you chose to let it go, you were the one that allowed it to be knocked from your head. Again, once you own it, you can deal with it.

4) You need to restore it by faith, which means praying something like: "Father by faith today I take hold of that crown that was removed from my head in that circumstance. I reach into it and I take back my crown out of the hand of the enemy and I put it back on my head in Jesus' Name." It is done by faith so you must believe that what you are doing is true. The Bible says it is going to happen.

5) You need to reaffirm by prayer the restoration of that crown: "Father, thank You for the crown of righteousness that is on

my life. Father, thank You that it has been restored. Father, You impute righteousness to me, that when I stand in the spirit world, that crown of righteousness is displayed because I am a son of righteousness." That is how you reaffirm it. You use your own words but that is how you reaffirm something in the spirit. Speak words that create an atmosphere for that reality to become your own. It is called 'confession of faith'.

6) You need to rebuild what you had. When Jerusalem had their walls torn down they had to go and rebuild them. They put the gates up first. They knew the importance and spiritual significance of gates so they always restored the gates first. In the same way, you need to go back and restore the Soul Gates that were hurt, destroyed or influenced by you losing that crown. When you have done that, build the wall of protection over it again. Decree that this thing will not rob me of this crown again. You rebuild them by worship, by meditation and by corporate and personal encounters with God.

Something that will do you a lot of good is to go on a 24 hour prayer watch. Just drink water, lock yourself away and pray in tongues for 24 hours non-stop. If you get tired, go and have a shower, go back into your room and pray for twenty-four hours vocally in tongues. After about three hours into it you may sound a little less exuberant! But by six hours you will start to feel so good spiritually. By twelve hours you will want to shout with a spirit of rejoicing! This is because you are starting to draw on a different source than you are used to. You need to push the boundaries. The crowns get established more firmly on your head when you push the boundaries of capabilities in your life.

These crowns are very precious to us as believers. They are very important for us and play a vital role in our lives. God wants us to wear our crowns. We need to wear them. I love them. I have been before the throne and watched the elders throw their crowns down. I have gone there and I have thrown my crowns down as well. It is the most amazing, exhilarating feeling to give something back to God that He has given to you! The twenty-four elders are only symbolic of the sons of God. Elders speak of mature ones. God wants us to become mature sons of God, so that when we come before the throne and we have something to give Him, we can say, "Daddy, this is the representation of what you have given me, and I am giving it back to you with joy! Because I know that when I give it back to you, I am going to get it back polished, gleaming, with more jewels in it!"

Unless you learn how to exercise authority in preparation you will never use it when the circumstance requires it. When preparation and circumstance meet, you have a divine miracle. You need to prepare yourself. You prepare yourself by wearing the crowns, by using them and by doing these things we have been talking about.

ACTIVATION

Let's start by spending two minutes praying in tongues. Then, while continuing to pray in tongues, recall a circumstance in your life when you know you lost something of the life of God inside of you – either through natural circumstances, through the hand of man or through your own choices. Sometimes it is our own sin that creates an environment for us to lose our crown because we can remove it just as well as anybody else can, since we are still human.

Then I want you to go back to where that happened and pull on that crown again. I want you to go and pick that crown up that you lost because it belongs to you. The greatest thing is that no one else can wear it but you! No one else has the right to go and pick it up except the devil because he is the one who is often behind it being knocked off. So you are going to go back, pick that crown up and stick it back on your head. You can choose any one of those crowns and just practise. There are times when I practise taking my crowns off and throwing them before the Lord, then I go and pick them up and put them on my head again, going through the process of practising like that.

So I would like you to stand on your feet, close your eyes and put your hand on your belly. Do not try and find Jesus 'out there' and pull Him down, but find the glory of God that dwells inside of you. Focus on your belly, where the presence of God is and draw on that while you pray in tongues. After about two minutes of praying in tongues I would like you to focus on an area of your life where you may be aware that you have lost a crown. If you do not know, or are unaware of any crowns, then a good one for you to focus on is the Crown of Righteousness because often when we struggle with sin, that crown gets removed from our lives. Go back to the last point where you felt the flow of that anointing or the remembrance of what it was like in that place. Then stand there and begin to repent for losing your crown. You are the one that has lost a crown, you have sinned. So I want you to go and stand there and repent while you are praying in tongues.

"Father, I repent and turn from that place of losing my crown. Father, I go back to that point in my life where the crown was removed from my head through the circumstances that were beyond my control or through the circumstances and things that I have chosen.

Father, today I turn and return to that point of the place of losing that crown. Today, Lord, I own my sin in losing my crown and allowing it to be removed from my life. Father, today in Jesus' Name I repent of it and I repent of the influence and power where I lost the rhythm and flow of that anointing in the Name of Jesus. Father, today I repent of its control and power over my life.

Father, by faith in the Name of Jesus, where that crown is sat in the realm of the spirit, I reach down and I pick it up again. Father, by faith today, I put that crown upon my head. Father, I receive that crown back upon my life. I receive the relevant anointing back upon my life. I receive that realm of government back into my life.

Father, in the Name of Jesus Christ, I decree that I carry this crown today. I hold that crown before the Lord today. Before the realm of the spirit I decree that this crown rests on my life in Jesus Name – Hallelujah Jesus!"

Do not worry about where you have lost kingdom life or what you have struggled with. Spend time praying in tongues and engaging the Kingdom of God within you. Then enter into the presence of the Lord. Once you have engaged that arena of His Kingdom (I do not go anywhere 'to and fro' or into my timeline or in any other arena until I have engaged Him), step into the glory, then step back out into this arena with the glory and begin to pray into your life. Pray down the pathway of your life and into the circumstances of your life and start to look at it through time and space.

I would begin to move my focus around until I can locate where I have lost something in my life. I recognise the loss by what has happened in my life. Then I begin to repent, reach through time and space into the reality of that time and pick up my crown, carry it back through into my room, where I am today and while I am still in the spirit, by faith, put it back on my head and receive back the mandate that God gave me to receive. Then step back into Heaven, take that crown and present it to Him as an offering.

When you give it to Him, He gives it back to you, but this time it is glorified in His presence. Then put it back on and come back down here. Now you carry a glorified crown. It is a simple process. We can be present here, yet present with Him at the same time. You can be present with the Lord in the spirit and facilitate your life and then come back here and everything has changed, because time and space has been changed by the glory. It changes because when you step into Him you step out of time and space. You step outside of the whole of time and it moves as the spirit world sees that a son has turned up. It scares the living daylights out of the demonic world because they live inside of time and space.

You can practise this activation anywhere you like. It changes the atmosphere, because you have just gone into the spirit, done something spiritual and received a spiritual reward, whilst you are still on the earth – isn't it amazing!? It is not hard to do something in the spirit. When you do something activated by faith, it is released on your behalf, because God wants to give it to you. Amen.

About Ian

Ian Clayton is the founder of Son of Thunder Ministries and passionately pursues a life of understanding and getting to know who the person of God really is.

Ian travels itinerantly by invitation throughout New Zealand, Africa, America, Europe and Asia ministering, teaching, equipping and mandating people to become sons of God.

Ian's heart in founding Son of Thunder is to have an avenue to put strategies and keys into believers' hands to enable them to actively participate in the reality of the realms of God's Kingdom and to experience the empowerment of life as the spirit beings we were created to be.

Ian trains and equips believers to give their lives in a persistent, passionate pursuit of the person of God, enabling them to discover that their lives are about the preparation for oneness and unity with God for the purpose of becoming mandated and authorised ambassadors of His Kingdom.

His passion is to reveal to the sons of God the purpose of the power of the attorney of God within them, removing the sense of powerlessness and hopelessness that is often attached to many in the body of Christ when they are confronted with the reality of the spirit world that surrounds them.

www.sonofthunder.org

www.sonofthunderpublications.org